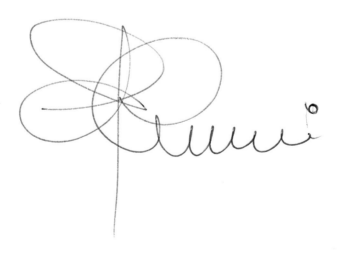

VOYAGES
to
Serendip

My Search For A
Better Place

SEAN CURRIE

Dedicated to the voluntary successors of the remarkable Henry Blogg, who I was fortunate not to meet during these voyages.

As always, for Jaruwan

Print ISBN: 978-1-54398-059-2

eBook ISBN: 978-1-54398-060-8

Voyages to Serendip-My Search For A Better Place.

Printed in Garamond.

First edition published 2019.

Printed in the United States

Contents

Introduction

I HAVE a story to tell. It's the one about a boy becoming a man; a story that untold numbers have considered since the dawn of understanding. Look around, not everyone makes it. Coincidently, much of my account centers around employment at sea, but it might have occurred anywhere. Uniquely, the ocean exposes the fallacy we have any control, and that feeling of insecurity in some way sharpens the awareness of our vulnerability.

Many have related their own account on this subject. Perhaps the first was Richard Henry Dana, describing a two-year voyage from Boston to California and back in the early nineteenth century. Books like his, and many since, have influenced my decision, but only the choice to convey the tale, not the manner in which I have written it, nor the story I tell.

Each time a memory is recalled it's vulnerable to amendment, and I'm satisfied my recollections are incomplete. The book, then, is a kind of ancient, fragmentary archaeology with pictures returning to me piece by piece, or an incident recalled like an insect suspended in amber, with notable gaps glossed over in ignorance. On the understanding inevitable errors would sooner or later offend, I have fictionalized everyone's name, excepting historical figures, and created the occasional composite character.

Writing is a solitary business, but during this long process I was offered much good advice. I have to thank people, too many to name, so I will nominate my wonderful friends Judy Solivan, Lina Donoso and Puja Shrestha to personify them all.

Finally, it is a well-learned lesson of life that kings lose their realms, the famous exhaust reputations, politicians fail their office, and the rich squander their wealth in a misbegotten quest for happiness. Asking too many questions as to why life is the way it is wastes the time undertaken to reveal an answer of little importance. I'm sorry for people who remain alone. I understand. The key to life is being content with what you have, especially if it is the love of another. This, and a modest place to live, will give you more serenity and happiness than all the monetary riches and fake adulation in the world.

1

Beginnings

1977

I am tormented with an everlasting itch for things remote.
—Herman Melville

AFTER EIGHTEEN years, nothing noteworthy had ever happened to me. All that changed here. Three thousand miles from home the heat hung heavy, compressing the air, fogging my sunglasses when leaving the air-conditioning. We stood on the stony dock on a scorching July day in Ras al Khaimah, one of the United Arab Emirates, you know, long ago called the Trucial Coast. I hear it's now a tourist destination, sun and sand for the unadventurous, but in 1977 there was little to value; an abundance of hardscrabble ground, that new blacktop upon which we had bussed from Dubai, a collection of breeze-block buildings and empty lots. It didn't rain, and was perhaps the last place on Earth for spring break.

A dozen of them, by which I mean the white men, stood around like casual professionals. The Arab, "the agent", stood at ease in his ankle length, white *thawb*, unsullied by the dust. It was the beginning of a journey I hoped might make a man of me. Age was the identifying

characteristic: no one started old in this business; you had to be innocent. Three months after my eighteenth birthday with no experience
and no confidence, guilty only of a yearning to visit the un-English
places of the world, I took the next tentative step.

But I'm getting ahead of myself. It all began a few months earlier, in
a suburban English high school, the stuffy sixth-form study overlooking the cricket field. I was awaiting exam results, indisposed to uni-
versity, and coming to the larger realization I didn't desire living near
London anymore, another commuting drone; in and out, like breathing. In later years I'd conclude measured self-analysis a virtue, but then
it felt like procrastination. I had run out of time. My England was
changing. The aftermath of the sixties and the permissive society had
come home, leaving a pallid, provincial, plastic type of country, caught
between Europe and America. Punk bellowed boisterously while anarchy was imminent, followed by a winter of discontent and the miserable Thatcherite revolution. Suffocating from normality as my nation
grieved in a snapshot of despair, I wanted out of the commuter belt and
the soft predictability of the Home Counties.

There on the table lay the *Careers Book*, our school's lonely contribution to commercial advancement in the real world. I flipped the pages
again, each dreary leaf promoting the stalwarts of British industry. I
had read it before and nothing stirred any enthusiasm, like watching
black-and-white television while everyone else had color. Then, closing
the book, quaffing my tea, I saw it! The back page shouted out like a
Technicolor cinema advertisement I had somehow overlooked. It portrayed a man, an officer on a ship's bridge, binoculars to his eyes, scanning forward. The sponsor disclosed nothing, other than an address in
London. Blind to his view, I knew it wasn't suburbia. He was seeking
the exotic, for the unmapped; and I needed to be him, to mature.

The behavior required to distinguish a man, how one handles life, both yours and those around you, cannot be gained in a classroom. What I had avoided for so long became obvious; the first steps were employment, escaping the meaningless conditioning of school and moving out. In that moment I craved to see the world. Impetuously I penned a letter to the advertiser who invited me to their large, Portland stone-clad building on the South Bank near Waterloo, spookily reminiscent of Orwell's Ministry of Truth. Well, I shouldn't bore you; someone in the Records Department offered me a job, deck cadet in their extensive oil tanker fleet. They said sign here, so with some astonishment, I signed "John Smith"; that's my name. Needing a way out of the humiliating mess called life, I was scurrying to sea as an apprentice, the industry's lowest rank, because I didn't want to blink and miss the next twenty years.

MY NEW employer sent me on a two-week "Induction Course," the career equivalent of bungee jumping. It all felt so out of context, a primer to another life with a rich and famous history racing towards transformation. The hands-on material was more useful, including survival training at an indoor swimming pool. A poor swimmer, I comforted myself that few could swim any distance that might conceivably be of use in a deep-sea career. We learned the benefit of life jackets, and how to right an upturned life raft. I gathered the North Atlantic might be a bit more challenging, but I imagined it a greater incentive.

I borrowed money to buy a uniform, and an ophthalmic surgeon attested my eyes should remain reliable for ten years. A week later, enjoying the freedom of preemployment, a telegram arrived, like a late-night knock on the door, with notification to join the tanker SS[1] *Lampas* near Dubai. I hid my dread of the unknown, while a daily

---

1   Steamship.

commute to London briefly appealed, but this is one of those life decisions you make. Growing up has a price called anxiety.

I loved my mother in that curious, English, almost-unemotional manner. She was born into a time of austerity, hard work, rationing and sacrifice. She seemed to have grown smaller as I grew older. I recollect little of her warmth. She was like my own queen, slightly distant, but always there, which is what every child most needs. On departure day, she drove me to the station and waited for the London train. We embraced, perhaps, for the first time with any feeling. The train pulled out, and I gazed rearward through the open window to see her looking suddenly frail, her arm bent in farewell, and her eyes wondering where her youngest son had gone. I raised the window and turned my back on that life forever. I revisited, but I would never stay—the world was calling.

At Heathrow, reassuringly, I encountered another cadet. Harry Dobbs, a handsome man an inch short of six feet, with tousled dirty-blond hair, was somewhat too convivial, which I took to be his way of alleviating the anxiety. I noticed he dressed better than me and didn't suffer the discordance of my lowly estuary accent. From the North Country, he grew to be my friend, if you can believe the provincial paradox of England's strained regional interactions. Neither of us understood the coming challenges. We overnighted at the shockingly cold Hilton Dubai, and they drove us next day, along with a second mate and ten crew members, the two hours north to Ras al Khaimah.

JULY 24, 1977, I stood on the dock waiting to join my first ship. The raucous supply boat—a rare splash of throbbing color—grumbled into the Persian Gulf,[2] a ten-minute ride from the sapphire-blue harbor, as the breeze ameliorated the heat. Out in the wide-open water we aimed

---

2   The UN uses this standard geographical designation, but recognizes the exonym "Arabian Gulf."

for the black, rectangular object ahead. Our destination loomed larger as the boat chugged on until it filled the horizon. Staring up as we closed, a giant yellow shell emblazoned upon the towering red funnel glowed down upon us like a radiant corporate sun, while I questioned Archimedes' principles of buoyancy. Could something this large possibly move?

A large aluminum ladder droned down the silhouette-black, cliff face of steel until it hung a yard above the placid waterline created by the *Lampas*'s lee. One by one we climbed. Attaining the summit, breathless and with cramped calves, I stepped upon the colossus and gazed about in awe. It was green, everywhere dark, grassy green, like a golf course fairway, encompassing my entire field of vision. The bow, and starboard deck, lay hidden by distance and camber. Astern, the towering white accommodation block loomed with two dozen rectangular window-eyes. The second mate, a shortish, hail-fellow-well-met sort of chap, having tried to explain the evening before, took a deep breath and uttered:

"Big enough for you?"

To imagine man could create something so vast and solid proved otherworldly and inspiring. Any nautical notion or semblance of a maritime history had disappeared with the coming of the supertanker[3]. We shook the hands of strangers and watched others depart. Harry and I hung around uncertainly, like actors who hadn't read the script. Half an hour later, somewhere inside the behemoth, I found my cabin; sparse, anodyne and dominated by creamy Formica. Touches of wood, a miniature fridge, a full-size bed and a bathroom added comfort. It gave the impression of a room that humans had never occupied, with a complete absence of descriptive aura. The whole package screamed

---

3   The *Lampas* was a Very Large Crude Carrier (VLCC).

"institutional," but at least that meant clean. I sat alone on the faux-leather daybed and recalled Samuel Johnson's seafaring dictum:

> *No man will be a sailor who has contrivance enough to get himself into jail; for being in a ship is being in a jail, with the chance of being drowned.*

Someone assigned me a watch, "twelve to four," which I discovered denoted inhuman working hours and dislocation from other life. For the unaccustomed, the arrangement taxed the young body; sleep became a luxury. In due course, we first-trippers, lost and overwhelmed, self-consciously modeled our tropical white uniforms and felt ridiculous. Without our knowing it, the *Lampas* departed. Anyone not looking would be hard-pressed to tell, save for the faint hum of air-conditioning and the slightest vibration. It was not as I had expected. I understood the mercantile concept of loading a cargo and carrying it somewhere, but the details escaped me for now in the confusion of a new language. I sat in lowly solitude, steeling my psyche, feeling like a man who's opened a flat box of furniture with no instructions.

I ate food, stumbled about the accommodation of closed doors and identical passageways, bumped into people I didn't know, and tried to sleep. They called me to work at nine that evening. I never acclimatized to the shrill waking night call. We had arrived at Jebel Dhanna, what or where I didn't know, but began work stationed aft for mooring operations. In the intense darkness the floodlights created a canopy hiding the unknown beyond. The stern appeared a vast, open space; green, naturally, and occupied by giant, sizzling machines. The winches, steam driven, wheezed and hissed as they breathed, belching heat into the air, as if we needed it. I was tired, innocent and alone. It had been a long day and I felt so uncomfortably out-of-place wearing my pristine white coveralls (called a *boilersuit*) and hard hat, like a boy trying on a man's clothes.

The second mate, unruffled, slipped into the routine as a worker dons a familiar outfit. Wisely, he advised I stand aside and learn. Deliberately, the giant ship's wires were unreeled to a mooring boat far below and pulled to buoys unseen in the distant darkness. Every man, save me, understood their role. As each wire—the width of a soda can and hundreds of yards long—fastened, the winches reversed and heaved the slack onto reels until achieving the desired tension. They called them 44s, denoting their diameter. The process dragged like root-canal surgery, completing at three in the morning.

Wearily I asked, "Can I sleep now?"

Apparently not; standbys were an addition to watch time. Finally, at four a.m., I found my cabin, showered and fell asleep. I awoke at eleven. In daylight, the curtain of lights drawn, as everywhere in the Gulf, one viewed the glistening azure sea, a hazy auburn horizon and cement-gray mountains behind at an undefinable distance. On deck, I saw nothing except a black hose sucking oil from somewhere deep in the Earth. I had come to sea with a longing to visit the exotic: Hong Kong, New York and Valparaíso. Jebel Dhanna, in comparison, was the parking lot on the edge of town to those glittering lights—functional and uninspiring.

A day away the island of Halul lay offshore Qatar, joint bottom of the interesting-port table. Famous for its pearling industry at the turn of the century, its name might evoke visions of Hawaii, all Hula-Hoops and surf, but in reality, it's a flat, square-mile sandbank, surrounded by an ocean of hazy blue water. From seaward where the *Lampas* weather-vaned about a large buoy (called a single buoy mooring, or SBM) whence the oil rushed inside us, scant interest for the eyes existed, save a collection of gray storage tanks and a few low buildings. The afternoon sun on the hot, hard deck made everything untouchable.

Working meant endless physical exertion. On a cargo watch of four hours, the cadet's role comprised monitoring the level of oil in each of the thirty tanks. That required walking, continuously, around the enormous deck, monitoring each tank's float gauge readouts, radioing the result to the control room, each passing minute ticking away in slow motion. By the end, soaked in sweat, feet aching, I stank of the acrid, sulfurous inert gas expelled as the unseen black gold rushed in, pushing us deeper in the peaceful water. We drank cool water, more water and inhaled the salt tablets. Halul felt like a trip to the moon on an exceptionally hot day. Once onboard the supertanker, expectations of the next port hardly existed.

Predictably, I questioned my choice of employment; I could have been at home, shopping in Tesco's, paying my hire purchase demands, living in a comfortable ordinariness. I had notions of a seagoing life. I expected to visit exotic locations, have a woman in every port and the occasional *apéritif* and, hey! I didn't mind a fair day's work, but I never thought I could be this tired and persevere. My young body ached as I began growing to fill a man's size.

HARLAND AND Wolff assembled the *Lampas* with some style and brutal splendor in 1975, at their unmatched shipyard in Belfast, famous for the *Titanic* and her two skyline-dominating yellow cranes ("Samson" and "Delilah"). It was the jewel of our shipbuilding crown, the only yard making the new supersized ships. One can visualize her size as three football pitches laid end to end, representative of her length and width. She derived her power from stark simplicity: one engine, a steam turbine, with an engine-room dominating boiler, and one propeller. These attributes resulted in a single purpose, to carry 300,000 tonnes[4] of crude oil over long distances at a constant speed of 14 knots. The raw momentum was undeniable. Above the engine sat a large apartment block that accommodated thirty of us in air-conditioned comfort. I can't complain of the living standards. Everyone had their own cabin, food was English and plentiful, and there was abundant fresh water, plus a comfortable lounge with a fully stocked bar, and a compact but deep, pool, the builders' thoughtful touch. These were profligate times before reality set in.

The father of Marcus Samuel, founder of the corporation in 1897, owned an antique shop in Houndsditch, which specialized in importing shells; hence the name. Correspondingly, a tiny lampas triton shell appeared lost in a glass case embedded in the wall near the mess rooms, like the only trophy she ever won.

SITTING DEEPER in the ocean with two million barrels of unprocessed oil, we departed the Gulf, the constructs of an alien society dropped over the horizon, and our world condensed to within the steel box. Rotterdam existed eleven thousand miles away. They took Harry and me off watch to work as day labor, toiling from eight to five with the crew, attending the morning meeting at the paint locker where work was allocated. The days heading south consumed the curse of the first-tripper, chipping rust spots with a sharp hammer, and feeling the despair of viewing the immensity of the deck and the futility of fighting the inevitable chemical reaction. It conveyed the impression of work to occupy men, like breaking rocks, but finally, it was a chance to settle in, and ponder again the decision I had taken. I could at least sleep now.

---

4   A metric tonne; 1000 kilograms.

The daily routine revolved about the three-meal eating schedule where stewards served us, embarrassingly, silver-platter style. We could drop by the comfortable officers' lounge in the evening, like an upscale, honesty cocktail bar replete with a few wives who rode along as supernumeraries, and tax-free twelve-cents-a-can beer. I learned new routines: lifeboat drills, fire exercises, elevator trips to the engine and pump rooms. In good weather the inert gas blanket expanded and the pressure valves banged all day straining to contain the bomb inside. On Sundays the captain (universally called the Old Man, except in his presence) inspected the ship, as if making my own bed would change the world. The *Lampas* offered an immense feeling of security as the engine drove on, while the bow pushed serenely through the ocean rushing hypnotically past, a dozen feet below the railing.

The long, punishing painting days endured without reason, the modern equivalent of scrubbing the deck. The British crew shared all the ambiguities and tensions of their reputation, appearing hard-bitten and cynical, with a latent hooliganism ready to erupt. The bosun, leader of the deck crew, was a good man, though, and taught us seamanship while spinning yarns of the most sordid personal details. He was animated, disciplined, funny and gifted—as all leaders—with the ability to take initiative. The pumpman, a short, Scot curmudgeon, wore his sleeves removed to better display his tattoos, like a character from *The Vital Spark*. Despite his stature, he had a jumbo temper that no one wanted to see get away from him. His overwhelming theme related to a better life before, while inserting two expletives in each short sentence, by which we youngsters were shocked, then amused, and which we subsequently mimicked, as if to assimilate his manliness.

I enjoyed gulping fresh sea air in the muffled quietude forward on the fo'c's'le, seeking unseen patterns in the chaotic water, while dolphins rode alongside. The movement through the sea had its own beauty: the color, the freshness and serenity. My skin burned from the sun's unrelenting rays in the especially brilliant skies, but they sold sunscreen. Harry, although fair-haired, just tanned, like a Californian. Movies played twice a week in the lounge, and that wonderful feeling after work of a long shower, a clean white shirt and my ever-growing familiarity for the first cold beer of the day. They planned a crossing-the-line ceremony to humiliate us teenagers, but the Old Man, typically wrapped in barbed wire, suppressed unnecessary indulgences. In my anodyne cabin the loneliness overwhelmed. I wrote letters to family and friends to convince myself those relationships might somehow survive. Like an anxious prison inmate, I feared my siblings and school friends might forget, and the voyage was a step into oblivion, the dichotomy of running away while craving the chains of home.

REACHING SOUTH Africa, the *Lampas* shipped building-sized waves. She sat low, drawing seventy-five feet of water, and the Cape rollers surged along her green expanse as the supertanker shrank in the seas, causing havoc only to be repulsed by wave-breakers before the manifold and accommodation block. Standing in the lee at deck level produced a pliable spectacle both fascinating and unnerving, as the waves first lifted then dropped away from large sections of the hull. The usually imperious ship undulated like a semi-hard stick of candy as it hogged and sagged. We slowed at Cape Town, allowing a helicopter to land fresh food and, expectantly, mail; some evidence that someone cared, or even remembered I existed.

I endured the routine. Since Harry and I were in the same boat called beginner, we had each other for companionship and an outlet to voice concerns, but some we kept to ourselves. I had been a prefect in a good school, a member of the rugby team wearing colors. Here I was, lowest of the low, deck labor with the uncontrollable misery of homesickness and ignorance—everything so new, so altered, like recovering from amnesia. It's a process, becoming a man, and I was staggering, hardly bounding forward. The voyage so far provoked deep introspection. Lacking the constitution for suicide, I wrote a letter to my father explaining my error and the intention to quit in Rotterdam. It made it onto the Cape Town helicopter, and then the weather settled as we cleared the continent and headed north towards the sun. Astonishingly, the deck held a dozen dead flying fish, as if to question the absurdity of it all.

Europe disappointed. Once near England the radio boomed in, maddeningly reminding us of home and the alternatives to the choice I had taken. The weather became, naturally, overcast and we all donned more clothing. After six weeks of long, sunny days we were now in the blustery weather of the English Channel, like an over-steeped pot of tea. Sleep became a premium again, but the night watch astonished as the *Lampas* plowed determinedly through the busiest shipping lanes in the world. I couldn't grasp how the second mate understood it all, the nightly mass of lights. I watched and brewed the coffee and avoided getting in the way, like an expectant father.

Rotterdam looked flat and industrial, a confluence of rivers spewing into the North Sea in a continually altering jumble of rivers, polders, and streams, finally constrained by the Dutch with the construction of "The New Waterway," in 1863, validating their mastery of the seas that embraced them. We were so far out the pilots boarded by helicopter. The *Lampas* labored to wheel about corners, but hours later we proceeded into Europoort, a marvelous man-made, ever-expanding harbor. Four tugs placed us astern into Dock 103, providing my first opportunity to walk ashore; artificial or not, a chance to smell the land. It smelled like crude oil.

My father was a good man, beginning work at fourteen, digging graves. He resembled the actor Jack Hawkins, handsome and enduring, but I'd always thought he'd needed the alcohol. Before departure, I received the only letter he ever wrote me. I reckon he felt he'd done enough getting the runt this far. He told me to do my best, which is all anyone can do. But it was effective, as if an old man had recited Kipling; it conveyed courage and resolve. So, I stayed. By a happy coincidence, I received my first paycheck: eighty-nine pounds per month.

Cast back to the ocean, we returned to chipping and painting, studying and learning the Rules of the Road,[5] thirty-four regulations on the conduct of ships in relation to others. They became my constant companion, although a mental divide existed between the words and their application. Once a month we stood before Captain K. and recited a rule or two, a tension-overload struggle for perfection without meaning. He was humorless, shockingly aloof, and without a single identifiable emotion. He never experienced indecision or procrastination, but sat before me in rotund contentedness, with a devastatingly pained grimace he had developed over the years. He remained in his three-room suite with his wife, submerged in boredom, surfacing twice a week for a movie. He didn't please, but did his job, and ensured others did theirs. His was a simple calling, with only one duty: responsibility.

I LONGED to see the world but Nigeria transpired to be unpropitious. Forcados and Bonny were ports so far from land I wasn't sure it was land. With not much to see and less to admire, I endured roaming the deck as the oil tore in from the unseen sprawl of Africa. My employer's historical performance in Nigeria has been far than stellar. The trademark

---

5   The International Regulations for Preventing Collisions at Sea 1972 (COLREGS).

atmosphere of moral weightlessness that Big Oil brought along raises the conundrum for the seaman contracted on a voyage to he knows not where. He has no choice, no vote, and tends towards ambivalence concerning certain awful places he might visit. But we were safe and cozy in our air-conditioned steel apartment block, remote from the cares of the people of the land, setting aside the depravity we had been sent to exploit. The *Lampas* loaded two million barrels of crude oil in the pouring tropical rain as the lightning shocked the sky red and yellow until our hair stood upright in the static.

As with all drugs it's almost impossible to pinpoint when I crossed the line. Over the years I have gained a more robust accommodation for beer; not something I'm proud of, and I don't blame my father's genes, but I realize the condition began here. Alcohol was an ever-present and accepted aspect of our daily lives. It was the solder that fused people together.

I had to study. My first navigational lesson concerned the compass, a revolutionary piece of equipment essential to all ships since its invention. The *Lampas* had three. The magnetic served as a backup, never to be used except in the unlikely event of the other two failing, wandering around seeking a nebulous magnetic north, instead of the true one, and affected by the errors of deviation and variation. The electric gyros spun seemingly forever while the *Lampas* rotated about them, unaffected by those demons, being more accurate and reliable. There are many singular and related methods of determining a ship's position, but the humblest and most reliable is to take simultaneous compass bearings of two known objects. Drawing the lines on a chart, one's position was where they intersected. I did it, and was hooked on navigation and cartography.

The trip progressed, like the *Lampas*, with drudgery and monotony, as she never-endingly pushed through the water for weeks at a time. In my antiseptic box the solitude felt poisonous and I recognized the dearth of personal effects: the pictures, mementos and knickknacks that might tenuously have bound me to other people and real life. I would change that the next time.

HARRY AND I signed off the *Lampas* after four months, a wonderful release, akin, I suspect, to being granted parole. Johnson's prison dictum omitted the gratification of having committed the original crime, but it remained a release. Our satisfaction was more ephemeral; we were paid, yes, but we understood it to be a stepping stone, a difficult and unsettling experience. I became a seaman to search for something; I had lived the voyage day by day and accomplished that. My emotional discipline had been strengthened. That was a beginning, but serendipity was a distant enigma. We took the long ladder descent to the launch in Ras al Khaimah. I departed longhaired, tanned and fit, with calloused hands toughened from the chipping hammers, but I was free.

On reflection it might seem graceless of me to criticize the *Lampas*. It wasn't anything I expected. I barely perceived the world, and saw no postcard moments. I guess I had removed the rust spots and painted a six-yard box worth of three soccer pitches, akin to playing tennis without a net, but I had broadened my perspective an astonishing amount. As for the ship, it kept me safe and comfortable, and not that long ago, traveling thirty thousand miles at sea would have been considered a remarkably risky exercise. I wasn't seasick because the *Lampas* never rolled. I traveled some watery areas which my school friends would never see, but instead of the magnanimity that follows struggle, I had a feeling of having missed something, and a niggling sense it wasn't as good as it could have been.

They built the *Lampas*, most likely at enormous cost, to do one thing and do it well. In many respects it was the same as working in any other place, except for my internal examination of isolation, worry and dread of the unknown. She was the white goods of the shipping world and I had had my nautical perceptions realigned. The voyage's momentum was such I never had time to react to its lack of reason, only the sensation of work.

I had begun, not as a quest, but as an escape. Things might have been different had I possessed some social skills, but I was an ornery child. Going away was hard, and coming home easy, but it plagued me with as much self-doubt as a Catholic, which I wasn't. I understood I might never renew the relationships of the ship again; these men had gone. Arriving home, I noticed a few assessments; my mother was happy to see me, and I was pleased to see her. In later life I have tried to understand how my leaving must have touched her. My father shook my hand firmly and commended me for its coarseness, like a good union man. He'd been abandoned by the corporation after a half lifetime of loyalty, returned to physical labor and home-brewed beer, so I considered it my obligation to use the schooling I'd been given. The people had grown older. So had I, but it was as if we had grown at a different rate. The familiarity of suburbia was comforting, but mostly I remember the silence at night, broken only by the train passing a few miles away. It was so quiet I was afraid to breathe, but I could sleep without the shrill phone calling me to work. It was good to see friends again, and I remained under the illusion that those long-standing relationships would endure, even as they rode the train to the city and I tried to explain my employment. I sensed there was the inkling of a change as I ruminated on my first obstacle, while realizing there are few shortcuts in life. I thought I needed to find something on this voyage, but it turned out I needed to find me.

Thirty-five days later a telegram arrived.

2

The Able Seaman

1977–1978

That it will never come again is what makes life so sweet.

—Emily Dickinson

ON AN overcast day in southern England—a month before I joined the *Lampas*—Elizabeth II took part in another festive occasion commemorating her Diamond Jubilee. She boarded her yacht, *Britannia*, and began a two-hour cruise from the grand harbor of Portsmouth, dressed in a white outfit highlighted with dark blue accents simulating something faintly nautical. Thousands lined Broad Street and Clarence Esplanade. The royal yacht glided by as people waved and cheered, then progressed to the Spithead roadstead, where English monarchs had reviewed their fleet since the fourteenth century. This was Elizabeth's third and final extravaganza, before the role of the navy evolved and the government secured a grip on the economic realities of life.

They anchored the 118 warships in three broad lines stretching seven miles from Southsea to Cowes, accompanied by hundreds of leisure craft jostling for a better view. Each vessel, freshly painted and dressed overall, looked festive, but purposeful. From *Britannia* they pronounced it "a magnificent sight" as the Queen motored past.

When *Britannia* reached the western limit, she rounded two visiting commercial vessels hiding in plain sight at the fleets' extremity, the 270,000-tonne BP supertanker, *British Respect*, and the SS *Opalia*. An editorial of the Fleet Review claimed:

> *...the Shell tanker...Opalia had what was possibly her full company on deck, fallen in as smartly as any other ship that day.*

The *Opalia* was infamous as the fleet cadet training ship at Spithead. All employees knew of its distinctive nature, like an annoying television personality. The telegram instructed me to join her in Gamba. Two days before Christmas, three other cadets and I flew out. Still eighteen; stronger and fitter, but far from home and about to encounter my first experience of Africa. Here we were in Brazzaville airport beside the Congo River, for goodness' sake. None of us felt like seeing the Republic of Congo, and, as it happened, the Congolese didn't want to see us. We spent the day sitting in the transit room, with its dull green concrete floor, dirty two-tone flaking-paint walls and a surprisingly young man dressed in unmatched fatigues, casually fingering a large automatic weapon hanging from his shoulder. We sat, waited and feigned nonchalance.

Early evening, we rode a flight to the town of Gamba in neighboring Gabon, surprised to learn the *Opalia* was loading offshore. I had hoped for more than SBMs, viewing countries through binoculars, as if never quite arriving on vacation. Near midnight we boarded a small boat surging up and down on a steep, confused swell alongside a short jetty jutting into the South Atlantic. It was a precarious commute, scaling a loose rope ladder above the heaving boat. The bouncing vessel droned offshore, spray lashing over us until we reached the tanker, low in the black water, creating a comfortable lee. The familiar caustic taste hung in the air; crude oil, like jamming a wad of Vaseline up your nose.

A dozen faces stared down from the deck and took up that old English ditty so familiar to drinking rugby players:

Why were they born so beautiful?
Why were they born at all?
They're no fucking use to anyone.
They're no fucking use at all.

Happy bloody Christmas! The low freeboard facilitated easy access via the pilot ladder. After shaking hands, our predecessors departed, and we hoped they made it home to celebrate. Hours later we departed hot and humid Gamba and journeyed north for the winter of Europe. They assigned me a small, irregular-shaped cabin right forward starboard, contiguous with the main deck. I shared it with a young Welshman named Glyn, and we didn't get along. He was slighter, a first-tripper with a nationalistic anger and fiery attitude to annoy me. This trip was not for solitude, and besides, confinement without intimacy is no fun at all.

Built in 1963 at the Cammell Laird yard in Birkenhead when ships were ship-like, the *Opalia* had graceful lines. An oversized white accommodation block curved across the stern chasing a long, narrow body. Above and behind were two tall, elegant red smokestacks, each adorned with the obligatory corporate logo. In 1975, with a burgeoning tanker fleet requiring staff, Shell had the bold idea of converting her to a cadet training ship. Instead of the usual deck crew she had twenty-eight students arranged in four companies rotating their working hours.

Two weeks later I'd uncomfortably settled in and a winter chill suffused the ship. Le Havre is an impressive port on the north side of the Seine estuary, famous for the to-ing and fro-ing of ocean liners in years past, but by 1978 that business had long gone. Our trade remained, and the *Opalia* was there discharging her heavy, hot cargo of Gabonese crude oil, heated to improve the viscosity by forcing boiler steam through coils arranged a few inches from the tank floors. The law of thermal motion did the rest.

During our stay we took what they once called "annual stores." Maritime tradition dies hard; this one was characterized by a column of trucks arriving from London. We put in some mighty labor taking on food, electrical spares, engine parts, ropes, paint, and more paint, but most abundant, cases and cases of beer. We manhandled the lot deep into the *Opalia*'s interior; a full day's effort. In appreciation, the captain organized a bus taking a dozen volunteers forty-five miles north through the lush, flat meadowland of France to the ancient town of Fécamp. It's famous for the Palais Bénédictine with its ornate and finely wrought façade reminding the visitor of a faraway fairy-tale land. But, instead of chocolates for children, they manufactured Bénédictine liqueur. They gave us the grand tour of production and the monks presented us with gift-wrapped bottles upon departure. It was an agreeable day out for which any tourist might have spent good money.

Harry Dobbs was a man of insouciance, seemingly understanding that if he didn't care too much then providence would pull him through life. In typical fashion he had spent Christmas at home and joined us in Le Havre, like a man who leads you into a revolving door and comes out second, leaving you standing alone. We departed a dreary, January France for somewhere more exotic: Venezuela. The dull routine of maritime life between ports returned; maintenance. The *Opalia*, lacking a deck crew, used cadets in an educational ploy positioned between experience and exploitation. Not everyone chipped the deck; some manned the bridge watch, while others studied, which didn't take long to realize was like throwing a double six in port.

Punta Cardón turned out to be an enormous refinery on the Paraguaná Peninsula in Venezuela on the southern coast of the Caribbean. Historically this place and the region to its south, leading into Lake Maracaibo, ranks right up there for significance with the Persian Gulf. It is the world center of heavy, viscous oil, billions of barrels lying deep beneath the dusty soil. In the 1940s Standard Oil built a refinery at Amuay, and next-door Shell built a competitor, at Cardón. Between the two developed the modest town of Punto Fijo, which as you might expect, is affected by the two, and the multitude of visiting tankers. It caters to them with agencies, inspectors, chandlers and other suppliers, but Punto Fijo was most renowned for its friendly womenfolk. I was "studying," so exempt from any moral implications, and desperate to sate my malnourished teenage libido, I joined others on an evening ashore of rest and relaxation. Two large, obsolete American sedans, trailing outsized fins, carried eight of us gripped by a collective urge, the short, bouncy ride past the breeze-block and corrugated-roofed slums near the refinery to the pleasant residential streets of town, and The Mamis, an establishment I consider unfairly termed a house of ill-repute. Remember Homer's counsel?

...for no one else has ever sailed past this place in his black ship until he has listened to the honey-sweet voice that issues from our lips; then goes on, well-pleased, knowing more than ever he did; for we know everything...

At a walled compound encircled by fruit trees and serenaded by buzzing cicadas, we pulled in through the gates of the sirens home, drawn like iron filings to a magnet, and entered the neon-lit enterprise. The irony of the establishment's name might have mattered another time, but we wanted beer, music and girls; each abundant inside to sate some fundamental primate need. Female sexuality, I have since concluded—without any evidence—reaches a summit according to a women's innocence or experience and the "sweet painted ladies" of The Mamis were considerably more skilled than me. Something adolescent in me surged to the surface. By late evening, I had experienced the warmth and welcome that melted my juvenile frustration, from a golden-skinned Latina after a clammy and personal encounter, as the fan whirred above and the bass thrummed in the bar beyond the wall. It was a fun and enabling experience; a dalliance with the world's great pleasure industry. Punto Fijo was, for one night, more memorable than suburban London, a visceral and affecting escape from adolescent hell.

Naturally, I honed my chipping and painting skills again—all ships rust—but I learned the use of guyed derricks. Why waste money on hydraulics when you have a dozen ungloved pimply teenagers ready to pull the wires, risking slashed hands from a barb, and then calling it character building? I learned rope mooring operations, tank cleaning and myriad other duties of the Able Seaman. I spent hours steering in a straight line, comparing myself to the automatic. She carried a sixth of the *Lampas*'s capacity but possessed few of the hydraulic and electrical benefits. That meant we opened and closed the hundreds of gate valves manually, by hand if we were fortunate, but with a large wrench if it resisted rotation. We monitored the flow of thick black oil with sawed-off wooden floats on measuring tapes from a hardware store. It was antiquated but reliable in all conditions. The days were hard, and longer days were harder. At the conclusion of one aching, extensive day, Harry and I dragged a cumbersome ladder back to a storeroom, then, together imagining the next twenty yards of up-and-down toil, gave up in roguish bonding and threw it into the sea.

We carried the Venezuelan oil to Europe, five thousand nautical miles away. The nautical mile, strangely, began life as a minute of arc along a meridian, the invisible lines running North and South on a globe. Observing the Mercator[6] chart, a navigator will step off the distance with dividers and compare it to the minutes of arc on the margin. In 1929 they redefined it as 1,852 meters. It took us about fifteen days to reach Europe.

PERNIS IS an odd but attractive suburban village west of Rotterdam. Similar to many well-kept Dutch communities, the red- and white-bricked houses with steep gables dominated, interspersed with tall trees and small, pleasing gardens lining the brick-paved streets. It's an agreeable place, but surprisingly adjacent is the largest refinery in Europe, Shell Pernis, which transforms four hundred thousand barrels of crude oil into refined products each day. In the spirit of the high-labor-ethic Rotterdammers, this juggernaut sits boiling oil, like a roaring monster behind the fence. This ability to assign room is peculiarly Dutch, caused by the lack of space, I suppose, and their working ethos; when you buy a new shirt in Rotterdam, it comes with the sleeves already rolled up. We arrived with fifty thousand tonnes of Venezuela's finest.

I liked Rotterdam and returned often. I appreciated the Dutch approach of diligent work and a beer afterwards, and their liberal attitude to life. When you entered a convenience store to buy a Pepsi, below the counter were *Newsweek*, *Women's Own* and the front cover of

---

6   Gerardus Mercator invented his projection in 1569. It's used almost exclusively in the maritime world because of its ability to represent lines of constant course; in effect it makes it possible to visualize a globe on a flat chart. Where would navigation be without it?

a magazine showing a young lady with a penis between her glossy red lips, like a shocking splash of violence on a landscape by Rembrandt. I believed this an appropriate mind-set. To work on deck at night was akin to a free ride at Disney as the nearby refinery lit up the sky, the glow warming us, while the hissing and cooking noises of the vast industrial complex rumbled away the hours.

But Europe was cold. We spent hectic days slow-steaming along the English Channel while cleaning cargo tanks. The *Opalia* lacked a fixed cleaning system, but had an abundance of cheap cadet labor. We toiled day and night in freezing, penetrating, windy weather dragging the heavy hoses round the deck, and lowering the high-pressure cleaning machines into each tank. We finally wrapped up the spinning-plate workload when each tank was considered acceptable to load, where-upon, the vessel sailed into the River Seine.

THE FRENCHMAN commanded, "Port ten."

"Port ten," I replied, whirling the large, eight-spoked wheel to the left.

The *Lampas* had a half-moon, eight-inch wheel for true steer-by-wire of the giant rudder, but the *Opalia*, being of older design, even with hydraulics, required human energy. In time I stabilized the head, "Steady oh-four-eight degrees."

The Seine is a challenging waterway, needing frequent adjustment of the heading. I was doing well coping with his over-exuberance for corners when, like a whopping and avoidable pothole, I saw a vessel approaching fine on our starboard bow. Hearing "Starboard ten," my mind mistakenly perceived a danger and spun the wheel to port, not seeing the cement barge being overtaken close on the beam. It's a classic helmsman's blunder, aiming to reason, interpreting the pilot's thoughts instead of unquestionably following his commands. We missed the barge, after much shouting, gesticulating and random piling on, but that's growing up. They say you haven't lived if you have no regrets, but I admit I got it wrong: seriously wrong.

More importantly, I was ashore again, walking alone, content to avoid the imprisoning cabin. Petit-Couronne sits on the left bank four miles downriver of Rouen. It was a dreary place in February; industrial and ordinary, and a long way from any tourist postcard. A mile from the dock gates stood a school, apartment blocks, a drugstore, ordinariness and gloomy skies. I strolled about the melancholy town and savored the sense of existing as if by accident in other people's lives. I imagined how they might live in their modest boxes. Was it so dissimilar to suburban England? The cuisine might have been finer, but by some logic this ordinary town has lodged in my memory, and I suffered the same sensation in other, disparate places. There is in many people a yearning to live on the other side, and I so wanted to be someone else. Maybe I might live one day in this small, anonymous French town, marry actress Marlène Jobert, and guzzle Calvados.

HERE BEGAN my second nautical rite (after the equator): the North Atlantic. We set off with a golly-gee-wow expectation for America. I had grown up reading Nicholas Monsarrat, but the *Opalia* wasn't a tiny warship, and though not a supertanker, she was sizable enough to ride the bleak, stormy seas and relentless swell rather adequately. What struck one was the ever-monotonous grayness of the ocean, day-after-day howling winds and the endless scudding clouds, never a chink in the sky's armor to allow a brief respite of blue. We felt the water, stretching to a sheltering sky, seep into our bones. "Seas" arise from the local wind pushing the water into short, steep pyramids, briefly lingering before tumbling down, breaking as their tops blow away in a crescendo of spume. "Swell" is the much more potent power of far-distant weather, its energy developing over hundreds of miles, and results in a lazy heaving ocean, superimposed on the seas. This ocean had waves substantial enough to bump and heave against the solid mass of steel as it crashed through the wintry water, the occasional whitecaps breaking across the bow, or along the main deck, hurtling into the facade of the house, dissipating its energy in thunderous sound and vibration.

Fighting the Gulf Stream as it gushed past Florida, and a series of low-pressure systems sliding off the North American continent, sailing ships used to set south to the Azores, then west to follow the favorable trade winds to America[7]. Steamships have the choice to follow a shorter northerly route and resultant poorer weather, as we did that late winter. As the breakers crashed against our cabin bulkhead they played "Philadelphia Freedom" in the bar each night and we sang along in drunken karaoke fashion. The music may have heartened us but the weather didn't. Our steel home gracefully pitched, yawed and rolled in the short Atlantic swell, but tankers are naturally stable in rough weather, from the weight of low cargo and an effectively watertight structure. For Glyn and me in our tiny cabin we heard, but much more, we suffered the sea's energy as it came crashing downward on the accommodation house and the heavenly shrouds of water rolled over so many lonely wrecks of an earlier time. It was a strenuous and hard-hitting three days in mid-ocean which promised a brief bonding between the two of us in adversity, but the friendship soon soured again as we approached the city of brotherly love. It was for many our first visit to America. We may not have been seasick, but we were homesick and unsexed. America held a fascination for anyone growing up in England

---

7   The route was also a function of navigational limitations, i.e., their inability to find the longitude.

in the seventies; all that excess in contrast to the austerity of indus-trial action, blackouts and our IMF-panhandler status, a place where happiness derived from the purchasing power we lacked. While the UK suffered every ailment of the changing times, American television promoted an altered, excessive, fun-loving lifestyle. It may have been a lie, but it was an escape from the cheerlessness of home. I had crossed the North Atlantic.

My introduction to what Orwell might have called predatory cap-italism was, after the roller-coaster ride of the Atlantic, a pleasant pas-sage into the Delaware River. But it's still a long, convoluted route to the Sunoco refinery, just south of Philadelphia. With limited time on the twelve-to-four cargo watch, I managed an outing to the local mall, living the pleasures of satiated consumerism; buying what I didn't need and eating when not hungry. And that's what we thought of America: shopping, pop music, oversized and too much food. We loved it!

We settled into a demanding pattern running thick, heavy black oil between the US, the Caribbean and South America, discharging, tank cleaning, loading again; all a bit of a blur, really. Puerto La Cruz caught the eye as an agreeable Venezuelan port. Indigenous crude oils flowed through extensive pipelines from the country's interior to the refinery for export. The metropolis of half a million rested at the foot of large, subtropical mountains that led to the busy, vibrant city fronting the beach. The machines of industry lay hidden, so the beachfront along Playa Paseo La Cruz attracted those enjoying the nightlife and warm water. To go ashore was a pleasingly lengthy stroll on a balmy spring evening, taking in the fragrance, humidity and incessant bug sound of the tropics. There are few nobler activities to raise one's spirits than walking ashore in a new land with a clean shirt and a pocket of dollar bills. The waterfront turned out to be a discerning location for the noble pastime of girl watching, while guzzling beer and enjoying an evening meal not available on the *Opalia* menu.

OUR LATER trip to Chesapeake Bay was most auspicious. Its watershed includes a population of five million people, but from the river there was scarcely any sign of habitation. It's a pleasant journey, bounded by tree-filled green hills, interspersed with an occasional grand house and quaint wooden dock. The river narrows when it reaches Washington, D.C., and splits into a labyrinth of tributaries as it extends deeper into the West Virginia and Pennsylvania heartlands. But this was not a pleasure cruise and the *Opalia* tied up at the Piney Point Terminal, close to a pretty beach of genteel houses. The terminal seemed lonely, and the trees concealed its ugliness. It was a place to find seclusion, so there was little to do. But my employer, in another affirmation of generosity, stepped up and treated us well, supplying one of those yellow, boxy school buses to take a dozen of us on a trip to the capital, seventy-five miles away. They were profligate times.

Washington symbolizes a living postage stamp for me, a place where history comes charging at you. It's a government city without the abject commercialism that mars so much of the nation. The limited building heights, wide-open spaces and greenery welcome the visitor with walkability. If you keep to the central zone around the Mall, the rows of buildings themselves tell a story steeped in its short history and the nation's ceaseless struggle for freedom and liberty, which I found inspirational. My own capital, London, experienced a revolution a century before, but the British neglected to enumerate the consequences—a fair legal system for everyone, security of the person, protection of property, a right to say how we're governed and freedom from arbitrary taxation—nor proclaim it in the infrastructure. The British fudged in this respect, declaring their rights inherent and ancient, so there was scant need to trumpet them. But in a mist-veiled meadow between Windsor and Staines, at a place called Runnymede, there is an acre of land given to the people of America, along with a few hidden testaments engraved to commemorate a meeting between King John and his feudal lords, representing the vague, distant beginnings of the essential foundation of our shared society.

THE *OPALIA* was aptly sized for trading to the US, a country richly invested with many fine rivers, but lacking the depth for larger ships. She was a "dirty" tanker, denoting her tanks could never again be sufficiently clean to carry petroleum products. No, they burdened her with black oil, in particular the dreaded No. 6 fuel oil. Once within a tanker's pipelines it's impossible to remove, and the ship will spend her life on this trade until her demise. But it's a noble business and does its part in keeping the modern world turning. I had later occasion to gain knowledge of refined products and other exotics; it takes time to live.

1963 was an extravagant and prosperous time for shipbuilding. The *Opalia*'s steel house had lashings of Formica, but also pleasing touches of dark, solid wood and brass fittings that increased in measure the higher you climbed. Reaching the captain's deck, an opulent dual curving staircase led to his quarters, built from a gilt-edged formula that had long gone out of date. The ship was not new, and exuded an odor of having been well lived in, sprinkled with the perfume of household detergent liberally strewn by our daily mandated cleanings. The officers had their lounge and the small crew—a few petty officers—had theirs, but the center of all boisterous entertainment was the cadets' bar with its failing lounge chairs and sofas, a scene of mayhem and merriment. It had the English dichotomy, a veneer of politeness underwritten with brief flashes of violence. We had a fully stocked bar with everything except absinth, like a scene from the cantina in *Star Wars*. The food was robust, English and plentiful.

We were the labor that performed the daily graft; mooring and unmooring, cleaning, painting, operating valves, loading stores, manning the helm, sounding the tanks, keeping a lookout and everything else a trained Able Seaman did. It was a valuable education, like total immersion in a new life, and afterwards you still had to clean up, dress in uniform for dinner, and study. But we were young and full of energy, so we drank and partied, engaged in occasional argy-bargy, barroom fisticuffs, and rascality of many descriptions. The cadets' bar was a drinking establishment of peers, liberal-minded, where good ideas were introduced and then discarded, where young men defied logic or reason, exemplified by a cadet named Goody drinking twenty-four beers one night: just breaking the record. Anyone could philosophize on any subject and often did. Neither Plato nor Spinoza could have matched Harry Dobbs: "There are only two types of people at sea, wankers and liars." We were the same age, on the edge of something, when one year made all the difference. It was a time of youthful exuberance, and life intoxicated us.

THE CARIBBEAN was fun, but we were addicted to the commercial drug of America. Texas. Now, there's a name to cherish. Few of my friends of old would stroll for a beer on a Caribbean island and then cruise to Corpus Christi. The city allowed me a chance to study, but not on the *Opalia*. The ship stifled freedom, everyone accepting their duties amid mutual support of a social system that had evolved over the centuries, and my cabin rendered those necessary private moments impossible in the sexless confinement. Harry and I spent a meandering afternoon engaged in the American pastimes of shopping and eating, then ventured back ashore to experience the nightlife, mingling with the young Corpus evening crowd. At a nightclub of no name, Harry effortlessly acquired the company of two charming ladies with his knowing spontaneity and hint of vulnerability that women fell for, as I played the supporting role. They drove us in their aging car to someone's apartment, where we snuggled on the sofas listening to music.

The night progressed euphorically, like inhaling amyl nitrate, when unexpectedly the conversation turned commercial, so Harry and I respectfully declined. The financials of the enterprise did not offend, only our inability to fund it. But the nice Texas ladies were sympathetic enough to return us home with a sweet goodnight kiss. Perhaps the date had not ended climatically, but it had been a day out. Our money had been well spent, and I began to see the world in color after too long in black and white.

ORDERS CAME in for the big one: New York. The Ambrose Light Tower, an ugly pipe turret resembling a half-completed oil rig, identified the pilot station. Embarking the man, we then entered the channel into Lower New York Bay and the anchorages near the magnificent Verrazano-Narrows Bridge, Robert Moses's final grand monument to the city he shaped. We anchored at Stapleton in the Upper Bay on a sunny May afternoon with the trees of Brooklyn to our east, Staten Island to our west, the roaring bridge behind and in the near distance, standing tall and proud, the skyscrapers of Lower Manhattan.

What an evening for fledgling young men beginning new lives! Outside, beers in hand, lolling on the rail—leaning, never sitting— we spent the hour chatting and taking in the vista of the New York skyline. From the harbor, the city borough projected a magnificent impression, a rising phalanx of shimmering lights dominating all and everything. From this distance it was quiet. When Henry Hudson first found this harbor, could he have imagined the experiment of diversity that would ensue? The one place to visit since leaving school was this peaceful anchorage beholding this breathtaking sight; few got to witness this glorious display, surely more awe-inspiring than anything nature might conjure.

The following day a pilot guided us through the curiously named Kill Van Kull waterway between Staten Island and Bayonne, traversing the heart of industrial New York and New Jersey. We passed under the unsightly Goethals Bridge, all purpose and drudgery, as if designed by a committee, the separate sections not quite blending in architectural harmony.

Passing the giant Exxon Bayway refinery at Linden, we arrived at the Hess terminal in Port Reading. Within hours of arrival I was ashore with Harry. No hindrance from security, just a nod from the uniformed guard, a cheery wave and instructions on how to find a cab. This was a destination that might later appear on a "bucket list," and here we were with free tickets. We hailed our transport, a brash, yellow Checker cab, and began one of the eminent taxi rides of the world, joining the New Jersey Turnpike, "counting the cars" on the vast road, a heady twenty lanes wide, astonishing us little Englanders. We sped north, ever nearer the looming city, into the Lincoln Tunnel. After a few minutes of thundering noise and darkness we emerged into the cacophony of Manhattan: car engines, blaring horns, people shouting, bells ringing, everyone going somewhere: our eyes spinning left and right, striving to embrace it all. We materialized near the Port Authority Bus Terminal on Forty-Second Street, so the cabbie dropped us there as a point of reference and transport home. We set about walking with no plan and no map, just enthusiasm, youthful energy and a sense of wonder.

One cannot see Manhattan in a day, but we walked, cabbed and rode the confusing subway system where we could. New York in 1978 is sometimes romanticized as if a frontier town, with its lawlessness, widespread homelessness, poverty and large areas of the city abandoned by local government. The mayor knew of the city's near insolvency and set to the slow rebuilding that took so long to bare fruition. He saw, as did any visitor, the graffiti of the subway and saw in it, not youthful neighborhood art, but the manifestation of a city out of control. Riding the subway, for the unwary, seemed a perilous undertaking, like an amusement park horror ride, but our companionship reassured us. We saw the gleaming marquee lights of Times Square which advertised not art, culture or even entertainment as we knew it, but sexual freedom, voyeurism and unruliness. In any moment of unguardedness, one might be solicited with varieties of vice. "Have a nice day!"

We were content to roam at will, experiencing whatever minor event or landmark we stumbled upon, struggling to encapsulate it, with our one, guaranteed touristy goal being the dizzying height of the World Trade Center's mighty twin towers. Upon arrival at the base, we, like anyone else standing before them, were mesmerized by their enormity. I have minor megalophobia, so I lowered my eyes, wincing at its devastating presence. The Twin Towers were something from another world, so tall, straight and unemotional. Their wonder was height, not much else, but what a height! We paid for the exhilarating, ear-popping ride to the summit, and tried to see as far as a man can while attached to the ground. New York was sumptuous and snarling and it became a gold standard. The only thing missing was a giant ape.

THIS VOYAGE broke any patterns that might have set in. It was a return to school, one of the boarding variety, but goodness, they made us work hard until it became painful. I was well practiced in endless fatigue. What made it so meaningful was that we, the cadets, were salaried labor that ran the ship. One does not become a seaman just by going to sea. The ship couldn't function without us—we were not supernumeraries taking lessons—the lesson was the work itself. We were ordinary young men doing extraordinary things. For that it was invaluable because I knew I had achieved levels of labor others could not. As Harry once philosophically articulated, "Ninety-five percent of life at sea is a load of shit, but you only remember the other five percent." This trip encompassed a large proportion of that small percentage, due to the trade we engaged in, and let's be honest, the generosity of my employer. I didn't enjoy bunking with another man, but I didn't spend that much time in the cell; I have a much profounder visual memories of the cadets' bar and the places we journeyed to. Fortuitously, there was no time to reflect in solitude, so the excursions' only shortcomings were the result of an excess of sexual energy.

I was no longer what I was; I was a man of the ocean, although the young suburban child still remained deep inside, like a benign cancer I needed to be rid of.

3

Spinning My Wheels

1978

A leader does not hazard his legions through ways of danger by himself untried.

—John Milton

I RETURNED to Rotterdam too soon, having spent a scarce month at home as my childhood rapidly disappeared, but that was the agreement; I earned a week's leave for every month served at sea. I had met the near-strangers-once-high-school friends, and we gathered for a beer, but something had changed. Females had infiltrated the group, an event I might have found promising, but I had meager time to catch up, and no talent for exposing them to my almost nonexistent charms. Everyone knew the secret except me. It's startling what you miss when away; the gossip, the politics and the relationships—they had all begun to morph into something new.

I was strangely enthusiastic about my employer, which feels bizarre through the hazy spectacles of nostalgia. I was proud, finding satisfaction in being a component of the commercial giant. Bigness is the purpose of a corporation and they had achieved that long ago, and the glow of their success beamed down upon the proletariat. The prior carefree, but hard-working voyage hadn't sated my want for travel. New York didn't disappoint, but with the restlessness of a nineteen-year-old I wanted to see—oh, I don't know—Hong Kong, Cape Town and Valparaíso.

Without impressment, I joined the SS *Acavus* late one June evening. She lay low alongside an unidentifiable dock in the mass of industry that is Botlek. The ship looked timeworn and sad, constructed in Germany a year before my birth, one of sixteen little *A*-class "clean" 19,000 tonners the corporation possessed, coming with a reputation for stimulating voyages to unknown locales. Luckily, I hadn't bought lottery tickets.

It was one of those humid nights so dark and heavy the clouds squeezed close above. Everywhere was wet and clammy. The bright lights of the port obscured the scene with their brilliance, while the small ship, lying close alongside, appeared somehow part of the larger industrial complex, as if joined by more than the black rubber hoses throbbing with life. Gazing despondently down from the dock, I saw the tanker's deck, tiny and confused, shining in the glare that obscured its greenness. The hull sat deep in the water, unseen, while the accommodation blocks streaked rust on dirty white. The reek from the open gauge hatches climbed, hung in the air, and overpowered—gasoline!

The tanker had evolved into one ubiquitous shape by the mid-sixties, regardless of size and purpose; comprising a large rectangular box subdivided into oil-tight compartments. The bow encompassed a smooth point, while at the stern they attached an engine room with a propeller, and atop that an accommodation block. The *Acavus,* however, remained a contrivance from another age, with few straight lines. From the lengthy wedge-shaped bow that stretched back onto a dark green deck to the amidships accommodation block, rakishly rounded at its forward end, then staggered back to the aft deck which ran to the subordinate curvy second house above the engine room. Atop the aft house sat a stubby red funnel adorned with the omnipresent mollusk. At the time of building, for intractable motives, deck officers lived amidships and engine officers and crew were consigned aft. By 1978, this appeared anachronistic, inconvenient and unsafe and did little to foster amity or bonding to a common cause. The deck officers, attired in clean uniforms at sea, were seen as distinct or worthier, an inappropriate inheritance from sailing days. Solitude and loneliness are strange but inequivalent bedfellows. I prefer the choice of when to be by myself, and unlike the previous voyage I now, gratefully, inhabited my own cabin.

The voyage began Africa-bound. Dakar is the capital of Senegal, an oddly shaped country on the chart aptly resembling a grim face in profile. The city lies at the most westerly extent on the Cape Verde Peninsular, and at the end of that sits the port, organically grown over the years; the last piece being the North Jetty mole that holds the oil tankers—banished to the outer limits, a stone wall away from the Atlantic rollers beyond. Dakar didn't appeal. It had a green-brown unfinished air the populace accepted. From colonial times everyone spoke French, and the English didn't learn foreign languages. I expected to see Europeans strolling in white suits, modeling pith helmets and swagger sticks. I walked, like a strange apparition for the locals, to a few open-fronted eateries (restaurant is too grand a word), drawn by a rusty Coca-Cola sign, amongst the pungent smell of garbage, where they sold unknowable parts of animals. It might be easier to list the worthy aspects of Dakar, but they escape me right now, although the mosque looked suspiciously well-kept. I had a free ride there, and still wanted my money back, but it put my situation in perspective. I was no longer a giddy, foolish young man beyond caring; I had seen poverty close up.

We set seaward, seeking the twentieth century. We washed the old ship down and settled into the comfortable routine, hoping Abidjan, four days further along the coast, might be an improvement. It was French and large, which I hadn't expected. Though not the capital of the Ivory Coast, it's the financial heart. It seemed dark, polluted and industrial, lazing in the magnificent natural lagoon of *Ébrié*, and worryingly had a reputation for yellow fever. I carried an obligatory record book of inoculations; arms like pincushions. We pumped gasoline into a pipeline that disappeared who knew where. We had arrived with a purpose, like aliens from another planet, and I was working anyway. What I always disliked was the call in the night, the bang on the door and the stumbling into clothes, the shock of the lights, the noise outside and the competing stench of the city and petroleum.

A FUNDAMENTAL process of maritime life is mooring to a fixed object, like a dock. Those on the bridge might be concerned with the vessel as a whole, but on deck, up close, one gains a better appreciation of the unpleasant forces involved. Here, in the hands-on world, I sought to show I could be a worthwhile, functioning member of a gang where experienced seafarers led. It helped that our outfits comprised torn short-sleeved shirts and shorts; everyone dressed individually, no longer donning the corporate boilersuit. We knew our reputation in the grand fleet: strictly second eleven. Few of the public perceived our presence and we didn't wear team jackets.

She had plastic ropes[8], stored below while at sea, reducing sun and salt damage, and avoiding loss to a rogue wave seeking anything unsecured, like a thief in the night. The power for our irregular party

---

8   Polypropylene or nylon.

came from the boiler bubbling away deep inside the engine room. The winches warmed through to alleviate shock, letting them creak, bang, cough and clear their throats after inactivity, like a heavy smoker waking in the morning. This was the hopeful time of the operation, the gang lolling about, speculating of a new country, experienced can-do men seeking anything remotely of interest in the port. They didn't see it in Abidjan.

We made a tug fast, the pilot's little helper. Once nearly alongside, the enthusiastic sort flung a monkey-fisted heaving line to shore, watching it bounce on the dock: the initial interaction, our first hello. We ran lines as directed, the Old Man ordering on the radio, the dock men shouting their own conception of how it should all play out. The ABs, like the well-practiced professionals they were, set off about the routine, sending out ropes. Each might weigh a tonne, but the weight is stretched over the drawn-out length. My confidence with ropes grew quickly. They had a friendly disposition, soft and human-sized. I hated wires!

It was essential the crew view me as one of them, and not the unready bystander of a year earlier. To manage, a man must accomplish that which he instructs others to do. Making fast to the dock is one of the last maritime endeavors still pleasingly human-like. It required a few men: the winch driver, the man on the drum end and another to hold a stopper working in union, without practice or planning. As the rope tightened, the winch slowed and everything tensed, men and machines. We didn't need the heavy rope slipping now. It had morphed into a rubber band pulled between dock and ship[9] as the mate clenched his fist closed and the winchman held fast. The AB on the drum clasped the rope taut. Any slack and it would jump and render,

---

9   A polypropylene rope will stretch up to 25 percent before breaking.

the tension lost in an instant, the rope slinking about the deck, its coils seeking something to bite.

I stepped forward, the weakest link, collected the loose ends of a stopper[10] shackled at the foot of the bits, and turning hitches over and under the rigid mooring rope, encased it like a truss. I held the remaining rope in a controlled clasp and stepped back, my arm outstretched. The winch backed slowly, and I held the weight of the entire mooring rope in my hands, as another fellow stepped forward—"Don't bloody let go, young'un"—and in fumbling, clumsy exertion, ran the loose end inboard of my stopper around the bits in a figure-of-eight motion until they secured the weight. I released the stopper and it jumped from my hand and unraveled on the deck. The whole affair was akin to running with scissors, but a cadet who couldn't step forward assuredly would not survive this employment. We moved to the next rope and I felt better for it.

And Abidjan? In 1978 I would beg you not to bother going there.

TIME IS a curious phenomenon that eludes easy explanation, but passes aboard ship in a commonsense manner. Nations incline to select political time for social reasons. For a ship on a long, slow passage, two factors require consideration. First, the political time between the origin and the destination, which is four hours between Abidjan and Curaçao. So, on our eleven-day passage, we adjusted the ship's clocks four hours backwards.

Secondly, for navigational expediency, it's handy to keep the relationship between longitude and the ship's world roughly in alignment. Going west we know the sun will reach its zenith later each day. When this occurs significantly after noon on the ship's clocks, then it's an occasion to retard time to align generally with the sun. If the clocks go

---

10   A two-tailed piece of messenger rope, each tail about six feet long.

backwards there are twenty-five hours in the day, and since we're working a watch system, who's going to work the extra hour? Bafflingly, each of the three watches during the night is stretched by twenty minutes. Arcane, but it works.

UPON ARRIVING in Curaçao, the entrance to the Schottegat was one of the most attractive places I'd seen. We reached for the bay through a narrow cut (the Sint-Annabaai) beside which cluster the candy-colored historic Dutch houses of the capital, Willemstad. The streets are full of galleries, shops, restaurants and bars. Outdoor dining is popular. Throughout the old town, the architecture is rich, with wonderful examples of eighteenth-century Dutch colonial building styles, while a clever pontoon bridge connecting the two sides of the city powers in and out of place. With year-round balmy temperatures, gentle breezes and low humidity, Curaçao is an agreeable location, like a perfect Dutch model of Amsterdam on an endless sunny day. A little further inward the magnificent Queen Juliana Bridge—tallest in the Caribbean—spans the entrance.

But further still, past this picturesque scenario, one sees the contradictory and unfortunate blot on the landscape. They built the Isla refinery in the Schottegat in 1918. Twenty-odd years later the insatiable Allied war demand for gasoline and aviation fuel (the light fractions of the refined barrel) transformed the petroleum markets, creating a large surplus of heavier fuel oil and asphalt. With no method of recycling, the refinery, in an extraordinary affront to the coming green revolution, simply dumped the excess heavy fractions in a quiet limb of the Schottegat. Eventually, they accumulated 2,000,000 tonnes of asphalt and 24,000 tonnes of chemical waste. Rarely was a short-term expedient to resonate as a long-term legacy. The asphalt lake, or Asfeltmeer, remains today cranking out poison, causing an ecological nightmare for the modern island trying to attract hundreds of thousands of tourists. Yes, the refinery and its employment over the years sustained the economic life, but I sense today they wish it, and its hidden legacy, would go away.

In 1978 it was usual and customary for a seaman to walk ashore and enter a foreign country to saunter amongst the natives, without let or hindrance. The spread of world terrorism and the drug trade has curtailed that simple pleasure. I was among the final breed considered ambassadors of free trade and not suspects of a phobic society. Curaçao was renowned for the Campo Allegro, a large plantation-like brothel out near the airport, but near the refinery north gate, if I remember correctly, were inviting bars where the weary sailor could wander. They discouraged the girls, but the small shacks nearby glowed red and purple from open doors, and that glorious aroma of cheap perfume in the hot, humid night pervaded the dusty road side. Just being close was sometimes enough.

SO, WE set off to another Africa with the memory of a missed encounter and the blissful solitude of my cabin to dream, with nothing but sea for sixty-five hundred miles. The clocks were turned forward. Captain P., a diminutive, bearded man who wore, incongruously, a gray uniform instead of white, was considered mad by every man jack. He had minor interest in the running of the ship, but made regular forays to the officers' bar in good weather to drink whiskey and play his pennywhistle. The noise irritated like fingernails on a chalkboard, but what could we say? It had the air of a sketch comedy, a showcase for an annoying man with nothing in his life. Departing Curaçao, he resorted to his normal standard, which wasn't very high, declaring, "Call me one hour before Durban," and that was the last anyone saw him on the bridge.

The South Atlantic is a generally fine ocean for sailing, being devoid of tropical storms,[11] although winds can be notoriously ferocious as the latitude increases. We traversed the equatorial doldrums and had a grotesque crossing-the-line ceremony for the pollywogs, or first-timers. Nothing to see here other than drunken men dressed tactlessly as females, one as King Neptune, lots of slippery, awful food, and a few bad haircuts. Alcohol was abundant, but it was a hollow and tasteless charade. The expensive British crew were facing an uncertain future, like an old shop with a going-out-of-business sign in the window. Some of the fleet had already substituted cheaper crews; Filipinos and Indians mostly, but that's progress, or a heartless way of rendering someone's livelihood obsolete, depending on your perspective. The atmosphere was nervous. There was a feeling of going through the motions, laced with an undertone of contempt for a bygone era. They were members of an ever-decreasing union, and many stood around looking sad, remembering happier days.

South of the doldrums came the southern trades, fresh breezes, like switching on a fan after stepping from the sauna. The ancient engine droned on. Near thirty degrees south the easterly trades backed, and gained strength day by day as the thermometer dropped. Into winter we plunged, the small-scale ship, fully laden, sat low, and the seas grew darker, green and gray until the sun disappeared following the gloomy, ominous, hurrying clouds, like a brilliant friend hiding behind a curtain. The swell grew longer on the starboard quarter until its waves broke along the rail and the ship corkscrewed and vibrated and the propeller broke the surface as the bow plunged down, then up again.

---

11 Hurricane Catarina in 2004 is the only one in recorded history.

The novelist Jean-Claude Izzo declared correctly that "storms weld the crew together." It mattered not where you worked or slept or the stripes you wore, the sensation was the same—no pausing or lying still, no relaxing again. On and on it went. Walking or standing was a constant physical exercise and tormented sleep became a rolling endeavor necessitating an unconscious recovery position, listening to the sound of newly loose objects rolling in the dark. Eating became arduous and tasteless, and work cumbersome, especially for the engineers living in the thunderous din of machinery, in an unrelenting artificial day. It continued unremittingly, like a never-ending roller-coaster ride. Fatigue set in. For the deck department it meant a thrice-daily trip down the flying bridge to the mess room, timing the run, avoiding the occasional sea breaking on the rail, crashing against the tank hatches and causing a high wet spume of ocean to cascade over the deck, flying bridge and anyone caught in the open. The *Acavus,* a tiny coffin in the vast vista of the sea, droned on at 12 knots along one of those freeways of trade that keep the modern world turning.

I had rounded the Cape of Good Hope before, but while the *Lampas* ground itself through the huge swell with all its power and size, brushing aside the seas through sheer brute force like a bull at Pamplona, the *Acavus* rolled, twisted and turned amongst them, becoming a part of the ocean. Standing in a lee, I took in the immensity of the rolling blanket of solemn, gray water, fearing the enormity, below which were so many ancient graves of those who had succumbed or lost power—the sea had just opened and swallowed them. At thirty feet above, the horizon is enormous with nothing save the ocean enduring forever, and I realized how much we needed that engine to keep spinning. I would loathe to be without power in seas as this, alone and vulnerable—launching a lifeboat would be unimaginable, and nothing like the swimming pool exercises. If I died out here, no one would know.

DURBAN IS the second-largest city in South Africa, in the province of KwaZulu-Natal. The weather was subtropical and fine for the tourists. We arrived late August when it was pleasingly warm after our long, gloomy passage. Today, South Africa has shed its self-inflicted political illness and is cosmopolitan, I hear, but in 1978 that evident malady was ripe, and we wanted no part of it. I believe I trekked ashore, but the seaman cannot protest where the charterer sends him while his right to visit those places is ancient, predating such political afflictions as apartheid. We didn't vote, and we had no choice. Durban is, however, lost to the limbo of forgetfulness. I was to visit the country a few years later and have nothing but fond memories.

Leaving unremembered Durban, the *Acavus* battered her way north through the Mozambique Channel against the Agulhas Current. We targeted Kenya, and passed the island of Zanzibar, where Stanley based his expedition to find Livingstone by walking through what is now Tanzania. Cartography became my intellectual drug. I addictively studied charts and contemplated the history that transpired upon them at an earlier time, like reading a book of antiquity and adventure. I remained a young apprentice with daily duties on deck with the crew, but when an opportunity arose, I attended the bridge for a brief dose of navigation. I so wanted to become an officer of the watch, the man on the *Careers Book* cover.

Mombasa lay on the eponymous island surrounded by the Tudor Creek and the Kilindini Harbor. At the northwest lies the area of Shimanzi, where our employer had operated since the early twentieth century. We tied up across from the Kenya Ports Authority and regarded the Soviet vessels through binoculars, as if members of a visiting Cold War sports team. Discharge of the gasoline was slow and interrupted, so we ventured ashore in northeast Africa, a world away from Dakar. In our modern, interconnected world, we shrink whole ancient peoples and traditions to the size of a map, but I hoped that this employment might one day equip me with a fuller consideration of her inhabitants, rich and poor.

Mombasa was a large mess of a city, old and new at the same time. It suffered, like many others, from bad government, but wore its colonial past better than some. It was also cosmopolitan, and a tourist mecca for those heading inland for the delights of safari. We didn't get that far, just a taxi to the famous Casablanca Club. We might have walked, but the industrial area south of Shimanzi is only for the fearless, being hot, humid and bug-ridden. The commodious club occupied two floors; a place too full to bother about the customers. Nonetheless, we consumed with enthusiasm. The priority, primarily, was to escape our floating prison, no matter how agreeable—and the *Acavus* was a gentle home—the urge to get away counted, to see genuine people engaged in tangible human activity, like actors in our own play. That we attended an exotic bar in a dark and vibrant city thousands of miles from England added to the allure. We felt safe and comfortable drinking beer, watching the girls—from goodness knows where—plying their trade. I like women; they're a wonderful example of gender, but a melancholy mood invested the voyage. The beers were enough.

STRAIGHT OUT of Kenya I received news to sign off at Suez for an impending appointment at college. Gerardus Mercator's genius, his ability to project a globe onto flat paper, had a drawback: the distortion of land masses over large areas. Africa is immense, fourteen times larger than Greenland, yet they appear roughly the same on a Mercator chart. But in the real world, on the surface of the Earth, it was twelve days round the Horn of Africa to the Canal.

The Suez Canal is one of mankind's eminent civil-engineering accomplishments. It's estimated they employed one and a half million workers, many digging with their bare hands in unbelievably oppressive conditions. The cost, like every other civil-engineering project, was over budget, while it took a long time to be internationally accepted. Skepticism was rampant, but I believe we can now report its benefits have been wide-ranging and long-standing since opening in 1869.

Initially, the Canal Company struggled to recoup the costs, so to solve the problem they invented their own system of tonnage, effectively, their own tax system. Until then the world had a standard measurement of cargo carrying capacity conceived by the British admiral George Moorsom, who measured the enclosed space of a vessel in cubic feet, divided it by a hundred and invented "gross tonnage" (a measure of volume). Deducting the non-revenue volume, he calculated "net tonnage". The Canal Company's measurement always derived a larger volume, but hey! it's their canal. The engineering bonus for canal building in Egypt was that they didn't need locks. It transpires the north and south ends are the same height with the sea flowing in and out imperceptibly.

From our point of view, the Suez Canal was another working challenge, with slight reward. The experienced men advised me to lower my expectations and keep a sense of humor. Upon arrival we anchored, awaiting the northbound convoy, and the anxiety grew. It meant people boarding who were not of us, so we locked our cabin doors and set aside the daily routine. Early the next morning, my feet itching to be away, we weighed anchor and set off northbound, another undistinguished ship in the procession. My recollection of the transit is limited; in fact, I am getting the impression the whole voyage was somehow illusionary, I remember so little.

The first hour one saw buildings, like any other place, of moderate height, none of any interest, but recognizably Arabic. They lacked contrast of color, almost everything a dirty sandpaper, filling me with disillusionment. Later the view became plain and anonymous, the water greenish blue, the banks a continuous sandy dune, the horizon everywhere hazy as the pale yellow turned progressively light blue, but unrelentingly bleak; so boring it defies clearer description. Now and again we spotted the scars of the last war, or perhaps the one before that; recognizable military hardware, but unrecognizable in detail. An abundance of energy and effort flowed into the Suez Canal, but I can't say it was much fun. It was bunk of the lowest level, like eating a meal entirely of Jell-O.

By early evening we reached Port Said, the northern terminus. I never settled into life on the *Acavus*. The British crew seemed from another age within which I didn't fit, and I feared getting too close. I'm sure they resented me and the future I might have; they certainly didn't like my undeveloped attempts at sarcasm, nor my forthrightness concerning British unions and my still developing political opinions. The muscular, but past-his-prime, white-haired bosun thought I was "a pretentious teenage git on a soapbox," and he was right, I was surprised to find myself thinking. While in solitude and contemplation I deliberated the conflict with the reality inside my mind. Well, no, it wasn't exactly the coalface, but the voyage's joyless, going-through-the-motions mood could not be ignored. The ship slowed. I shook hands with two people, departed down the pilot ladder onto the agent's launch and disappeared into the city. I fretted venturing out alone in such an alien atmosphere, so hunkered down for a quiet, relaxing evening and let the sea drain from my body. When you really need a drink, you can't find one.

The next day I wanted out of Egypt. It felt foreign and unknown, like a vacation you sought to cut short. The agent took me to the airport through unimaginable traffic; any concept of rules, regulations, or systems didn't seem to matter. The chaotic situation reached its zenith in Cairo, one of the most populated and impoverished cities of the world, where the inherent impulses of human behavior outperform any semblance of road rules. I held on, thankful I didn't own the car, and tolerated the ride; at least it was slow and, in its way, entertaining. At check-in I found no available seats for London, so I asked for any flight going to Western Europe. The *Acavus* had been a short, slight, forgettable voyage, but sometimes that's enough. It was very much like working.

I distinguished a change in myself. It had begun with the pumpman on the *Lampas*. The ship possessed no politically correct police. Men assembled together regress to an earlier social time, our perceived masculinity exposed in abundant profanity, but I needed caution in regular society.

I arrived home in mid-September and set out to college two weeks later, to South Shields, a dreary coastal town hanging on at the mouth of the River Tyne, five miles from Newcastle. Once a major industrial region specializing in heavy industry, the Tyne was about as rust-belt as was possible to be in the late seventies. There had long been a nautical college there, but the current buildings screamed twentieth-century English modernism. Out front stood a white nautical mast and flag, and just in case the sign didn't say everything, they had an anchor supported by its crown and stock. It was a large college specializing in nautical academia. Students attended from all over the world, but were predominantly British, studying for the three certificates that defined the career ladder in the Merchant Navy. Like every other industry, it had abundant rules, regulations and procedures. Certification is based on international standards, which the British thought, with some justification, they exceeded.

College had good and bad days. It was regular life, I suppose, sleeping every night, interacting with the ordinary people of society, but it was very much centered on our own group. Shell had a dozen cadets on the course, so we naturally coalesced, like vacationers on a bus tour. I shared a room with Harry and another guy, but we were young and enthusiastic, we had money and we had energy. The academic schedule revolved around the important subjects we would need later: navigation (celestial and terrestrial), ship stability, meteorology, communications, cargo handling and those collision regulations I had been cramming. Practical work involved passing the "Efficient Deck Hand" certificate, a sort of theoretical Able Seaman.

I didn't enjoy my time in South Shields, primarily because I felt so foreign amongst the broad northern accents. I grew accustomed without liking it. The winter weather in northern England was miserable. By early March it was all over. I called my employer and queried my next appointment. At college I heard everyone's tales of adventure (the 5 percent), and I knew any ship name beginning with the letter *L* was penitent, so, being pretty excited about the prospects I asked for anything else.

They told me to join the *Litiopa*.

4

Oil and Water

1979

One cannot answer for his courage when he has never been in danger.
—Francois de La Rochefoucauld

THURLEIGH, BEDFORDSHIRE, where my mother was born, is about as middle England as it gets, geographically and characteristically. The people are sensible and slightly dour, but reliable; the sort you want on your side in times of trouble. We used to visit the family tree, but I lacked passion for distant clan loyalty. It's a pleasant village in the English way, with an air of tranquility and steadfastness.

The Americans had acquired a base there in late 1942, as men and arms poured into England. On a gloomy morning the following January, sixty-four B-17s took off and headed east-northeast on their thirty-first mission into the Nazi fortress of Europe, dropping 138 tons of high explosives on their secondary target, the U-boat submarine yards at the Wilhelmshaven naval base, near Bremen.

Scanning black-and-white photographs of the young American aircrews, I saw they bore a resemblance to me in 1979. They smiled for the camera as anxious young men do, but there were fundamental distinctions. They were drafted in the millions, an entire nation supporting them, and I arrived alone again, a volunteer. I labored in a dangerous profession, but I admit, not as perilous as theirs. Two weeks before my twentieth birthday, British Airways flew me to Bremen, my first visit to Germany. After a night in a moderately uncomfortable pocket-sized hotel, we—me and a few others—drove out to coincide with the *Litiopa*'s arrival. From the center of Wilhelmshaven, we were taken northeast past the site of the former Reich Naval Shipyard where so many had died from those plummeting bombs thirty-six years earlier.

The two-thousand-foot jetty stood on the edge of a bitter North Sea, just to the west of the mighty River Weser, remote and desolate. It was a cold and gusty first day of spring, triggering a physical and emotional indifference within me. The dread and novelty of joining a new ship had eroded, while my life was idling, like an orchestra tuning up. I recognized the one person in our party less experienced than me and saw in him the flat stare I once had, the fidgeting anxiety I had suffered, which in two years of sea life had set in motion some beginnings of maturity.

The bus arrived by the giant ship dominating the environment, sitting like a black steel fort on the water's edge. No one cheerfully unloaded the luggage. This wasn't romantic oceangoing of old when seafaring was a calling. No, we were young professionals, well paid and tax free. We were there to pay the mortgage, not to discover the world, bringing oil to everyone—hydrocarbon man. Not that I didn't want to return to sea after my five-month sojourn in the miserable South Shields; in some sense I did. It had been an academic diversion, a chance to mix in the real world, but Northumberland might as well have been a foreign country. Right or wrong, I had thrown myself into this career to foster development. To first succeed meant making money. I would never borrow again, or depend on others. The life-style in England no longer appealed; I'd been to Africa, the Caribbean and America, and I wanted more. It was time to revisit the sunny, fair weather of the crude oil trade. As we laboriously ascended to deck level, the terminal crane hoisted our gear in a net, like a giant bird delicately feeding the monster.

I recognized no one, but after a while the chief mate—the ship's manager—allocated a cabin and assigned me the eight-to-twelve watch. The corporation had taken delivery of eighteen *L*-class supertankers in the 1970s, replacing an earlier generation. They improved the aim of moving vast quantities of energy efficiently around the world; they were larger and more cost-effective, like every other business upgrade. I understood what confronted me. The *Litiopa* was full-sized, but no longer awe-inspiring. A melancholy gloom pervaded the ship, with all of us bearing in mind four months of somber, dreary travel ahead with modest chance of surprise. I settled into the cabin, Formica-like clean, but at least mine, while I added a well-scrubbed respectability. Privacy was essential; the familiarity of naked men in common show-ers had never appealed. The seafarer's cabin is a lonely place, but that very isolation is essential when working with others in confined con-ditions. I now sailed as a senior cadet, stumbling between enthusiasm and despair, yet understanding more than I did two years earlier. My salary reached £208 per month. I wasn't wealthy, but I could afford my own beer. About the only other purchase would be the odd tube of toothpaste.

The half-empty *Litiopa* exited the rebuilt Wilhelmshaven, through the long-buoyed passage north of the Frisian Islands. It's a treacherous setting for large ships, surrounded by shifting sandbanks, buoys and abundant fishing boats restricting our room to maneuver. I stressed too: locating the vital spaces onboard, learning the routine and rhythm of the vessel, accumulating the sights, smells, dissonances and details that formed its heartbeat. The work revolved around a never-ending rigid timetable of professionalism where everyone knew where and when to be at each hour of the day.

With each new hand shaken came a hope for a positive response, but I waited for the sullen reply of the odd character to ruin the voyage. For a humble cadet it only took one. My first visit to the officers' lounge, stepping in and confronted by two uniformed men:

"Ha! Look, it's a Muppet!"

Well, that wasn't very nice, although I understood where it derived. It's the kind of remark you expect from a six-year-old. Striding forward I encountered the fourth engineer behind the counter and his grinning fiver on a bar stool. The fourth was a grizzly-esque, athletic man with a rectangular face and well-scorched skin. I asked him to pass a beer, but he refused. "Are you a member?"

I didn't like any of his humor, but he was comfortable intimidating people. Decision time, John. Stand your ground or walk out and face four months of the consequences. I pointed to my epaulets. "Well, why are you standing behind the bar then? This isn't my first ship."

He stared down with narrowing eyes, his face a darkening sky below a cascade of curly black hair. I saw no point in confrontation, but remained resolute. He leaned back and reluctantly passed a Heineken.

Few people liked "Wick," especially when he over-imbibed. He was a man who could empty the bar on a movie night. He broke the code, the semi-militaristic discipline without resort to manual capacities of authority. His fiver, a toad-faced 75 percent copy, dressed like him, fashioned the same hairstyle, and followed him everywhere, like a duckling. Perhaps the boy Wicker was lonely as a child. Either way, I set to avoiding him.

THE *LITIOPA* plowed a giant bow wave southwest through the traffic separation schemes that attempt to promote order in the confusion of northwest European waters, heading to the enormous Europoort anchorage. In my spare time, I unpacked, played my innovative music cassettes, and taped up a poster of Farrah. It might have been Betty Grable in 1943. Cause the cabin to quickly be mine, an extension of me, rather than an anonymous cube for a rotation of personnel passing through. The next inhabitant echoed the previous one, leaving our translucent strips of Scotch Tape where our home comforts and fantasy women had instilled some meager comfort. Europoort and the English Channel passed in a dreary, overcast haze of work and stimulating drudgery. I exhausted my appetite for correspondence with the outside world as I focused inward, as if hibernating. Heading further west-by-south, the *Litiopa* had a quarter of its cargo yet to deliver, and one final European stop to make.

A year earlier, off the extreme western tip of France, near the rocky landmass of Ushant, the *Amoco Cadiz* suffered a steering failure inbound to Europoort. After prolonged attempts to tow her to safety under a Lloyd's Open Form[12] contract, the sheer weight and momentum of the supertanker proved too much for the tug struggling to save her. The vessel ran aground on Portsall Rocks, three miles from the coast, and spilled 1.6 million barrels of crude oil. Media coverage made much of her Liberian flag of convenience, but it had little influence. The *Amoco Cadiz*, like the *Litiopa*, had one engine and one

12   An almost universal two-page standard document for a proposed marine salvage operation. It's "open" because no amount of money is stipulated: payment is determined later in London by a professional arbitrator. At the top of page one is a statement of the contract's fundamental premise: "NO CURE—NO PAY."

giant hydraulically powered rudder; if either failed, the consequences near land would inevitably end in disaster. Events go wrong at sea, like everywhere else, and the resultant oil spill was the largest ever. Ushant didn't then have the defense it does today. Radiating from it is the first traffic separation scheme inbound approaching the Channel. Some say you can't draw lines on the sea, its vastness free to everyone, but on the chart, there they are, plainly delineated, clear lines of order in the confusing chaos outside.

We headed toward the Gironde estuary with half a million barrels of environmentally dubious hydrocarbon energy for France. The estuary forms the entrance to the ancient city of Bordeaux and the Aquitaine. Near its wide opening, at the limit of a lonely road wandering through the luscious green farmland of the Médoc peninsula, lies the small community of Le Verdun-sur-Mer. The village, fronted by white dunes, had a small boat harbor, and a ferry that crossed to Royan five miles away. It wasn't the grandest Atlantic resort, but as a Francophile, I might have enjoyed a stroll ashore had the opportunity arisen.

However, the diminutive, pretty commune had an aberrant, darker side for the visiting supertanker, and it was to fill me with dread of this place. Our stay was fleeting but demanding because of a natural phenomenon called a tidal bore, where the front wave of the incoming tide travels against the outgoing river flow. Bores are uncommon, but occur when tidal ranges are large and the funnel shape of the waterway creates a sudden increase in water level. Anything floating, whatever the size, rises with the rapidly incoming wave. The *Litiopa* lay floating and waiting alongside the pier jutting a thousand feet out into the appealingly wide, open estuary.

Forewarned, the protracted mooring operation continued through the day, the longest standby. Whatever happened, the ship must be safe, and so we proffered fourteen lines to the spirits of security. When the bore rolled in that evening, the springs would take the full force of its creeping anger. All our 44s ran out and tensioned, then two additional, mandatory, shore-supplied wires—incredible 72s—were heaved aboard. The two newcomers hung in a lazy curve, like overweight cables on vacation, rather than straining taut in support. As darkness fell, it didn't comfort to glimpse the shining steel-gray strings holding a hippopotamus. Cargo discharge began, as it always did. Everyone wanted the cargo off and ourselves out of the pretty but treacherous Le Verdun, with its pervading sense of dread and unease.

About ten o'clock that tranquil night, the bore crept in, imperceptibly, like a returning serial killer. Nobody heard or sensed the stranger amongst us, but the wires gently stretched their sinews and tightened. We had positioned extra men on deck to man winches spaced a thousand feet apart. The *Litiopa* had sixteen wires laid out to the pier, as flexible arms to hold us, but the supertanker was a mighty object and once moving possessed a momentum of such incredibility that naught could hold her. It lay her bare to the callous tide, out of status alongside the fragile pier. She needed to be free, in the open sea, powered by her giant engine, plowing through whatever seas nature might produce, but now she lay vulnerable as the determined water rose and sought to carry her away.

On that immense, shadowy deck, while easing the aft springs, we heard one of our 44s part forward with a remote, fearfully ripping crack, two football pitches away. Men tensed, shuddered inside and hoped no one had stood nearby. Standing close to the shiny-dark wires was now perilous. Wires barely stretch under tension—maybe 2 percent—before they unravel, then with a devilish, sharp report they yield. Their individual wires would snap free, the structure might hold, the broken strands standing erect like a fearsomely barbed cat-o'-nine-tails. If it stretched further, the deadly open-ended steely weapon would suddenly be loosed upon anything or anyone in the vicinity. It was a wicked night on deck, the stuff of nightmares. It troubled me. Not the fear of embarrassment or ineptitude—I'd met plenty of that—but in actual fear for my life and the terror of being found out, of everyone knowing I didn't play my part. Fear is a terrible emotion. They don't teach you about flailing 44s at college.

Arriving forward, the broken wire lay idle on the deck, evoking a dead silver snake, having kissed its deadly shot and missed its prey. The broken end had swept over the side, lost forever, to join countless eyes lying beneath the pier pilings, a refuge of so many dead wires. We eased a few others, the winches jerking like electric jolts, struggling best to judge which had the most tension; a challenge without touching them. Everyone was watchful of the menace surrounding us. Another spring parted violently on the aft main deck, the sound not so much loud as unique and unnerving. An indecipherable voice from somewhere in the shadows bellowed the anxiety we all felt under the dazzling flood-lights, while the pumps threw the oil ashore.

It terrified me. Was this feebleness of character, or survival? The forward wires stretched as the ship rose with the bore, until those 72s, like big brothers, held us. The breast lines, hopeless as usual, impaled themselves into their storage drums, not only rendering them ineffec-tive, but jamming them deep in place. We required stopper chains[13] to hold the weight of each embedded wire, then the winch paid back until it unjammed from its own grip. I wanted to assist, but like riding a bull at the rodeo, that night wasn't for amateurs. Greater experience, and dare I say it, courage, was demanded to step forward and hold a chain that night. Only my imagination could contemplate the result of being

---

13   About a five-foot length of half-inch chain with a short rope tail.

near a wire if it broke and took to the air in vengeance. Unexpectedly, this growing-up idea was going too fast, as if I needed to reconsider a parachute jump.

The demon had crept in, worked its menacing deed, and slunk away in the darkness. At midnight I escaped the adrenalin-pumping, joyless watch for my comfortable bed and the safety of ignorance, like a child hiding under a blanket, contemplating if a life or living were more important. I learned something about myself that night, a night of unrelenting and unbearable dread. Turning off the light, I snuggled down in tormented sleep, while Farrah gazed down in contempt.

WE ABSCONDED from the pier that never wanted us and departed Le Verdun. The *Litiopa* headed out into the wide-open spaces of the Bay of Biscay and stretched her steam-driven muscles, not so much sailing as fleeing. I despised my dread and ineptitude of the previous night, replaying the images in my mind, trying to justify my fears. The truth crushed like a heel, but I could finally settle in and enjoy my new seaborne routine. After Le Verdun, predictability was back in vogue.

The *Litiopa* appeared, prima facie, akin to the *Lampas*, built by the Mitsui Engineering & Shipbuilding conglomerate in Chiba, Japan, in 1977. All shipyards instill their own peculiarities and idiosyncrasies. In size and cargo capacity she was the same, as the buyer ordered, but with one amendment: a stunning, startling, complete lack of bridge wings. It gave the vessel a stubby air of incompleteness, like a nearly finished plastic Airfix kit a child had tired of.

I settled in to the safe routine of life at sea on a supertanker. When empty, that meant tank cleaning, day after day, week after week. Before the events that transpired at Prince William Sound in Alaska, tank cleaning was a two-part, dirty affair. The shortcomings of the tanker's simplicity included the thorny question of how to overcome the lack of deadweight required to immerse the propeller with no cargo onboard. The answer, since ships first took to sea, was compensatory ballast, and for tankers, water—free and abundant—could be carried in the cargo tanks. The insidious drawback, and you might be ahead of me here, is that water and oil don't mix.

Tank cleaning in 1979 began while discharging, rerouting a small quantity of oil into empty tanks via small pipelines at high pressure through "washing machines" (rotating nozzles) that jetted the oil against the internal structure of each cavernous tank. Someone gave the operation the ugly acronym COW (crude oil washing). The veritable gun effect of oil striking steel caused the black scum to recombine and become usable oil again. As the washing medium—crude oil—and the freed dregs fell together to the tank floor, they were suctioned back and discharged with the cargo. COW required significant extra work, but was, and remains, incredibly effective.

The second component of cleaning—designed to replace "dirty ballast" taken onboard in port, with "clean ballast"—was accomplished by water-washing at sea. Cleaning a tank with COW took an hour, but using seawater, the same process might take twelve. It went on and on, day and night ensuring the guns accomplished their runs, scouring the deck below our feet, like a roaring monster within. Recollecting, this seems so spectacularly wrong, and you can sense it becoming ugly. The goal after washing, and you might need to close your eyes here, was to separate the recovered oil from the water. There's no stone wall of integrity surrounding the subject.

Once the oil and water regathered together—called, worryingly, "slops"—the ploy was to decant and refund the water whence it originated. As you might imagine, this water is not the wholesome variety that Flipper played in. We stood leaning against the rail, viewing the decanted dirty water-mix as it gushed into the sea, as ethically weightless as playing golf on the moon. We waited until adjudging it too filthy, or our morality overwhelmed us. It was like that, delivering shareholder value. The operation completed, we offered the remaining slop, mostly free oil, to the subsequent charterer. In my youthful innocence I took it in stride, the accepted practice of the trade. What made it tolerable was the enormity of the medium we were working with, the seas' global rinse cycle, which we believed too enormous to damage. It was an operation best watched from behind a curtain. But don't indict us, the soldiers on the front line; look in the mirror.

AND THERE was Africa again. Before any vessel enters a port in Nigeria, it must be inspected thoroughly and extensively. So well inspected that it requires eight men of unknown obscure bureaucracies drinking cocktails in the captain's office, presenting page after page for his signature. The charade continues for an hour, until the vessel is approved, at which moment he presents each uniformed representative with four hundred cigarettes and two bottles of alcohol, preferably Scotch. We loaded two million barrels of light crude oil offshore in the shimmering West African heat, with the far-off hazy coastline the only sign there might be life. I may be wrong, but I sense I never missed Nigeria up close. It sadly represented the paradox of a country rich in resources dying slowly of flawed politics. We sailed out and found nothing but sea.

Large ships—the titanic ones—do not belong in port. They're too ungainly, unusually confined and absent their element. It's a problem that developed too rapidly to be solved. Oil tankers grew oversized so quickly the terminal building business strove to keep up. The year I was born, the tanker *Universe Apollo* was the first to pass the 100,000 tonne deadweight figure, and yet here we were in my nineteenth year and they had quintupled that capacity, like a boy outgrowing his clothes, a consequence of ships living in an almost unlimited playground, the ocean. Working on supertankers, I prized the deep sea. In port everything happened in slow motion, until those giant pumps spun. Then life became a nonstop whirligig of activity until the tanks were empty and we were free again.

IF I was going to squander months on a supertanker, I decided to relax and enjoy the ride. Being a senior cadet now, academic learning became an imperative beyond chipping and painting. I had some rudimentary knowledge of navigation and it was time to understand bridge watch-keeping, when not cleaning tanks. The eight-to-twelve is a comfortable life. The forenoon watch was an eventful time of shooting the sun while people visited the bridge to gossip, gaze about, inquire of our position or check the weather. After lunch, we exulted in the luxury of a free afternoon, time to sleep, dream in the manner young men alone do, or deal with monotony and solitude in one's own way. It's a long afternoon, and precious for it. We drank cocktails before dinner, and then a few more before returning to work at eight for the "first watch."

Entering the bridge at night, one passes through the chart room, a good place to pause, assess the active chart and ascertain where approximately we might be. Hopefully, the prior watch has made coffee. The bridge is pitch-black, like slowly waking from a dream. The windows define themselves, then the red console lights. It takes up to forty-five minutes to gain night vision, but it's comfortable in fifteen. I longed for the time when it would be mine, the sensation of controlling an immeasurable sum of money and power. It was an easygoing occupation to become comfortable with, especially in the deep sea where the entire world is contained in a windowed room and the all-encompassing horizon, so ethereally flawless when moonlit. I was gradually becoming the man in the advert. At night we sought lights as they sought us. We strolled outside for fresh air, lounged in the "pilot's" chair, or read something on the chart table, or glanced at the instruments, just like you might while driving your car across a wide, flat, never-ending desert.

I liked the third mate. He was destined to one day command; I could measure his demeanor and resoluteness, the stolid look of a man who would back you up. We had plenty of time to learn enough of each other in the way men do, i.e., uncomfortably. Thoughtful discussions of feelings were absent, and we knew all we needed to know by the second night. He hailed from the suburbs, like everyone else in England. His wife, Karen, was agreeable, too, in the manner you might expect a young woman might be; the only female in a ship of men. They were a couple who might have seemed more at place if he took the train to London every day. I'm sure they had 2.2 children. Their lives checked all the clichéd notes efficiently, and yet here they were, at sea. In some irrational manner, the *Litiopa*, with little resonating in her wake, was like commuting to work.

In 1979, long before satellites became useful, we could not fix our position at night beyond the visual or radar range of land. We used the notion of dead reckoning, the tried and trusted method of traveling the world since men first set sail, until the invention of the chronometer in the eighteenth century. Dead reckoning requires a starting fix and projecting a future position based on the assumed course and speed. The watch held other routines. The *Litiopa* had two gyro compasses, spinning seemingly forever, hidden away in a closed room somewhere remote. The concern with gyro compasses was that although they almost never malfunctioned, if they ever did, how would we know they were drifting off somewhere other than true north and the automatic steering was drifting astray with them? You can see the problem.[14] For peace of mind, we verified the gyro each watch by taking a compass reading of a known object unaffected by anything on the ship, or the Earth, and compared the result with the calculated reality. I liked to choose one of my favorite stars, like Sirius, the brightest in the sky. The difference between the physical and calculated bearings was the error. Well, it passed ten minutes.

At midnight, the three of us met for drinks; the engine room being unmanned, so we could avoid Wick most of the time. Women at sea were a curious phenomenon. They had a reputation for creating ill luck because, supposedly, they distracted men, but I welcomed them. The myth was that inattentive men angered the seas, which might seek revenge. Naked women, however, calmed the seas, which was why wooden ships of old boasted a bare-breasted lady on the bow to shame the stormy oceans. The *Litiopa*, rather predictably, had a large yellow Shell where a lovely lady had once been; naked women replaced with a corporate logo. Yes, the eight-to-twelve is a soothing and social existence.

It was a strange time for the world: the Pol Pot regime collapsed, Philips demonstrated the compact disc, they certified the eradication of smallpox, and UK inflation reached 17 percent. As customary in our safe, steel box, the outside world held limited interest—the ignorant bliss of the seafarer. It was comfortable to seek isolation; working, sleeping, never any cessation to the predictability of routine. Why get involved with ideologies and politics which we could neither affect nor

---

14 There was an alarm based on the magnetic compass, but that wanders around with its own inadequacies and needs to be verified too.

participate in? It encompassed our whole world within the ship and the horizon surrounding it. If nothing entered this bubble, then we knew little, and cared less. Ports came and went; a lost memory of long stand-bys, bright lights, hot, burning deck watches and sleep deprivation.

Eventually, we went where all supertankers go. The Persian Gulf resembles a bottle that keeps gushing from the neck, yet is always full again. The bottle-neck is Hormuz. What worries the world, then and now, is if someone tightens the bottle cap. Every day, you might stand on Quoin Island in the strait and watch all that oil steam past, outbound for Japan, Europe and the Gulf of Mexico. Cheerlessly for us, inbound all minor pleasures were sealed; beer and Farrah. The seafarer, ambassador of freedom and trade, consigned all vestiges of civilization behind and bent to local custom. A week after I'd joined the *Litiopa*, Iran's government became an Islamic republic by a 98 percent vote—a pretty good majority—and overthrew the shah, which was why the price of oil was soaring. The ayatollah was back after fifteen years in exile and blotted out what few freedoms the shah had allowed the people of Iran.

Numerous export terminals awaited our empty ship. Mina Al-Ahmadi, inhabiting the southern section of Kuwait, was no better or worse than the others. Built by expat Europeans and Americans, they laid it out in a grid pattern, so regular and predictable, which just made it boring. Giant tank farms surrounded the town and the main road leading to the port. It wasn't a place anyone wanted to go ashore; sand and sunbaked earth, once remote and isolated, not a sign of commerciality or appeal. No amount of money could conceal the triteness within. The crude oil was pumped from a few miles at enormous speed into the *Litiopa*, but they made her for that—she could take whatever Kuwait, literally, threw at her. But loading crude oil at high speed was a stressful business, hoping those valves held. If they failed, or a mistake occurred, the ensuing disaster had unimaginable legal consequences, and no one wanted any part of sharia.

THIS WAS one of those voyages which dragged on and on, where nothing much happened; the *Litiopa*'s reason for being. Times were changing. The Shell UK fleet reached its zenith in 1975 when it totaled ninety-six vessels. By 1977 that number had dropped to sixty-eight. Why did they even own ships? Plenty of independent tanker owners existed, large and small, and truth be told, they probably carried oil more economically than Shell, or BP or Exxon. No, the Seven Sisters remained in the carriage of oil business for a few noteworthy reasons; they sought to be in shipping for the market knowledge that came along with it, and they didn't want to be held hostage by a diverse, competitive industry that had a habit of breaking rules.

I took a short flight home to England from Europoort, and what? Familiarity or unfamiliarity? It was as if my life had entered a new phase. I no longer felt at home anywhere, much as a nomad does. I had gained a disparate mix of naïve vulnerability and steadfast resolve, and a torrent of highly unsettling dreams concerning Le Verdun. I still bore the frustration of the supertanker voyage. Anyone who ever thought life's too short to live the same day twice has never been to sea on the *Litiopa*. The men aboard were mostly decent and professional, with a couple of exceptions. Although individually qualified, we failed to fashion ourselves into a compelling whole. I doubted whether I could perform another *L*-boat voyage. They were suitable for the comfortable married man, like the third mate, who viewed the trip as an elongated day at the office. He knew what was coming as soon as he joined. But I didn't have a family. If I would do this, I wanted to see the world.

I wanted to achieve something that people in the suburbs not only didn't understand, but might be jealous of. I wanted to shock people. I wanted to go to Valparaíso.

On the *Opalia,* Harry and I had spent a long evening in the bar drinking with a Scotsman named Campbell, who was dissatisfied with the corporation, the sea, *L*-boats, and maybe life, for all I knew. Like a man with a loaded gun heading to the sixth floor, he wanted to acquire his license, become a third make and run a Shell tanker onto some rocks. I assume he never did, and I'm not condoning those thoughts, but I understood where they came from; the *Litiopa* was about as much fun as a tax audit.

I told my employer: no more bloody *L*-boats.

5

Miscellany

1979–1980

Men go to sea before they know the unhappiness of that way of life; and when they have come to know it, they cannot escape from it, because it is then too late to choose another profession.

—Samuel Johnson

I LOVED France. I could now travel there on my account; a short and choppy ferry ride to Calais. By 1979 people crossed to buy cheap crates of wine and exotic cheese, a consequence of European membership. Britain and France have a quarrelsome history dating back to before each became the nations they are, and both struggled to position themselves within the new European superstate. We joined the Common Market and left the sad days of warring entanglements behind us. The more adventurous aspired to closer proximity, and I had seen Marlène Jobert movies; French women were liberal and exotic.

Thus, here I was on the Côte d'Azur. Could anything be finer? Well, yes, just a smidgen. I didn't mind spending a few days lingering in such salubrious surroundings while waiting for my next ship. The only problem was her name: SS *Lyria*. That's *Lyria* with an *L*. I'd tried to sway the corporation for something more stimulating. I'd cajoled, even demanded. Finally, I'd begged. But they possessed plenty of these behemoths, with large accommodation blocks handily quartering half a dozen cadets. Looking back, it disappointed me. But, as they say, work is a four-letter word and my marginal bank account had dwindled precipitously. I had to go. Time to bear responsibility and repress my cynicism at the foot of the ladder.

Port-de-Bouc is a commune of twenty-thousand in southern France, twenty miles west of Marseille. It had an exceptional waterfront peninsula jutting into the Mediterranean, where we stayed in a quaint hotel for a few days, living amongst the amber-roofed, pink-and white-colored buildings awaiting the *Lyria's* arrival into the port of Fos-sur-Mer. It was a dreamy time, walking the streets between the blue sea and green hills watching games of *boules*, hoping to see Brigitte Bardot. They served us grilled langoustine, butter, fresh, crusty bread and wine for dinner. I imagined my English peers: "What, no chips?" The weather was as good as expected. The people were as beautiful as the town, and I wondered what they did and how they lived. They were like me, but altered, as if from a postcard of another life. How might I ever live here?

But it was another *L*-boat, as if I hardly knew the name. Each one was seeping into the next, like oil flowing over a levee. It came with permanency and monotony. There would be the comfortable, Scandinavian accommodation block; clean, sparse and fashionable; the quiet, hushed journeying, hardly any noticeable progress; the same repetitive routine. The days rolled by; the weekly work routine, Sunday lunch, cleaning the cabin for inspection, the lifeboat and fire drills. Everything happened without shock or surprise. We took ports in slow motion, fearful of the immense kinetic energy of this enormous object moving. I needed hands-on experience but we scarcely visited any-where, so how could I learn?

THE RANK of bosun is remarkably ancient. Shakespeare used the character in *The Tempest*. Formally "boatswain," the abbreviated term is now customary. He is the foreman of the deck department, orga-nizer of the practical, and the highest-ranking non-licensed member of the complement with a role both supervisory and functional. He is frequently the leading man that others turn to in an emergency, or anchoring, or lowering the guillotine of an auto-kickdown (AKD) stopper used for securing the bow by chain to a single buoy moor-ing. He didn't maintain watch-keeping hours, but was available around the clock.

Dave "Ben" Cooper served as bosun on the *Lampas* when I joined back in Ras al Kaimah. He had entertained us with stories unrelated to a past generation, but expressing a new commitment to the corporation, tainted with sexism and smut. He'd regale us girlish young men, bereft of muscles and chest hair, with his wet-dreamed accomplishments, as if in crudity he exposed our youth, innocence and unpreparedness for a career at sea. We might now consider his conduct harassment, but then it was just another piece of the jigsaw called growing up. He was maybe thirty-plus, tall and recognizably dependable, congenial yet assertive, the sort of man who steps forward when others step back. Unlike the now-extinct British alcoholic seafaring dinosaur, he had achieved the rank through meritocracy. Ben epitomized the new generation, a man who wielded his authority with good humor and respect for his knowl-edge, not because he outdrank everyone, or because the crew feared his physical presence. He had that elusive quality, leadership. Sadly, the problem, and it's a substantial one, was he and his sober British compatriots were too expensive.

As an answer to the thorny problem of loading or discharging deep draft vessels without building costly and cumbrous new ports, the single buoy mooring provided an almost magical solution. The buoy, roughly thirty feet in diameter and weighing perhaps 400 tonnes, contained a bearing system allowing the upper portion to rotate around the moored geostatic lower part. When secured to this revolving portion by a heavy chain, a vessel like the *Lyria* could weather-vane around aligning itself to the dominant environment, i.e., the wind or current. The flow of oil began somewhere mysteriously far away and arrived gushing through floating hoses into the tanker. Ironically, after the expense of such extreme technology, the hoses were attached to the manifold with sixteen nuts and bolts, hammered home by hand-wrenches after a few hours' labor in the sweltering heat. The SBM and the supertanker are twin links in the chain of systems brought about to sustain our addiction to the free flow of oil. They make possible the locating of refineries near markets.

Ben trained us in the basics of seamanship: ropes and knots. There are many, but if you ever consider a nautical activity, only four or five need strike you with curiosity. The sheepshank is one I have never used, and I can't imagine why anyone would, but the stereotypical sea dog Quint demands Hooper tie one in the movie *Jaws*. He did successfully, but never again because no plausible manner to incorporate it in the script could be found. The bowline is a worthwhile knot if you fall in the water and someone throws you a line inconsiderately devoid of a loop with which to embrace yourself. I never used it in vain, but the rolling hitch is a party piece an old hand might show to a young first-tripper—stimulating, but rarely useful. Then there's the half hitch, and its big brother, the double hitch, that account for 95 percent of everything else. These are all the knots you'll ever need.

The ship inched towards the buoy with unimaginable momentum. They called the forward mooring gang for a protracted standby. When a few hundred yards away, a mooring tender picked up a heavy nylon rope and dragged it closer to be hauled aboard on a drum end. Then came the perilous part. The vessel crept closer with judicious, and unfamiliar, bursts of engine power. Starting and stopping the *Lyria's* turbines caused everyone anguish. Those piloting from the bridge a quarter mile away relied on radio contact, with the ever-present fear of overrunning the buoy, an essential component of the local economy. After the nylon rope came the dreaded chafing chain, sparking and snapping like a rabid dog no one wanted to approach. It all came through the steel AKD stopper, and at that moment, with the tension balanced between the enormous weight of the *Lyria*, the subtle movement of the breeze, and those three or four turns held by an inexperienced cadet on the drum end, everyone held their breath at the tipping point—someone had to step forward and engage the heavy pawl of the AKD.

Meanwhile, I had been assigned to the chief mate, setting hydraulic valves in readiness for loading; "lining up," they called it, in some manner content not to be involved forward. I heard the usual muted mooring sounds from perhaps fifty yards in the otherwise near-silence of the night: the winch churning, radios squelching orders, the clanking of the chaffing chain as it rumbled through the round panama lead at the very apex of all that following weight, banging as each link clambered stridently aboard. Sometimes only experience can illuminate the subtle, nuanced variances of good order and catastrophe. I had been in enough forward mooring operations to tell that the incoming chain wasn't freely rattling through the stopper, but was grinding, struggling vehemently, like a chained felon being dragged to the scaffold. Too much noise, too much tension.

Something was not as it should be. Then the awful sound of exploding rapid-fire heavy clanking, followed by urgent shouts, a few sparks and dust filling the air, and I knew the chain had slipped violently back to the water below. More shouting! Silence, like the stillness of the room when the party's over. A fearful, unpleasant sound and, frozen at the foremost hydraulic box, I dreaded the news as a junior cadet came rushing back, my heart racing in fear of his words.

Unsettled, his face ashen, he exclaimed, "The bosun's been hit! Both legs!"

I got close enough to see, without getting too close, like half glancing at a fresh accident on the freeway. They grouped around my friend Ben's figure, lying prostrate and listless on the deck surrounded by anxious eyes. I sensed the vibration of the engine far astern as the *Lyria* slowly backed away, the mooring aborted. A boat came to take him ashore, and I never saw him again. A solemn tone imbedded itself in my mind as the night dragged on and the days followed. The rope holding the chain under tension had rendered on the drum end and let loose the flying steel chain about the fo'c's'le, striking Ben on the way, before disappearing back through the AKD in a rushing trip to perdition. A few of the crew voiced their disdain of a cadet handling the drum end, grouping us all in their contempt. It was hard to comprehend how the sea could be so hostile to humans the way it most commonly is. Winches and chains—no place for amateurs.

THE ISLAND of St. Croix is today one of the US Virgin Islands, but remote from the glamorous stereotype. It has beaches and hotels, though not as many, nor as well frequented as its neighbor, St. Thomas.

It had a problematic history over the centuries, changing hands between several Europeans empire builders scything their way through the Caribbean, crushing the imported other-peoples to make sugar. However, that history should not just be the grappling, pugnacious explorers and men in uniform, without mentioning the people who they brought and broke. Perhaps the most famous citizen was a lady named Annie de Chabert, born on the island in 1908. In contrast to any stereotype or constraint, Annie became a mother, political figure, church worker and civic leader. She purchased large property estates on the south side, away from the capital, Christiansted. In 1965 she sold a large tract of land to the American company, Hess Oil. A year later they had constructed a refinery which grew in volume until, in November 1979, when the *Lyria* arrived, its capacity reached six hundred fifty thousand barrels per day, making it one of the largest in the world.

We arrived from Nigeria, relieved to find a conventional port where we might walk ashore. In a moment of uncharacteristically good fortune, somebody of a generous demeanor deemed each cadet receive one watch off duty, which for me meant freedom from lunchtime until breakfast the next morning; a rare gesture of charity. What charm the island exhibited from our perspective had been sucked out by the refinery and aluminum plant next door, so we set out to Christiansted, a fifteen-minute cab ride over the low hills. No planning, no packing, no monetary outlay; there we were, the unexpected tourists.

The town's eighteenth-century style produced a mix of Caribbean and Danish: solid stone buildings in pink and pastel colors, with red roofs and cobbled streets. With a population of three thousand, it was a place that tourists who sidestepped the beaten track might stay for a few days. They found little to see, following the scuba diving lessons, duty-free purchases and beach. We walked around the King Street area and discovered naught we needed, so headed for the hotel bars on the boardwalk, overlooking the modest harbor and Protestant Cay. It was a dreamy, idyllic afternoon, so close to yet so far from the *Lyria*'s giant pumps engaged in their hectic, strident business.

We drank the sunny afternoon away with no fear of a summons to work, and since we were there with nothing else to do, we continued as the evening overtook the day. As the bar tab grew, I lost my tenuous relationship with reality. I sensed dinner occurred during the evening, but we ended up sipping Black Russians with the Caribbean waters lapping by our feet. By late evening I was intoxicated, perhaps more drunk than ever before or since. Through my hazy memory I missed the ground coming up to meet me, but remember sitting wearily on the curb—not quite in the gutter—as someone hailed a cab back to our floating home.

I made it back in drunken shamefulness, and onto the forenoon watch at eight a.m., like a bloodhound with a hangover. I staggered around the *Lyria*'s deck in a Frankensteinian stupor until noon, when the twelve-to-four found me lying down completely out of energy and interest. I sense what you're pondering. There I was with a free afternoon on a semi-attractive Caribbean island and the whole experience dissolved in seafront bars. In life, as in all deep mysteries, people are difficult to define. That's just the way I am, finding substantive satisfaction in such accomplishments. I knew I could never make a worthy tourist in the traditional sense, and ultimately spare time is time for doing what you want. So is sticking needles in your eye, but I wouldn't recommend that.

EVENTUALLY, I unenthusiastically endured the second of my two weeks of engine room familiarization. As the world of shipping hurtled towards a new era of corporate consolidation, they considered combining the two departments (deck and engine) in the forlorn hope of saving money; the cost of manning being second only to fuel in running the *Lyria*. It was nowhere near realization in 1980, at which time the engineers remained split between two contrasting methods of resolving the puzzle of spinning an enormous bronze propeller behind something that big. Steamships were my life so far, but they were a dying breed. The inexorable growth of ship size since the War, and then the closure of the Suez Canal, required propulsion units able to produce an incredible 40,000 horsepower, and only the steam turbine could accomplish it, but while consuming vast quantities of oil. The boiler burned fuel and then transferred the heat produced into circulating boiler water. They used the steam to power a turbine that produced the mechanical energy to spin a shaft and propeller.

So, I rode the elevator down eight floors. Opening the door, the overwhelming sensations were heat, noise and the smells of sweat, hot lube oil and heavy fuel oil. Then began coffee and a handover in the freezing control room, to which I lent nothing and understood less. Fifteen minutes later the fiver took me on a tour. Where better to begin than about a hundred feet across from the control room at the vast cliff face of the dark silver boiler, reaching from the burners below to out of sight above. Standing close was unbelievably, searing hot, but you could squint inside and see the roaring, burning fuel, and beyond that envision the tubes with their boiling liquid rising to a steam drum and onwards towards the superheater. I stepped hastily away to avoid burning my face.

We walked the gratings, our hands sliding along the glistening smooth handrails, to the feedwater pumps, the condenser, the giant main circulation pump, the evaporators and down to the turbine flat; everywhere the same dull, light machinery green, as if to soothe our psyches. There, the dominant sensation was a low, rumbling hum and the vibration of the gods; not violent, but smooth and enormously strong, the power to rotate the giant propeller. The gearbox straddled the shaft, and to one side the high-pressure turbine and the other the low-pressure turbine. From the rear of the gearbox sprang the shaft, twenty-four inches in diameter, spinning seemingly forever[15], mesmerizing and wince-inducing up close. Even with dozens of machinery pieces, the enormous engine room appeared nearly vacant, everything dominated by the boiler.

Automatic sensors and alarm systems covered many areas, but human hands and eyes still had a role to fulfill. All that machinery; a large, roaring steel bag of angry monsters, spinning, boiling, bouncing with electricity, steam and power. It was a hostile environment in which to work, no doubt, overseeing high temperatures and pressures. I respected them for that. It was no place for indifference. All engineers have dreadful stories of misfortunes in this place of controlled violence: stories of boiler explosions while firing up, overheating due to lack of water circulation, exhaust gases catching fire, high-pressure steam leaks (superheated steam, alive and active, burns instantaneously at 400°F), and electrical shocks. Danger was everywhere.

The age of steam was dying. Giant motor engines were coming, consuming more lube oil, requiring more maintenance, but more thermally efficient and, this was the kicker, much more fuel efficient. These engineers would have to move on, or relearn. But for my week in the

---

15 Even in port, they engage a small electrical motor to turn the propeller shaft slowly, ensuring uniform cooling and lubrication.

pit, everyone acted reasonably and a cold beer after the watch was as good as always, but it all ended up feeling hollow and slightly oppressive. I learned the engine watch was conducting oversight and about as much fun as jury duty. I had taken the decision to be a navigating officer and fortuitously, I had chosen the calm, relaxing darkness of the bridge, avoiding the glaring lights and noise below.

THE SHIP carried a complement of six cadets, which made for heady days undimmed by familiarity. There are social strata in all human life; the man and the woman, the light-skinned man and the dark-skinned man, the rich man and the poor man. Don't blame me; I'm just the guy on the oil tanker. We may have ideals, and mine are healthier than most, but the noblest of all is the abolition of these divides. I lived my life by this principle, yet occasionally failed the standard. Shipboard life required a certain level of innate discipline, beginning at the top and trickling down. The *Lyria* had no Royal Marines. Authority functioned with no one declaring or even recognizing it, which is some kind of praise for the British Merchant Navy in late 1979.

The cadets had a mix of experiences. As senior man, my working time revolved about watch-keeping, while the youngsters chipped and painted. I was apart from them, but on weekends we relaxed. Sunday entailed the captain's inspection, a tradition of time immemorial. For us young men, down below in our own corner of the accommodation block, post inspection became a time to unwind and be youthful and fearless again. We argued about things we didn't understand and, with excessive melodrama, we searched for the answer. Someone, somehow, discovered an alternative to beer, of which I was already fond. With hindsight I can't imagine that the gallon jars of white wine were any more frugal—the beer still cost fifteen cents—but it became the drug of Sunday afternoons, as we lounged around complaining, drinking, listening to music, and writing flagrantly ill-conceived songs.

I read Marx and identified with his explanation of alienation living in a society made of stratified social classes, much as the one I knew. I was a socialist when I didn't know it, then I voted for Thatcher purely on a misconceived egocentric level, but I still didn't understand how I was to better determine my destiny. I had gone down a route seeking nothing but random luck and wherever that might take me.

When we arrived at the Western Approaches, the BBC bellowed from the radio. We found the Pink Floyd topping the charts, and we lonely, alienated young men reveled in the recognition. Someone trekked ashore in Europoort to buy *The Wall* on double cassette and we found that writing our own songs concerning the estranged disaffection of life, much like drilling holes in a sinking ship, was no longer necessary. Sometime later, at the end of another criminally monotonous, four-and-a-half-month voyage, I signed off. Maybe I would request another *L*-boat. Well, right after hell froze over. It had been a troublesome journey, occasionally arresting, rarely enlightening, but often draining. Another year passed, and it had been a good one for the roses. For the *Lyria*, as dull as a trip to the grocery store, there was a happy, John-Smith-sized hole in the complement.

6

To the Rising Sun

1980

How much does he lack himself who must have many things?

—Sen no Rikyū

"YOU WANT me to go to Japan?" I replied to the telephone. That's more interesting. Sign me up for the Land of the Rising Sun. What did I know about the place? Well, my sister had a blue Datsun Sunny, and some found the novelty amusing, but it started every morning, while the English were fitting a square steering wheel to their best seller. Odd and distinctive, it was our initiation into Japanese car ownership. As for the nation, my understanding reached as far as the plot of *You Only Live Twice*, where Sean Connery, incongruously, feigned to be a Japanese fisherman. This was a step into the unknown, but *L*-boats didn't go to Japan, and that was good enough.

Japan and Great Britain discovered each other when the English ship *Clove*, under the aegis of the East India Company, sailed into the port of Hirado, in 1613. The two became the world's wealthiest island nations, similar in size, latitude and climate. They both suffered monarchies but the surrounding oceans, mostly, sheltered them from the political plundering and transgressions of their neighboring continents. The folly of their conceit meant that once rich enough to do so, each bossed and bullied others close and far, and were soiled and polluted by empire. In 1980, although both within the giant orbit of American influence, the popular and industrial cultures intermingled: Union Jacks, red letter boxes and pop music going one way, while cheap, reliable electronics and cars returned.

But Japan plays only a part in this chapter; the leading actor is the remarkable substance methane. I had just failed chemistry, even with my exam prowess and unashamedly stashing what I thought to be the appropriate formulas inside my pencil case. However, I understood the combination CH_4 was a compound of a carbon and four hydrogen atoms, while I learned my trade in the more familiar, and more chemically complicated, hydrocarbon world of petroleum. Right on schedule, my employer flew me to Tokyo. Most of what I heard seduced: technology, nice weather, Japan and cool, clean methane. My goodness, after two supertankers I was ready for a change.

To go east, I took a flight over the North Pole, pausing at Anchorage where they had a stuffed polar bear standing on its hind legs; a rare stunt in nature, I should imagine, but there it was, performing the feat for transit passengers in perpetuity. After a second, long flight I arrived in Tokyo, aching, tired, and alone. The agent greeted me with a bow and smile, and off into the dense, chaotic traffic we rode in a Datsun Cedric with doilies on the headrests, along the newly congested roads, amongst the gleaming buildings of the megacity. I was alone, sleepy and frazzled within a metropolis of ten million persons. Where would I be without the agent? What if we encountered Godzilla? That's the wretched lot of the seafarer traveling alone, relying on others while trapped amid two houses of safety, like a baseball player marooned between bases. They set me down at a spotless business hotel, the name of which eludes me. I had a decent steak in the restaurant with four potato chips arranged in a pyramid—I should have ordered rice. People were friendly and wary at the same time. I reciprocated with my usual awkward charm, but we exchanged few words. I made a mental note of the rather fetching young ladies receding from sight, no matter which way I swung my head.

The next morning the agent drove me to the Chiba Prefecture. The novel and distinctive surroundings impressed: the cars smaller and cleaner, the roads narrower and better organized, the signs written in a kind of slashing-pen hieroglyphics. Our destination, Sodegaura, was famous for its Japanese-German village and flowers, but we drove deep inside the heavy industry, oil refining and chemical processing area built on reclaimed land neighboring Tokyo Bay. Alighting from the minibus at the pier, I stood, breathed in deep, and, transformed from my touristy sojourn, fixed my mind on the toil ahead.

Wheeling my bags along the pier, a gentle rain began in that English style; clean and freshening. I inspected the tall side of this strange black ship, alike, yet unlike those before. It lacked heft, riding unusually high, having just arrived with a full cargo. The hoses through which the cargo flowed were braided metallic, not the typical synthetic rubber, while they underlay the whole manifold with sloping wood upon which a constant stream of water flowed. Inexplicably alien-like, it was slightly menacing. Summiting the gangway, I stepped onto the SS *Genota*, clean and modern, meeting a diminutive man in a dark blue boilersuit and hard hat; recognizably Chinese. Seafaring is an international trade common to men all over the world; it's as if we speak the same language, with distinctive accents. The British crews portrayed a microcosm of the society I lived in, and lessened the sense of adventure. I knew the *Genota* would be wholly contrary.

Departing Sodegaura, I settled in. The ship was modern and comfortable, the accommodation clean and slightly idiosyncratic. I had a fine and spacious cabin aft on the starboard side, so I unpacked and made myself at home; Pat Benatar posed on the wall. They assigned me day work to learn the infrastructure of the methane business, a trade begun by Shell back in 1964 transporting cargoes from Arzew, Algeria, to Shell Haven[16]. In an explanation too straightforward to be true, they extracted gas from the ground and cleaned it, leaving methane, and some trace elements. They liquefied it in a process too complicated for me to understand, and unnecessary for this tale. But I did know that converting methane gas into a liquid at constant pressure requires enormous cooling, when it becomes liquid natural gas (LNG), a clear and colorless fluid existing at minus 163ºC (-260ºF), which is amazingly, extraordinarily cold. The process shrinks the volume of gas six hundred times, making it simpler to store and ship. In this state, LNG will not ignite, a fact that never lulled us into complacency. When reaching its destination, they transformed it back into gas and supplied the homes and industries of Japan.

The *Genota* performed a liner trade, a fixed schedule planned months ahead, supplying one of three terminals in Japan. At the outset, the thought of a prearranged timetable was troubling; one could just about schedule the date and port to sign off. Upon the southern terminus of the route sat the Nation of Brunei, the Abode of Peace. A natural gas industry developed in the early 1960s and my employer had been there ever since. I decided there and then to knuckle down and show enthusiasm in light of all the novelty. I wanted to learn the business, and I longed to experience Japan up close.

---

16   Shell Haven was mentioned in Samuel Pepys's *Diary* of 1667.

A PASSAGE took seven days in each direction, adjusting the speed to arrive at daybreak, which I considered civilized scheduling. The only other modification transpired if one of the seven fleet vessels dry-docked, in which case the other six would accelerate to maintain the timetable. Mostly, like any other tanker, they rode along at 14 knots. These were agreeable, pacific waters to sail, with a pleasant atmosphere of commonly fine weather if you avoided the occasional typhoon.

They built my new home in France, in 1975, incorporating many fine technical enhancements necessary for the cryogenic nature of the trade. LNG causes serious harm to humans, but also damages mild steel. If a leak occurred on exposed pipelines, a sound remedy involved spraying the area with firewater, which speedily froze and sealed the leak. This explained the constant flowing water at the manifold. The real problem with LNG, however, was when it reverted into a gas.

Many declared LNG safe, but even at minus 163°C the liquid boiled, ready to release an enormous cloud of flammable methane. Despite all that water surrounding us, fire is the most feared occurrence on a ship. So, the *Genota* had an abundance of firefighting equipment, including, incredibly, 5 tonnes of exorbitantly expensive liquid nitrogen. Our home, with "LNG" written large on the side, gained everyone's attention when we entered port. They tested igniting small volumes of LNG and the results were spectacular. Nobody had ignited 75,000 tonnes of the stuff, but they assumed the result might be on the Hiroshima scale.

A ship arrived off the mist-shrouded coast of Lumut and hoisted the G-flag[17] with clockwork inevitability at dawn every two days, for years and years, keeping the gas liquefaction plant producing and the ravenous consumption of Tokyo Bay sated, as Japan powered itself to world manufacturing domination. Every two weeks we arrived as the morning

17   "I require a pilot."

haze lifted, revealing a distant, dark green tree line and a conglomeration of silver domes and chimneys engaged in the exotic industrial process we neither understood nor cared about. But the summer-day smell of land and the sight of birds gratified, while I'll never forget the hot, thick tropical air of the morning.

SIX OF us attended stations forward and aft, which despite the technology was conventional. They'd done it before, like ordering fast food at the drive-through. The ship maneuvered from the northeast and pivoted, dragging an anchor into the berth, a three-mile pier astern melding into the distant shoreline. Once in position, we ran wires out to mooring buoys. It was basic work; it was daylight; we were wide awake and professional, and never took the operation for granted. We lived longer that way. After a few hours, on schedule, the *Genota* was all fast in the exact position, her stern abutting the extensive jetty.

Oil tankers commonly transfer cargo through a manifold situated amidships. *G*-boats were special. The elaborate mooring operation had placed the *Genota's* stern cargo decking beneath an enormous steel-and-aluminum praying mantis of a loading arm. It towered high in the air like a king-size Meccano set, surrounded by cool white pipelines hovering above. Upon completion of mooring, the structure—hundreds of feet in height—powered down with the delicacy of hydraulics and its male connection impaled our waiting open female cavity. The two stainless steel units came together in glaring coitus, their hydraulic clamps oozed collectively, completing the connection with a hiss and clunk, mating us to the distant liquefaction plant. We all smoked a cigarette.

After the customary preliminaries that transpire upon any ship's arrival, the *Genota* loaded her water-white, precious, pure energy. Our five capacious empty tanks waited bare, except a few inches of bubbling liquid remaining from the previous cargo, kept to sustain the cold temperature. If they ever warmed, they faced the slow cryogenic shock of cooling down before loading again. And here's the economic winner for transporting LNG: as the liquid boils and evaporates, the gas can either be released to the atmosphere or directed to the ship's boiler, substituting for the thick, messy bunker fuel.

The pipeline from the mantis wound around the accommodation block onto the main deck, depositing its consignment to each tank; all very unsophisticated. We lingered on deck with the astonishing feeling of liquid gas being squirreled around us, but the work was unflustered. The deck lines suffered an aching metamorphosis under conditions the human body could never endure. Upon arrival they would have been blistering hot in the morning tropical sun, but as the LNG plunged inside, they tightened and contracted: their expansion joints shrank but held their rigidity. Ice crystals formed on the exposed pipelines as they cooled and the air condensed upon them, becoming a surreal jacket of snow in the tropics. We scooped and threw snowballs. A few indigenous scary insects, glowing radioactive green having evolved from the liquefaction plant, settled on the ice, safe in their silver booties protecting them from the cold. Lumut was hot, incredibly hot, the Brunei sun baked down, the humidity drained whatever energy we had. We drank water, and then we drank more.

The chief officer manned the control room for the entire operation as the graphs ticked around following temperatures, pressures and tank levels. In an emergency, we had the ability to shut down the shore pumps three miles away. A second, ample— "what happens if I press this"—red button could jettison the steel mantis uncoupling the *Genota* from the terminal, lifting the scaffold free, like the gantry during an Apollo liftoff, clouds of gas billowing uncontrolled into the atmosphere. In the event of a rapid departure, remote controls could release the stern wires while we would heave the anchor, pulling the vessel clear, like a slow-motion giant getaway car.

Cargo transfer lacked nail-biting action and was all the better for it. We completed at three a.m. every time and set sail for Japan, for an already known destination, and the known destination after that.

THE LOUNGE, my favorite place, was congenial, well-appointed and comfortable; my type of spot to relax after work. But I was waylaid one morning by the chief mate with evidence of the previous night's bar tab. I thought I handled it well, but the mate is the mate, and would truck no nonsense. He placed me on the eight-to-twelve watch, which, fortuitously, became a pivotal move. I returned to navigation, although truth be told, it was unadventurous, tracking the meridians north and south like a monotonous background pattern, every couple of days passing a sister ship heading in the opposite direction.

I have never tried to give definition to what I supposed undefinable. On this social watch, I encountered one of those rare people who transform your life while simultaneously crystalizing your thoughts. The watch comprised the third mate, me and the lookout, a Hong Kong Chinaman called C. Zau Ching, the kind of man who never grows old, with a fuzzy mini-bearskin haircut and an open, ever-smiling demeanor. The oriental and the occidental have had a fractured relationship over the years, and I believe they've always resented the knife and fork replacing their inconvenient cutlery. However, Ching and I were to improve the bond, in our own modest fashion. He imparted to me the middle way, while his unique mix of humor, personality and belief imbued in me a new capacity to consider impudent choices.

The Far East has been prevalent in Western popular culture since at least the early nineteenth century. Exotic philosophies, cultural and material exports made their way to Europe for hundreds of years with little issue. More recently, while Europe was allowing every suggestion of nationalism to be trampled by malevolent governments growing ever larger, Asian cultures flourished. They proudly related their warrior past, took part in centuries-old art forms, worshipped their ancestral gods, and participated in brazen nationalism. My England was struggling to find its place, fighting to maintain our interpretation of the sausage, while being transformed and buried under a new European superstate.

Here I was, working with a man from another circumstance and philosophy, and we had time to misuse on the evening watch; time to fill and time to discover, so we talked and talked while he freed my mind from suspicion and indoctrination. In what other business could this happen? Once past the ignorance, enthusiasm and awkwardness, I wanted to know of Ching's society, traditions, religion, family and life in Hong Kong. I soaked up his Eastern wisdom night after night and tried to explain my fears of failure, the need to learn and find another way. He transformed how I thought of the world, one of the turning points of my life. I learned to reject the mantra that I came first. When we played Ping-Pong, Ching won, naturally, but he exposed not one glint of ego or conceit. He played not for the score, but for companionship and the sheer athletic joy of hitting a ball well. With his guidance, I could define myself by character, independence and morality, rather than material standards. I was no longer an angry young man, nor a man who had too many things but little left of himself.

I considered this my post validation for coming to sea. I sought brief immersions in other cultures, to occupy another life, but with the option of scurrying back to safe old Albion when the trick was over. Ching taught me that this need not be the case, like a man made eloquent by his knowledge and experience. Maybe I could live another life in another place. England remained the only country I could remember as home, yet all I had wanted for so long was to leave. That his English wasn't fluent led to more questions and clarifications. Speaking with distinct accents somehow made understanding clearer because there was no requirement to seek some hidden implication. He said what he meant. Ching wasn't the drinking sort. I could now relate to someone who didn't rely on the bar. Almost every acquaintance at sea, if not while working, depended on alcohol. Without beer, Ching became my best friend for four months.

SPARKY, DEPRIVED of work in port, accompanied me ashore in Japan a half dozen times. We thought him strange, but then how could anyone be sane listening to Morse code every day? At the outset the sensation of walking into the country felt like everyplace and anyplace, but in this case, there did seem to be more of the extraordinary than the ordinary. I experienced that curious sensation of being on another, parallel earth again, away from the safe confines of the *Genota*, like walking in space without a lifeline, and for that, almost and always, exhilarating. It is a unique business where you can be working in an English environment one hour, and then abruptly find yourself deposited with little assistance in a foreign place. The lure of the unknown, yet semi-familiar enough to participate in, I found intoxicating and addictive. We couldn't speak the language, nor read the signs, but we negotiated a taxi fare well enough, and the expressions for shopping, eating, drinking and sex are common to every taxi driver the world over.

We didn't care about being distinctive in Japan, because, well, we were. The country is 98 percent ethnically homogenous. The Japanese pride themselves on their distinctiveness, but it's tinged with a considerable slice of westernization: baseball, clothing, fast food, chocolate and popular music, as if another, more luxurious, American invasion had occurred after the war.

Nearer the port, the buildings stood bland. A gray day made them grayer still, while concrete predominated over brick. But then the signs began, the businesses and apartment blocks. I found the electrical wires strung across every street offending, but below this unsightly mess, the Japanese took pains to keep their cities clean, and we respected that. We roamed the cities—Chiba, Negishi, Sodegaura, Senboku and Tokyo—small or large, the abundance of signs and banners were so many garlands of confetti thrown on a model village, but they drew one's attention because of their decorative sense, in the vein of all advertising.

We hooted in triumph when stumbling across an errant English word, as if the Japanese were unconcerned to conjure up an original one. With the signs hanging from strings above the road, or rotating in the gentle breeze, it wasn't what they revealed, or even how they appeared, but that they were unique. The English are a restrained people, and I supposed the Japanese similarly imbued, so perhaps extreme advertising was their expression of liberation, in the same way the English had football hooligans. At night the advertising glared from neon signs, like *Blade Runner*, which didn't quite fuse with the nodding, bowing and general graciousness of the people.

Once within the city center, bicycles proliferated, and those strange, midget trucks they use for carrying everything—*Keitora*, they call them—epitomizing an economy at work, an economy of small businesses, running…stuff, who knows what—from anywhere to everywhere, "just in time," as Toyota demanded. The cars were white, clean and never damaged, as if the state forbade driving a wounded vehicle; a blinding example of groupthink. The road markings were strange, but they meant to protect pedestrians in the narrow, shared streets clogged with signs. The roads remained tidy and smooth, so somebody must have paid taxes. It was a society protecting the ordinary citizen and fostering the common good. I was giddy with wander, my eyes and brain digesting the smallest, most mundane details.

We strolled about the city, taking in the plastic toy shop windows, the ramen restaurants, the cartoons, the pandas, the colors, the iconography, and any pretty ladies, naturally. We bought hand-wrapped Japanese dolls for family gifts because I'd seen nothing comparable. We sat in a coffee shop without understanding a word except the rigorous smiling bow, which we took to be virtuous, and the Sanka was fine. We sat, took our time, eyeing the young waitresses, as you do. Then we paid, received the change and dropped it for a tip, as you do. Five yards down the street she apprehended us and graciously, beaming while nodding, returned the change, perhaps ruminating on our eccentricity. Nobody tips in Japan. Ever!

I discovered an idiosyncrasy of some note: the Japanese were obsessed with vending machines. Now, I like them as much as the next man. They're convenient and cost-effective, though frustrating when the chocolate bar becomes trapped in the mechanism. They had cold drinks in three dozen flavors, hot snacks, cold snacks, spicy snacks, cigarettes, cheap plastic toys, newspapers, condoms, fresh salads, noodles, pornographic magazines, and even beer, for goodness' sake! Yes, apparently, they also sell used ladies' underwear, but those escaped my eye.

A sense of victory washed over us when we stumbled upon a McDonald's sign—something we could understand and eat. How do you ask for the menu when you've arrived from another planet? Helpfully, many restaurants had plastic representations of the selected menu on the street: noodles, vegetables, sushi or steak and fries. Yes, Japanese toilets were incomprehensible, but use the ones in the bar— at least they have a door. We tried the sushi shops where the unwary glimpsed the fresh, gray, raw shrimp lying ready to be quick-fried or steamed, perhaps. But then we sat at the bar, sipped our Suntory beer and they placed the still-raw shrimp on marble with a pinch of wasabi mustard. I spun away to eat another day.

We loved the pint-sized bars in the compact streets adjacent each shopping thoroughfare, with their flowerpots outside and "Asahi" sign in the window. They were clean and quiet and after a drink or two, the suicidal middle-aged businessmen, struggling to wring meaning and redemption from life, were fun enough, in a Japanese way. Beer took their fear away; then it took everything else.

We strolled the Akihabara district, Tokyo's "Electric City," where every shop sold an abundance of paraphernalia, tiny and large. Sparky sought something for his radio, so we ventured in and out at random seeking some specific widget, soaking up the toys, gizmos, radios and domestic appliances, all in a choice of six colors. They fostered and promoted the hi-tech gadgets for a world trying to keep up, and there we were at its epicenter. I gathered all the electronic brochures because each had a Japanese model on the cover—all of a sudden Pat Benatar seemed obvious and dated.

We roamed the Ginza, where its photogenic slickness detracted from its unabashed glitzy capitalism. We walked the busy streets of Tokyo at night, awash with the young in their revolutionary punk attire flouting the otherwise constant adherent conformity, or just watched the girls, all pigeon-toed and innocent, all batting eyes and firm flesh, yet flirtatiously turning to avoid direct eyeball contact. I was momentarily spellbound by gorgeous Japanese women, yet unfulfilled.

The deeper we delved, the stranger it became, negating my long-held prejudices. The Japanese preferred the delicate to the bulky, the simple to the complex and the natural to the artificial. Yet in all that wandering I heard no bamboo flutes or wooden gongs. No, I was in the bustling cities, so we tried the Pachinko parlors, like standing on the stage of a Yellow Magic Orchestra concert—*"Sock it to me, Sakamoto."* Noise was the overwhelming sensation as lonely people fed shiny steel balls into hungry machines, satisfying their gambling obsession. We tried; it was a cumbersome, awkward game, but the popularity of *Pac-Man*, *Space Invaders* and *Asteroids* had not dimmed its ubiquity. People stared, and we stared back, each trying to understand the alien other. The lights shone everywhere and, as always with advertising, excess for excess' sake, or perhaps just bad taste, everyone apparently ignoring the pornography of it all: the manga, *anime, Hello Kitty,* big-eyed girls like so much schoolgirl eroticism. We didn't look closely, but somehow it sank into our consciousness; the nauseating, saccharine cuteness of Japan, a profound insult, milking the lush green pastures of sexism, in 1980 a culture about as sensitive to women as Benny Hill. Every single element conspired to make it feel unique.

Yes, for the accidental sightseer, Japan was a glorious place to visit, with barely time to soak up one revelation before another one jumped out at us. The cities I never observed from a distance. I never knew their fine architecture or innovative civic planning. I never approached from a long broad freeway, or majestic bridge. No, I came from the industrial area, bland warehouses and boxed-lunch factories where real people lived and worked, like stepping into a television documentary. That's the profit of being a seafarer; your view of life was unobscured by the deceit of tourism, like walking through it by accident. I got to see Japan the way it really was, and I am grateful for that. A door cracked open onto another life.

I STOOD to sign off next voyage at Senbuku, when the Old Man relayed a message informing me my mother was in hospital with lung cancer. She had never smoked a cigarette in her life. No one asked my opinion, but they resolved to sign me off in Lumut, where no one ever departed a *G*-boat. I was concerned for my mother, naturally. I took the electric trolley ride down the three-mile pier into the country of Brunei, then a short flight to Singapore, then a long flight home. With hindsight, the voyage's only crime was that no obvious effort occurred—everything flowed with the rigidity of a checklist, like people working in a nuclear power plant. My mother's smile when hearing my voice and feeling my hand, from the strangeness of the hospital bed, was touchingly obvious. Naturally, she had affected me since my first hiccup, right up until her socialist views, reflected in the *Daily Mirror*, influenced my new, sensible politics. I remember taking the train with my father to see her, and all that stress and heartache was gladly without economic distress. She underwent all that terrifying surgery and rehabilitation and we never received one invoice. Like life itself, I couldn't admit it would end.

But for me it felt as if my life had entered a new phase. Japan opened my eyes to an entire world of excitement and I needed to see more. I never saw Ching again, but we have kept in touch these thirty-five years. He remains in Hong Kong with his wife and kids and, as far as I can tell, has had a full and happy life. I wonder if he ever knew he had changed mine. But this is the critical plot point of my story. Ching had ended my slough of despondency. I wanted to reach out to the world and find whatever was in my destiny.

7

Learning to Drive

1981

For the things we have to learn before we can do them, we learn by doing them.

—Aristotle

WITH THE generosity of my employer I returned to England from Brunei three weeks early. St. Thomas' Hospital is one of those prestigious British institutions the nation takes for granted, while publicizing the sins of its disagreeable architecture. But the hospital has been providing health care to Londoners—essentially free—since the twelfth century. It's on the South Bank, ironically, a brief walk from my employer. The rebuilding of the 1970s left it clad in white tile, which had the unfortunate characteristic of always looking in need of its next power wash. This, coupled with a location opposite the Houses of Parliament, led to its visual criticism.

My mother lay comatose on the hospital bed, having had a lung removed. It was unnerving to view someone I knew as resilient now made fragile; she held my hand, and I trusted it gave her strength. Oddly, I found myself hostage to the requirements of others: Shell and my mother's misfortune. The two had contrived to send me from one side of the world to the other in an extravagant display of corporate largesse. I wasn't ungrateful—I was eager to be at her side—but the alacrity of it surprised me. And my mother? She lived, deservedly, for another thirty-eight years.

In the fall of 1980, I revisited college in South Shields, as the grim winter set in and dragged us through it until March, instilling further misery, our demeanor matching the gray, gloomy skies. It was weather in which you huddled over and pulled your collar high. I had my own, bite-sized college box, a smaller version of a cabin. But no matter, it was comfortable, nearly new and clean enough. Harry Dobbs was there, so it was like getting the band back together again; I contemplated a sociable six-month stretch. I recognized a few others, and those I didn't I soon got to know.

I had completed the correspondence courses, but before me stood a long list of new academic challenges, accomplished without the aid of a calculator, and nautical matters that supertankers had ill prepared me for. Several episodes made this a propitious time of learning. First, the plan was to sit for the Class III Deck Officer license (Second Mate). This filled us with the realization we were to use our time earnestly and reduce social drinking activities. But I had bought a car—used, naturally—a navy blue Mk III Ford Cortina for £900, about as middle-England as it was possible to be. Some, like Harry, effortlessly connected to other genders, while for me, less educated in the mating rituals, it was the hardest thing in the world. However, guided by his word-to-the-wise understanding of women, I did well enough, and he copied my mathematics. The car provided the bonus prestige the female population held in some esteem. I began the protocols of dating Sarah-Jane, another cadet, a dark-haired bohemian type, all long scarves and flowing hair. She had not the ignominy to ask of love as I unhooked her complex mechanism. It was just sex, usually in the back of the Cortina, all groans, whimpers, exposed breasts, jammed zippers, splayed legs and ineptitude. It began complicated, but with practice became straightforward. Ching declared that pleasure is transitory, but the less I thought about it, the more I liked it. Strangely, although I didn't pretend to be very proficient, it never became boring. Romance and kind words rarely crossed our minds, but it satisfied to achieve the level of social behavior expected by my peers. One day she told me, "I remember my future life." Right then I knew the female mind worked differently, and more study would be required.

I had a proclivity for exam-taking, so I inhaled the learning jammed down our throats, focusing on what I thought might be required for examination, and neglected the rest. The secret is always to contemplate the examiner's requirements; clear and well-drawn diagrams are helpful, and as it happens, my specialty. I didn't intend to finish top of the class. Whatever scores you obtained, the only outcome was a license, or not. I consider myself pragmatic, or heady with cynicism, if you prefer. In March we took the exams, including Morse code, for heaven's sake. I passed everything; not, I hasten to add, with any concept of flying colors, but just enough. I spent the final two days coughing and spluttering in a steel, house-sized, burned-out box to receive a firefighting certificate, an exercise that made us realize how dreadful it might be for real.

When it was over, Harry and I laughed goodbye, as if we'd served a three-year stretch in the Scrubs together. I shook his hand and uttered, "Somehow I think we'll meet again." But we never did. Unjustly, I imagined his life dissipated drunk in a bar on a Goa beach, perhaps, but I tracked him down thirty-five years later. He never sailed again, but married and succeeded in a new life ashore in the more affluent suburbs of Newcastle. Few men could ask for more.

So, I had a license; I was an expert on paper. The cramming had paid off; it wasn't just drinking and copulating. I'd achieved the first goal, reminiscent of the man on the back cover of the *Careers Book*. The company called and appointed me to the *Leonia* heading for the Persian Gulf, as if I were going home again. I flew to Dubai with a fourth engineer; its weather and sandy bleakness no longer filled me with wonder. We took a fleeting car ride to Ras al Khaimah, and, late in the evening, boarded an old Westland Wessex, her rotors already whirring. We lifted into the air with a tremendous, deep-thrumming noise, the earphones doing little to ameliorate the deafening din. The exhilaration of vertical flight existed briefly as we set off northwest into the dark skies of the Persian Gulf. The aircraft trembled and clattered at the shock of defying the laws of gravity.

Ten minutes later, circling over the open black sea, we suffered the unnerving sensation of dropping without seeing, until the giant glow of the *Leonia*'s deck lights engulfed us, and we experienced the relief of landing. The door drew open as we sat atop the large "H." Within a few minutes we and our bags were out and, along with everyone else, we turned our backs as the Wessex rose thunderously into the darkness in a storm of savage wind and noise. A moment later it felt strangely quiet, like the peace after a passing tornado. We, and the standby fire crew, filed quietly aft to the comfortably massive white accommodation block towering above, as the aft-facing floodlights darkened one by one, allowing the bridge to see ahead. Here I was, back on the *L*-boats, in the land of Islam, as far from reality as possible, but this time the familiarity somehow reassured.

Captain B. was a genteel chap, understanding, experienced and comforting, like David Attenborough; the sort of man who oozed confidence and composure, yet was tainted with the idiosyncrasies of someone who lived distant from society. Like many seafarers, he was comfortable on a ship, as if he'd long ago crossed some cryptic line, and he knew the way to the bar blindfolded. He assigned me the eight-to-twelve, of course, but in the confined and busy waters, he spent considerable time on the bridge overseeing me. I understood his reticence. School might furnish the tools, but growing up you have to do it yourself, which today might be considered an imperfect manner to run a multimillion-dollar piece of equipment, but that's the Merchant Navy tradition. The *Leonia* headed into the oven of the Gulf. No time for unpacking or sleeping, just working and napping in between standbys. The crew was Hong Kong Chinese, so I was comfortable with that. I could break down the wall between me and Ching, but now, as officer of the watch, I was a little more circumspect, never again to make friends with "the foremast jacks."

Contemplating "responsibility," something strange happened. I felt unwell, but put it down to the climate, food and working hours. Distressed, I bared my chest to the chief mate (the vessel's "doctor"), and he diagnosed chicken pox. At Ras Tanura anchorage he confined me to my cabin, which was the nicest I'd ever occupied: large, comfortable, separate bedroom, lots of wood and easy chairs, and the low-humming refrigerator, ready to be stocked. A real doctor appeared by boat and confirmed it wasn't smallpox, and I was glad of his certitude. My confinement stretched for two weeks while on medication. More significantly, I couldn't work, which was an appealing benefit. I felt uncomfortable not contributing to the common cause, like I had a bit part in my own story, left indulging in solitary vices. I gazed occasionally from my large front-facing windows like a bored passenger wishing he'd booked the Rhine River cruise instead. Finally, we left the Gulf without charisma or interest, and the world was exactly the same as it was two weeks earlier.

OUTSIDE THE Gulf they freed me, and the *Leonia,* from captivity. I was ready and willing to work on the bridge deep-sea. The Old Man let me alone. I know, it's an emotional association with employment, but I was young and exuberant, like a cub waking from hibernation. I set in motion my routine of taking morning sun sights and fixing noon while heading south. This was what I sought, real navigation.

She was fairly new; Harland and Wolff built, a younger sister of the *Lampas,* with all her benefits and faults. And what about the thirty souls onboard, the lonely people who pass unnoticed through life? Well, the staff were professional, cynical and jaded seafarers employed because we were the best, or so we thought. We had British certificates and those centuries of seafaring mercantilism. Instead of commuting to work by rail, we climbed a flight of stairs or took the elevator to the engine room. We'd joined a formulaic voyage, with a fair idea when we could return to reality. The Chinese crew was on a ten-month contract, a long time absent from family or sans any intimate friendship. The new crews from the East; Hong Kong Chinese, Filipinos and Indians were replacing the Europeans across the world's fleets in a dizzying corporate slide to the bottom.

And me? I was finally removing the stabilizers. I had done my chipping and painting; a lot of it. I'd climbed masts, driven cranes, lowered myself on boson's chairs, held stoppers, spliced wire, steered ships and accomplished a thousand other modest tasks that qualified me. All I wanted now was to drive one of these monsters, feel the exhilaration of controlling power, the responsibility of pressing one of the engine-control buttons or twisting a switch to feel this mighty feat of maritime engineering turning. At the time I favored the steady day-to-day predictability. I settled into a life measured in watches, regular sleep, a few drinks and company for dinner, and the evening all alone, me and a watchman, the eyes of the ship. My new rank brought me a wage increase, too; £641 per month.

Those early nights we saw a few lights, and I felt comfortable rather quickly. I over-enthused as a novice does, plotting every radar echo and checking too many compass bearings; the anxiety of the beginner. The science of collision avoidance is both simple and complex; the fundamental maxim states that if the relative bearing is steady, then risk exists. Much depends on the range, and ships alter course, but it's a good place to begin. The world's oceans are large and surprisingly easy to become lost in. I gained a sense of how free it was, and how excellent the visibility could be at night. Seeing lights at twelve, fifteen, twenty miles was not unusual.

Then, on a black East African night, somewhere between Mogadishu and the Seychelles, an apparition crept into our consciousness, "very fine on the starboard bow." Two dim white lights, one above the other. So, here it was; just me and him, ready for a game of chicken. The radar displayed ten miles. Whatever I did, it would not happen with alacrity. The *Leonia*, fully laden, deep in the abyssal water and sluggish as a bear skating on ice, still churned along at 14 knots. Being young and indecisive, I fidgeted, picked up the glasses and looked again. I glanced astern, just in case. What to do? I needed no more bearings; he was fine to starboard of our foremast. The two lights remained unchanged but clearer, and I could faintly discern a red and green. Eight miles, closing, time to act before the rapidly approaching inevitability. I had the feeling of it all going wrong, the sound of grinding steel, the flash of flames and the blinding explosion. Do something, John!

In a jolt of blazing clarity, I deactivated the off-course alarm. Leaving the helm in automatic, I twirled the two-inch course correction dial and aimed twenty degrees to starboard. I stood leaning against the steering column, eyeing the lights growing brighter ahead of me. Nothing happened. I glanced up at the helm indicator and it showed the giant rudder turning 5°, 10°, 15° to starboard, but nothing was happening. My mind screamed, "Fuck! Am I crazy? Why aren't we turning?"

I hoped the fellow I would never see—inexperienced like me—on the bridge of that unknown vessel, didn't at that moment edge to port, keeping me just to starboard. For an interminable time, still nothing happened, and then the slightest change of vibration as the water surge from the propeller flowed across a broader rudder angle, too subtle for anyone to notice. Our darkened masthead moved and the lights of the other vessel drifted to my port, and the *Leonia* finally altered her head, sluggishly, then swifter. The nameless vessel flew twenty degrees to port, and we kept turning. I didn't want this monster to get away from me, like letting your pet rhino loose, so I eased the dial back to port, avoiding vibration. The *Leonia* kept straying to starboard. Was she ever going to stop?

Time dragged on until she finally reverted to our original heading. I settled down, and the stranger that passed in the night disappeared. My minor but first encounter completed, in as clear a textbook manner as could be hoped. I'd met risk of collision and followed the rules and did what I had to do, in what seemed like an ethereal moment where I was seeing myself happen. Well, it was hardly grand opera. The engine being unmanned, I enjoyed my beer alone at midnight with a contented air of budding proficiency.

We charged down the southeast coast of Africa pushed by the mighty Agulhas Current, a welcome free shove when we guzzled 165 tonnes of bunker oil a day. In December 1977 a strange event took place twenty-five miles off the coast near Plettenberg Bay. Crashing through choppy seas on a misty morning came the four-year-old supertanker *Venoil,* carrying 250,000 tonnes of crude oil from Iran bound for Nova Scotia. In a far-fetched, credibility-defying coincidence, at 9:39 a.m., the *Venoil* plowed into her sister ship, *Venpet,* traveling empty in the opposite direction. The *Venoil* heaved its bow into the *Venpet's* side, leaving a gash forty-five feet deep and 180 feet long, just above the waterline. Both vessels burst into flames and the billowing smoke was visible for fifteen miles. Happily, by taking to the lifeboats, and with assistance from helicopters, both crews survived, but the spill formed a slick six miles long and two miles wide.

The inevitable inquiry discovered the two vessels approached on nearly reciprocal courses (the difficult-to-resolve, nearly-head-on situation, as I had encountered). The fully loaded *Venoil* made small adjustments to starboard. The *Venpet,* empty on passage to the Gulf, incredibly, made small adjustments to port (as I had feared), whether believing he was only increasing the starboard-to-starboard passing distances, or, as many have judged, to cause the two sisters to pass close enough for a friendly wave, no one seems to have determined. Reality is seldom an impediment to human recklessness.

LEAVING THE Cape's radar range, we returned to deep sea, that long Atlantic passage to skirt the coast of Africa, and into the Western Approaches. I savored the final years of celestial navigation. In a short while the miracle of user-friendly satellites arrived and transformed everything, but in 1981 only three simple instruments were required to travel the oceans: the sextant, the chronometer and the compass. At that perfectly divine moment called noon, when the sun reached its local zenith, latitude could be derived without a clock, or even a vague sense of the time, but only the comforting grip of a sextant and the magic angle between me, the horizon and the heavenly body.

Longitude was different. It wasn't feasible for a ship to go to sea without a functioning chronometer and identify the longitude until the late twentieth century. The word *chronometer* was first used by the watchmaker Jeremy Thacker, in an effort to solve the problem set by the Longitude Act of 1714, promising a remarkably high reward of up to £20,000 for a solution. The British government realized the problem, and that the only sensible resolution—however preposterous it might seem—was a clock usable at sea. They tested countless devices and procedures, mostly unconvincing or impracticable. Jonathan Swift, in *Gulliver's Travels*, compared finding the longitude with solving the impossibility of perpetual motion, while my hero Isaac Newton considered it "the only problem that ever made my head ache." Despite the challenge, the marine chronometer, or at least its first realization as a portable but accurate timepiece, was developed by John Harrison in the eighteenth century. Ships have been using the decedents of his creation ever since.

Plenty of ships sailed the oceans before chronometers. They could determine their latitude as readily as I did at noon, but the astute reader will have noticed that half a position would never be enough. The British, as they cultivated their nascent empire, lost more men to not knowing the longitude than they did to battles in the seventeenth and eighteenth centuries, which goes to show how world-shattering Harrison's achievement has proven to be. The *Leonia* had two chronometers, safely tucked away in a sunken wooden cupboard as part of the chart table fixtures. The glass window above allowed us to view them, like sacred instruments, read without disturbance.

It's commonly thought the chronometer solved the entire problem of determining longitude. If we ascertain the time where we are, then the difference to another place (typically Greenwich) is our longitude, east or west. A rather convenient "exact" time to discover at sea is when an astronomical body crosses our meridian ("noon," for the sun). So, it might be convenient while taking the noon latitude, if we know the exact time of the occurrence, then we also have our longitude.

I once saw John Wayne determine latitude and longitude in a movie with one sextant reading, but I suggest the script contained some artistic liberation from reality. When viewed through the sextant the sun creeps higher, then hangs momentarily, before falling again—only after do you realize that was noon. No, for longitude in 1981 we needed a more complex and more accurate method that involved some celestial navigation. For now, I want you to know I loved navigation, both terrestrial and celestial, and the satisfying resolution of this puzzle can make your head spin.

WHEN I was ten, someone gave me a cartoon book detailing authentic British Second World War exploits. One story concerned a raid on the coast of France in February 1942. I gleefully digested the airborne commando foray, flipping the pages, reading of English derring-do: "C'mon, boys, let's go get 'em," as our pencil-lined heroes mowed down the scowling enemy in funny helmets, defending a large Gothic house before the French village of Bruneval. The raid was a success, taking key parts of the Würzburg radar array, and then escaping down the cliffs and returning home. The whole raid took only ten pages. My father had visited a few miles south thirty-seven years before me, stepping from a ship at Sword Beach on D-Day+3 of the Normandy landings as a young Royal Engineer. I so wanted to walk the cliffs in fine sunlit hours, saunter the overgrown defenses of the Atlantic Wall and imagine, as difficult as it might be, just what it was like in that time of bravery and lunacy.

Bruneval is a farming village on the bump in the coastline called Cap-d'Antifer, just north of Le Havre. The port comprised two berths lying nestled at the foot of the vertical white cliffs. There I was on the *Leonia*, standing on deck, looking up, and had I been taller, I would have seen that gothic house, now without the radar.

WHILE AT Cap-d'Antifer, my monarch, Elizabeth II, traveled ahead to Sullom Voe, officially opening the largest oil terminal in the United Kingdom on May 9. The first crude oil, Brent Blend, had arrived in 1978, but the place was still under construction. It was a cloudy day, and the Queen wore a knee-length, light blue coat and a white hat with matching blue band as she toured the facility. BP, the terminal operator, were later blamed for what transpired. The construction used a significant number of Irishmen (as has been common in England for some time), but unbeknownst to them, the Provisional IRA infil- trated the workforce and detonated a 7-pound device inside the power station—while Her Majesty strolled on royal walkabout. Few people heard the explosion, and it was not until evening that the police con- firmed the incident. Although the full force of the attack had been diminished—as much by the terrorist's own inadequacies than any- thing else—it remains the only IRA attack in Scotland.

By the time the *Leonia* arrived, the incident no longer interested the press. The Shetland Islands are stark and devoid of any vegetation other than wild grass, moss and lichen. Trees appear banned by fiat, but the extensive sheep population appreciates the pasture. The weather is oceanic, i.e., miserable. Since that first Brent Blend crude oil arrived in 1978, Sullom Voe has become one of the largest terminals in Europe.

We approached the strange, subarctic and ancient place, from the north. The pilots took us south through the Yell Sound, the sort of undemanding, yet tricky, navigation made obvious by the radar bouncing off the steep-sided, clear-cut islands. The water is exceptionally deep and there's little chance of running aground if the engine continues to spin, as it always did. The thousand-acre terminal's throughput has fluctuated over the years, but it keeps its pre-eminence in the world of commerce for one very important reason, which I shall explain.

There are hundreds of discrete crude oils, and they keep finding more. Each have their own characteristics, dozens of which affect the requisites of diverse refiners. Some are heavy, or dense, and produce the weightier components of the refined barrel. Others are light, less dense, and produce the more expensive components, like gasoline. Some crudes have more sulphur and are categorized as "sour," while the less sulfurous, ironically, are called "sweet." Some crudes are acidic, some have more salt, some are high in trace metals, all detrimentally affecting the refining process. Considering all these attributes of so many crude oils, how is it the financial pages quote only one price each day? Well, the assumption is, if you know the characteristics of each grade (called an assay), then you can ascertain its value in comparison to another, so a light sweet crude oil will probably value higher than a heavier sour alternative. The market, influenced every day by supply and demand, impacts everything, but crude oil is the world's most actively traded commodity, so no one can track every individual grade. The solution is to publish the market value of "benchmark" crude oils—typically ones commonly traded on a day-to-day basis. The benchmark determines the general market trend while we can establish each crude's value in relation to the benchmark by its individual physical attributes.

One of those benchmarks is Brent Blend. Others are the OPEC Reference Basket, Dubai, Oman and West Texas Intermediate (WTI). The only other defining factor of the daily price (after the market and the characteristics) is location. Benchmarks have locations where the price is established, and any other place of sale will have a transport cost involved. The geographical location for WTI, for example, is the lonely town of Cushing, Oklahoma, known as the pipeline crossroads of the world. The location for the benchmark Brent Blend is Sullom Voe, so it is the market value of one barrel of Brent Blend crude oil at Sullom Voe which is the price you typically see every day in the English newspapers.

AS WE wended our exit from the Voe, the latitude and cold made getting out of bed difficult. We set off for the Florida Straits via a great-circle to a point off the most eastern tip of Canada, a place unmistakably named Mistaken Point, for the sailors who mistook it for Cape Race in earlier times, turning north too early and running into treacherous rocks, like so many unmarked gravestones. Navigation was of the intermittent variety, since the North Atlantic's suffused gray monotony mostly hid the sun and stars. Great-circle navigation is the practice of navigating along the minor arc between two points on the surface of a sphere found on a plane that passes through the center of that sphere. Weather and inconvenient fragments of land can affect the credibility of a great-circle, and to be worthwhile, the track along the arc needs to be dependable. We could no longer draw the straight line on our favorite Mercator chart, since that projection has the benefit of fulfilling a constant course, the one thing a circle isn't.

One morning a few days before Cape Race, I pinpointed two objects crossing from my port side. In the vast shades of gray mingling sea and sky, I took a bearing of the dim lights to better appraise my responsibilities. It is a truth of oceanic life that one can steam for days, or weeks, without observing another maritime object, and when at last it appeared, there they were, on a steady bearing. I often wondered where people were going. I had a bad feeling from the start. It was a slow, drawn-out crossing situation. I kept strolling onto the wing as they came into focus: two large fishing vessels in tandem, butting at a good speed into the choppy seas, bouncing up and down as they advanced. Glad not to be a fisherman, I considered the options. According to law, I was to stand on, maintain course, and allow them to safely maneuver around me. But they kept on. Encountering another vessel at sea, each of which have obligations, is a curiously distant, yet personal affair. One's mind, by which I mean each watch keeper, at some level, must take the measure of the other, without ever communicating deeds or intentions. It's like playing chess by remote control. You can see the moves, but you never comprehend your opponent's needs, experience or competence. You believe yourself to be professional, well-trained and conscientious, but what about him? Here's the scary thought: Is he awake? Is he sober? Is he even there?

Lacking a cooperative giant squid floating up from the abyss seeking a high-calorie snack, I contemplated the alternatives. They were clear now, even without the binoculars, four miles distant. I took up the Aldis signaling lamp, a trusty method of gaining attention in dim light. It was overcast and dirty gray, so I gave them a few five-pulse shots. They ignored me, or their bridge lacked a human eye. Were they on auto-pilot and unmanned? I understood their nonchalance in such wide-open waters, but there we were, enormous and real, the super-tanker bearing down on them.

Slightly sullied by having to respond, other than standing on, I already knew how the *Leonia* handled. As if in some nightmare apparition of bad timing, the Old Man appeared for his morning coffee. He didn't like it either. I used the forward electric whistle (the aft steam one would have shaken the dead). Five blasts, still no response. I loathed the conundrum that faced me. It was awkward and unnecessary, but I understood the burden; I didn't need a Master Mariner standing beside me. It was his ship, but it was my watch. I hadn't called him, but now he saw what I saw, a situation developing badly, like a patient on life support. I told him, a second before he told me, in my most indifferent, proficient-like manner:

"Looks like I'm going to starboard, Captain."

Turning to port was against the spirit and intent of the law, and we no longer had sufficient room anyway.

"Yes, make it now, Third Mate."

OK, I paraphrased that. I put the watchman on the helm and began a long, slow, complete circle to starboard, a maneuver for wasting hours of our passage. The fishing boats continued their course oblivious, to Quebec, perhaps. *C'est la vie.*

We made it into the Gulf of Mexico, battling the Gulf Stream whose axis runs a few miles off the Florida Keys, so smaller ships creep inside, skirting the islands, catching the countercurrent. But the *Leonia* wasn't about to drive down that narrow back road; we were too big, too heavy, and too corporate to run the risk. I disembarked a few weeks later in Barbados, from where I flew back to England and placid domesticity. I might say "home," but I'm unclear if it was anymore. Home is where you're accepted unconditionally, but too many people had forgotten me. When I arrived, I heard Sarah-Jane had been calling, corroborating my sexual orientation was predictably middle-of-the-road. So, we cohabited in sexual congress, and watched cricket while the savage fiscal doings of Thatcher's government exorcised the England I thought I knew.

WE DRIFTED apart when time came to work again, but then Shell, as corporations do, made one of those small, bottom-line decisions that have a habit of ruining people's lives. I imagined the conversation around a large oval table:

"We need to resize our staffing potential," or something in that vein.

"We completed the eighteen-month study and with our right-sizing growth showing signs of negativity, we believe a slackening of employment demand may be beneficial," while pouring a decaf and choosing the donut with the sprinkles on top.

"So, what sort of negative impact do we need to consider?" spoke the overweight, middle-aged man at the head of the table.

The young, tall man standing by the whiteboard turned over a leaf revealing the number: 200.

I suppose it should have been a complete psychological devastation, but it wasn't. This wasn't a rehearsal, it was life. I was unemployed. They had seen me through college and financed my license, but when you receive such emasculating news you are bitter, if only for a while. Eventually, equanimity washed over me. I was twenty-two years old and unemployment rates in the UK were spiraling to a dizzying 12 percent. What to do standing on the edge, other than find a treasure map and dig, or step into the dreadful waiting jaws?

8

Into the Darkness

1981–1982

If we do not find anything very pleasant, at least we shall find something new.
—Voltaire

WAS THAT it, then? I once venerated my employer—more out of duty than devotion—but that was when they paid me. Everything I knew of seafaring and a maritime lifestyle derived from them. Oh, I'd heard of life in other companies, but Shell were the standard, leading us all to nirvana. I believed. The corporation manipulates everyone: customers, shareholders, but mostly, employees. Now they had hewn my psyche at the commencement of a career, as another corporation had my father in the autumn of his. When we were young, he explained the story of each trinket in his box of foreign memorabilia (ivory idols and Gurkha knives), and it impinged upon me a desire to travel. I never thought of it again until I saw the man on the cover of the *Careers Book*.

It might have been worse if I possessed responsibilities, but I had no one and no mortgage. Still, it emasculates because society no longer considers you a functioning member. To live in a capitalist culture, one needed to contribute; this remained the doctrine of Thatcherism. Sure, the UK had an economic safety net, but few believed it a legitimate lifestyle.

It is the very nature of the capitalist mode of production to overwork some workers while keeping the rest as a reserve army of unemployed paupers.[18]

And he's right, isn't he? I don't recall considering a profession other than the one I had chosen. I sensed that at twenty-two it was too late to change, which was inaccurate, but I took the new circumstances as a challenge to better myself. I had enough to avoid the soup kitchen, eking out an existence, and living off others. It was shockingly easy to do nothing, but at the core of my thoughts, at the heart of every conversation and internal consideration was the ultimate agenda: eventually I had to find work. I wrote letters to prospective employers, domestic and foreign, and Uiterwyk Corp. (of whose existence I was unaware) invited me to the city for an interview. I should have explored further, but clocks were ticking; the economic funds clock, the tax-avoidance law[19] and the frustration of living in England. I still had that urge to travel, to seek the unknown, a missing part in a young man's life that unemployment jarred back into reality.

Dutch entrepreneur Jan Christiaan Uiterwyk (1915-2005) had moved to America after the war, become a citizen occupied in international trade, and founded "The Company." He purchased his first ship in 1967, and at The Company's height owned fourteen vessels and chartered another twenty-five, running from the US Gulf Coast to the Mediterranean, West Africa and the Middle East. It was a liner

---

18   Karl Marx.
19   UK law allowed seafarers to earn tax free through a complicated equation of time in the country against time out.

business—regular routes with schedules—specializing in the style of port the new, burgeoning container ships didn't trouble with, carrying fruit, general cargo, boxes, cars, bagged food, personal belongings and anything else that could be squeezed inside.

Bevis Marks is one of the ancient narrow streets of London, nearby St. Mary Axe, which traces its heritage to the fourteenth century, for goodness' sake. Its glass and concrete edifices tower over the historic ways and roads with their wagon-wheel and footpath origins when the city was darker. The interviewer revealed they required a navigator on their general cargo ship, the MV[20] *Victoria U.* I had no experience of their business, but he offered me employment as second mate for $1,400 per month. The reasons he tendered the commission, I suspect, were because I possessed a British license and I'd served a worthy apprenticeship. If I were cynical, I might add I was bipedal. He called her "a mature vessel"; having once carried passengers, she had a well-appointed accommodation, and he was sure I would find it interesting. I accepted his remarks with skepticism, but it was work, and I needed it.

ON OCTOBER 5, 1981, I flew to Philadelphia. No agent greeted me on arrival, so I hailed a cab and we drove though the less noteworthy lots of the city to the mockingly named Beach Street. Darkness descended as we trundled along the uneven road, past broken railings, and the detritus of urban decay. We meandered towards the Delaware beside some waste ground, and arrived alongside the small cargo ship, all upright booms like giant straws in a gray bathtub, resting against the quay, her forward lines tight, hanging on the flood tide.

She sat alongside a lay-by berth for reasons I never understood, perhaps resting after exertion. Two days later we set southward. Everything was unfamiliar. I had a putty-colored cabin, which I cleaned to meet

---

20   Motor Vessel.

some kind of standard. It was small, functional, and void of any luxuries. I shared facilities in a bathroom down the companionway, except for a small basin in my room. She had a cosmopolitan complement. The young American chief mate I quickly liked, and the captain—who mumbled as if unsure of his own words—hailed from the Portuguese archipelago of Madeira. To know him was to wish you hadn't bothered. The engineers were British and Yugoslav, the electrician Burmese and the crew, dressed as if gathered by handing out flyers on a third-world building site, were Ghanaian. The aged chief, third and Sparky all had wives aboard, with Sparky's acting as chief steward; possibly out of boredom. Like everyone else, she did her job, but didn't do a very good job of it. The ship was old, dirty and cramped. A stark and military-like ambiance overwhelmed. I'm not a proponent of capital punishment, but if any ship needed to be put out of its misery, it was the *Victoria U*. And, naturally, she had never carried passengers.

WE NEGOTIATED a half dozen US ports, while meeting a schedule to load numerous cargoes from small, obscure shippers. Times were changing. The ubiquity of the container[21] meant shipping lines built vessels of ever more capacity to carry many more boxes to new outsized ports, rendering the docks of another age redundant. For anywhere not near one of these, the solution was to ship and truck—"intermodal," they called it—or find an obscure line like The Company still operating a niche business.

We skirted Florida a half mile off the Keys, catching the countercurrent; none of that corporate tanker nonsense here. The *Victoria U* was sometimes full, sometimes half-full, of an incredible variety of goods. At Panama City we loaded rolls of paper, cars, boxes, bags of food and

---

21 The container, or "TEU" (twenty-foot equivalent unit), has some claim to being the most influential economic invention of the twentieth century.

a hundred other packages of various shapes and sizes. In port I squandered time leaning over the open hatch coaming, appearing suitably concerned about a business as alien to me as midwifery. On tankers we often faced a continuous bustle of exertion and endless apprehension as the oil rushed in or out. Here, life slowed, and I contributed little until departure.

New Orleans had often played second fiddle to the mighty Texan, experiencing a commercial challenge when Houston built the Ship Channel, giving easy access to the Gulf. Both ports had a considerable concentration of petrochemical and other heavy industries, so the city lobbied the federal government for its own quicker, leaner outlet to the Gulf, rather than the twisting, turning, silting, giant river that personifies and circles it. Construction began on a bypass with a new deep-draft route, completed in 1965, called the Mississippi River Gulf Outlet canal[22], forever afterwards known to the locals as "Mister Go." There I was then, standing on the bridge with a pilot and helmsman, cruising along a wide canal with flat, wet greenery for miles on either side. It's straight and painless to navigate, its reason de jure. After some seventy-five miles the canal joins the Intracoastal Waterway, and heads left into the backyard of the city's industrial heartland, where we tied up at the end of North Galvez Street, as close as a ship could berth to the city center.

We spent days unloading boxes, then backloading other boxes. I had identified some startling comparisons with life before, both worthy and unworthy. On the debit side the *Victoria U* smelled, like any

22 Water breached the levees along the MRGO and the Intracoastal Waterway in twenty places during Hurricane Katrina in 2005, directly flooding most of St. Bernard Parish and New Orleans East. Storm surge along the MRGO was a leading suspect in the three breaches of floodwalls on the Industrial Canal. Three months before, a storm surge expert called MRGO a "critical and fundamental flaw" in the city's defenses. After the storm, an investigation showed that MRGO intensified the first surge by 20 percent, raised the height of the water wall three feet, and increased the velocity of the surge in the funnel region between the MRGO and Intracoastal Waterway. The canal was blockaded in 2009.

other industrial place, perhaps. But this one had a potpourri of odors: wood, cooking, rotting food, sewers and the strange smell of old, like your grandparent's basement. No one remembered what happened there long ago, but some sense of it remained, like a murder-mystery play after the curtain had closed. On the positive side, my mind draws a blank.

Being time to buy necessities, Sparky and I rode the bus to the Canal Street shopping area. I'm not a fun shopper, but the disoriented task in an alien environment made it surprisingly undemanding. Money squandered, plus a coffee and burger, we stepped out feeling content, a plastic bag of cheap goodies in hand, and our bellies full. I paused at the curb. Sparky, like an absent-minded professor, chatted weirdly as he did about nothing in particular, when unexpectedly I felt contact from behind and stumbled forward, into the thoroughfare, as a bus sped past six inches from my face. I wouldn't imagine I had time to think, let alone regain my balance, but in a precious split second a hand seized my jacket and held me in suspension until the rapid-transit wall of aluminum sped past in a rush of advertising and blurred glass. Then, with air before me, the hand released and the sign flashed "WALK." I exhaled and gazed around, groping for an answer, and tailed the crowd crossing the street.

Sparky hadn't noticed, jumbled as he was in the crowd. We strode across Canal Street and he asked if I felt okay; maybe he noticed my ashen countenance and weary, stumbling gait. I kept my thoughts to myself. Not a soul would understand anyway, like I'd just seen Bigfoot, but I knew something or someone had just saved my life, saved me from being swept away by the speeding city transport in a whirr of metal, flesh and blood. The incident redelivered life to me as a mysterious entity we all shared. Was it the hand of God? That line of thought raised more questions than it answered, but I couldn't let it go. I had been angry in my youth, but now I felt contemplative. Maybe one day, serendipitously, I might be hopeful.

I FELT I'd consigned something very personal on Canal Street, but even sleeping with a flood of unsettling dreams, the work continued. We squeezed through the Inner Harbor lock, built for another shipping age, and raced down the Mississippi—an incomparable, brown, winding sheet of barge-filled water—into the Gulf of Mexico.

Texas City, like perdition, I suspect, was ruthlessly unattractive, where the lights, smoke and flares of the gray refineries that dominate its southern half burned like a never-ending firework display. Mister Go's competitor, the carcinogenic Houston Ship Channel, is a widened and deepened natural waterway, created by dredging Buffalo Bayou and Galveston Bay. The shockingly industrial channel is lined with terminals and berths, including Exxon Baytown and Shell Deer Park. The Turning Basin was once the port's largest shipping point, and the most upstream place to which ships could traverse, although it had grown rather quaint by 1980.

The *Victoria U* slipped under the freeway and made fast to load endless white bags of rice adorned with the "US Aid" logo. The employment of longshoremen proved too expensive at night, so we walked along the dock to the International Seaman's Mission for a good, hearty burger. When I see pictures of the center today, the Filipinos and Indians, the only customers remaining to frequent it, seem so sad, as if all the excitement has been sucked from the industry. All that's left are the flags, a phone call home and God.

The following night's excursion escalated our imagination, as we circumvented the warehouses, traversed the railway tracks and turned onto Clinton Drive, where we found the gray, austere, boxy building: "Hong Kong Disco"[23] with "SEAMEN" screaming in pink neon from the roof. The girls were from Vietnam. I was content with the scenery wherever their origin. Houston, with fine weather, was congenial enough. Most of all I appreciated the high cost of American labor.

HDW Hamburg built the *Rotte* in 1960, a year after I was born. In 1979 she became the ship I knew, measuring 8,921 gross tons (which, remember, is a gauge of volume), and could carry 12,856 deadweight tonnes of cargo. Amidships sat a white house, wrapped around the engine room, and atop that a black, red and white funnel with a large "U" attached. She had three hatches forward, and two aft, each attended by a forest of wire-driven derricks. Right aft above the propeller were the crew quarters, dark and miserable, like room 101, where few entered voluntarily. She was conventional and seaworthy in a visual sense, if not always the legal one. She was long, slender and traditional, in a nautical manner; a dull sample of a dying class. The entire appearance evoked a boring, gray unpainted model, as if she were hiding, the only stark colors being the fading-orange lifeboats and the rusty streaks tumbling down the hull. She was a "common carrier" in the legal vernacular, carrying numerous small cargoes for members of the public, who booked a shipment according to internationally agreed-upon rules.

TODAY THE old piers have been remodeled as gardens and parks, which is possibly what the good people of Brooklyn desire, an alternative to the coming and going of rusty ships, the noise of stevedores, the grubbiness and pollution of business, and the interruption of their impressive view of the Manhattan skyline across the East River. In 1981, however, Brooklyn Pier No. 1 was a bustling, lively place during the

23   Established in 1975, now sadly gone.

day, but by sundown—lacking those expensive stevedores—it became dark and lonely. We were warned to take care sauntering ashore, but I'd heard that before and ignored it. I was twenty-two and indestructible. Two blocks from the pier stood the Watchtower building, and with my newfound contemplation of God, I sought some proselytizing literature, but they were closed.

The US Coast Guard extended the planned few days in Brooklyn after discovering defects during a routine inspection. It was satisfied the port lifeboat descended successfully, and its refusal to return was of no importance to them. Of more concern, the emergency diesel[24] wouldn't, well…let's say it wasn't up to code, so they barred sailing until it proved operational. I took the opportunity for another stroll ashore one evening into Brooklyn Heights, as the engineers hammered and cursed the generator. I might describe it as a gritty neighborhood, solidly working class. But I was reasonably cautious, and didn't I have the man above on my side? It drizzled; my type of weather. The lush canvas of street lights and looming buildings brought an anxious stillness to the evening and rallied my thirst. I achieved my only planned goal when I found a quiet bar, of the New York/Billy Joel style; plain brick walls, small windows, a door at the corner, and a "Miller" sign glowing neon, calling me into its warm interior, like Mother's open arms.

The bar had a pretty good crowd for a Saturday, and before I downed my first beer—which, for those who know me, doesn't take long—a tolerably attractive young lady with well-worn self-assurance had sat beside me, as the businessmen got stoned. Not close, not practicing politics, but I noticed plenty of other seats at the long bar. As I ordered my second, she spoke, and, well, it's better than drinking alone. Of course, my thoughts turned carnal, but I was familiar with the ostracizing capability of the female sex. I went along with the pretense until

---

24 SOLAS dictates a vessel should have an alternate power source outside the engine room.

she finally outlined her business proposal, grounded on two easy-to-re-member values: fifty dollars and one hundred dollars. I congratulated her on the simple but effectively targeted business strategy and won-dered just how much cash I had in my pocket. It seemed unreal and glaringly obvious to look, until I paid for the beers and got to feeling all right.

FORLORNLY DEPARTING one of my favorite cities, I viewed the magnificent metropolis drop below the horizon, and set a rhumb line[25] for what Henry Morten Stanley named the Dark Continent, just east of southeast. A new chief mate had joined—older, English—which was slightly suspicious. He couldn't find a better job? Otherwise, it was the same complement. I had settled down to my standby station right aft, hidden in all practicality from the bridge, my ineffectual radio the only tenuous contact between them and us. I had the same three ABs each port. Initially, a wall existed between us, but at least they didn't laugh at me. Finally, they accepted me. When I had to, I would step up and assist with unraveling a rope, securing a stopper, or whatever else a helping hand could add while directing. Standbys were so much more relaxing; just small ropes, no wires, and if the ship moved, a few of us could heave it back with a rope on a drum end. We developed into an inelegantly dressed but effective working unit.

It's forty-five hundred miles from New York to Monrovia and I set-tled into an agreeable fifteen-day routine. The ship, now fully loaded, incorporated deck cargo including cars, one of which they chained beside the paint locker. Each day the crew cleaned their paint brushes on the wheels, then the fender, then the wing. I was grateful for no other obligations when the Old Man directed me to administer the

---

25   A line on a chart crossing all meridians at the same angle, i.e., a constant bearing, or a straight line on a Mercator chart.

medical duties. I considered this strange, since I had no proclivity for such responsibilities, nor had I any training, but he was serious. He always was. He spoke softly with a thin veneer of authority, which most people ignored. But that was his decision, unorthodox and controversial; not my favorite words. I took myself down to the hospital, saw it was clean, and unlocked the pharmacy: two cupboards of bandages, drugs and frightening medical instruments. I hoped no one became ill, for their sakes.

The old ship took to deep sea quite well, reveling in its own retro-ness. It grew less pleasant two days out of New York when the chief mate, perhaps not fully conversant with the pipeline system, transferred 150 tonnes of freshwater from forward to aft and it never arrived; lost somewhere in the bilges, tank bottoms, or another mysteriously hidden place. Suddenly we were bereft of freshwater for washing and cleaning. We didn't have a steamship's huge capacity to generate freshwater, but relied on dockside potable supply, so we each endured on one rationed bucket of freshwater for personal hygiene every day for the next two weeks.

The transatlantic voyage, at first comfortable and predictable, became tedious and wearisome. As the temperature rose and the ancient air-conditioning struggled, the most unfavorable aspect of the *Victoria U* silently scuttled into view. She suffered an unwanted pet called *Periplaneta americana*, or as you might know it, the American cockroach. They have a small brain, but then it is programmed to do only three things: eating (practically anything, evidently), copulating (prodigiously), and running from bright lights. They can move at a heady three miles per hour, ostensibly without losing speed when adjusting direction. And they appear in two manifestations. First, your eyes are taking in surroundings, without contemplation, when unexpectedly the wall that was bare, cream-colored a few moments before, now has a mark upon it, as if magically appearing from within the paneling, like a UFO. The second manner in which they reveal themselves is more alarming. It's dark, I'm asleep. There are only two hours before being called for the watch and there's a sense my skin is itching and it won't abate. Then it strikes me, so I open the light and the three-quarter-inch intruder scurries away to the nearest dark corner.

I had a standing operational procedure; can of chemicals in hand, awake and anger boiling, I tracked his last known whereabouts and squirted a stream of DuPont's finest death into whatever recess where it sought refuge. Never once did I allow them to contrive an escape. I can explain the roach in two words: infuriatingly unanticipated.

AND THEN we were there. Africa glowed on the radar, "in the empty immensity of earth, sky, and water," as Joseph Conrad wrote. I could see it through the binoculars. I'd visited briefly before, but that was in my corporate air-conditioned box with the yellow mollusk protecting us from the dreary reality outside. This would be another experience. At the risk of stating the obvious, Africa is beyond measure. As a child I devoured *Tarzan* and *The Snows of Kilimanjaro*. I knew they were fiction, and I didn't expect to see a giant, tanned, loincloth-clad white man come swinging into view, the local inhabitants playing second-fiddle luggage-bearers. But I just imagined it might be nobler, somehow grander or more cinematic. I thought maybe the acceptability of an eclectic group of Europeans gathering together for gin and tonics after a day of elephants, big cats and wildebeest would be tolerable enough. My sense of Africa had been clouded to suit my own prejudices, I admit, but Monrovia wasn't like that, and the tourists didn't visit because travel agents didn't recommend it. As a destination it looked better on radar.

Interestingly, Monrovia is one of only two national capitals named after a US president. Legendarily, the population was seeded by escapees and born-free blacks from various Caribbean islands in the nineteenth century. Three miles north lies the port of Freeport, where we entered through a deep and well-buoyed channel between two breakwaters, on the southern of which sat a shanty town, rusting corrugated roofs complementing an overhanging, heavy gray mist. The wharf, two thousand feet long, berthed three ships. This almost sounds respectable on paper, but the dull dreariness of the location and the realization that nothing appeared to be happening filled the visitor with aching apprehension, as if we had taken a wrong turn along the way.

We secured to the crumbling dock with large spent tires preserving our rusty hull from further damage. We sat for four days with cargo handled by cheap stevedores at a slower rate than I had believed possible. I couldn't imagine the economic sense in being there. The car remained by the paint locker, slowly taking on the appearance of psychedelic art.

Monrovia in 1981 functioned under military rule. Its government offices dominated the economy, so not the finest indicator of free enterprise. In the city itself they announced the electricity was unreliable, and I didn't long for a walk in a city without light, avoiding the poor and crippled I knew I'd encounter, ready to crush my idealism. The people lived on the margin, expecting no improvement and getting none. Famously, its main thoroughfare (I'm told a bustling wide road with a shabby, tree-lined median swarming with human vermin) has an address—80 Broad Street—which includes the registration of tens of thousands of nonresident corporations, including the owner of our ship. A few sought it out, expecting to see doors festooned with labels perhaps, but here's the twist: Africa's most famous street address, like the "Urban Spacemen," doesn't exist; all the mail is redirected to a warehouse a few miles away.

We had brought with us, in number two hold, four giant yellow haul-trucks, the sort you see rumbling around enormous holes in the ground, full of aggregate. Each weighed 40 tonnes, which wasn't a problem in Houston, and they assured us Monrovia had a crane to extricate them. It did, but it lay in parts, not expecting fabrication for some weeks. The only solution was to rig our 20-tonne heavy-lift boom and cut each bucket free, picking up the components separately in a health and safety nightmare. No one had rigged the boom before, but they attempted the challenge and I shunned involvement. It was well beyond my limited knowledge; all goosenecks, hooks, preventers, trunnions and shackles. I watched as the derrick strained all its steely tendons, pulleys and winches laboring, waiting for the inevitable failure and the unimaginable consequences. But, incredibly, it worked.

By some accounts, Monrovia has the distinction of being the world's poorest city; so, regrettably, it was a bold idea that hadn't worked out. Some places are good because they are bad, but this was just bad because it was bad. We departed the dark, matte, defeated city, somehow shabbier and more tainted than when we arrived.

Once on the African coast you feel like the flavor never disappears: the rotting, damp smell, the humidity and the uncleanliness. The third world just felt different, an uneasy collision of tribal origins and recent colonialism and its sorry aftermath. I knew our schedule, so I drew the 2B lines a few miles off the beach so we might spot the occasional lighthouse to support our position. I love navigation. There is a sense of wonder every time you choose an unfamiliar chart, smooth it flat and begin a leisurely gaze upon the water for obstructions—then browse the ports and towns along the coast. It's dispiriting to open the same chart again and again, but a virgin document longs to be pored over, scanned and considered, as to what this fresh corner of the world will offer into view.

Watching a coast as it slips by the ship is like thinking about an enigma. There it is before you, smiling, frowning, inviting, grand, mean, insipid, or savage, and always mute with an air of whispering, "Come and find out".[26]

I REMEMBERED Abidjan: dirty and French. My gang and I now formed a cohesive working unit, joking uncomfortably, like you do when mixed cultures and languages meet. They had done it all before, professionally, expediently and, it has to be said—even in our collective fashion of shorts, jeans, dirty T-shirts—fairly safely. We spent two lazy days watching the mysterious play of men coming and engaging in nothing at all. They employed gangs of a dozen for each working hatch. The ship's crew opened the hatches: employment too important to allow others. But once open, and all the treats inside to the tween deck exposed, the shore gangs descended, manhandling the bags of rice and bundles of donated clothing, the wooden packages and the strange-shaped unknown objects. All had to be unlashed and pulled toward the hatch opening for the 5-tonne derricks to reach in a union purchase,[27] all tension and straining.

---

26 Joseph Conrad.
27 A rig in which a pair of fixed derricks are used in combination, the wire runners coupled in such a way that the load is swung from a position vertically under one derrick to a position vertically under the other. It has the great advantage that a load can be moved laterally and vertically without having to adjust the booms.

The ports are where pristine Africa meets the Western world, and maybe that's why they are what they are. Behind the trees, meeting the beach, lay an immense continent I could only imagine. I didn't see the best of any place. There might have been something to explore on a subsequent visit, but I struggled through the first. Africa wasn't meeting my expectations, as if I'd bought a first-class ticket and been downgraded to coach.

THE PORT of Tema, Ghana, was new, and is twinned with the London borough of Greenwich, because the prime meridian that tourists straddle on the hill there is the same one that runs directly through Tema. So, interestingly, had I been bothered, I could have taken a noon sight safely knowing that the sun would reach its zenith just as the chronometer swept past twelve o'clock. The port was large: twelve deep-water berths, an outsize tanker quay, a dockyard, warehouses, and transit sheds. While coming alongside I spied a bent man roosting alone on a bollard between us and the adjacent vessel. Throughout the mooring operation he sat there, not noticing the operations occurring about him. He seemed half-asleep, and I didn't blame him. Standing down after placing the rat guards, I glanced aft, and there he was, still sitting, staring inward to the docks and warehouses—didn't everyone at the water's edge look to the sea? What did he know that I didn't? Or had he identified his goal for the day, finding the most comfortable seat in the port? Maybe he was waiting for a friend, or just waiting for something to change.

I was soon jaded by Ghana, as if it were a place deposited in some slow-motion other-universe. For entertainment, the gaily painted car was gently settled on the dock, alone and forlorn, like a Jackson Pollock piece that nobody wanted to claim. But at least the shipper got a deal on the freight. Our wildlife's larger cousins scampered about the dock in fear of no human. Tema was not worth the admission, and I had a free ticket. Nothing would take the edge off the grim denouement of our visit to Ghana. I felt useless in port. All I did was watch other people. That's what everyone else did, but the juxtaposition between the casualness of this employment and the edgy fear of tanker life was jarring. Tema was a drab and shoddy place, and a stroll ashore became hard to justify.

Heading east—happily skipping the infamous Lagos—into Douala, the African success story and largest city of Cameroon, its commercial and economic hub and the richest city in the region. In a dark past, Douala had the dubious distinction of being the center of the transatlantic slave trade, so it was nice to see the burgeoning city doing well. It used to be a German protectorate, one of only four modern nations to do so, as the French and British carved up the rest in an unseemly scramble for colored areas on a map; a somber reminder that nothing lasts forever.

The Wouri River begins a hundred miles upriver and flows past the city in a mile-wide, slow-moving torrent of brown, muddy water. The city sprawls along the eastern edge. Its long, continuous wharf stretched for miles with a dozen general cargo ships lined along it as we approached and slid awkwardly into the only gap, dipping the eyes of our ropes again. We hung about for three days, during which I walked ashore with Sparky and his wife into either Bonebong, Boneleke, or Bonanjo; it was easy to become confused. I thought it might be a half-decent port. Well, think again.

I cannot recall our destination of eating and drinking, but the world's great pleasure industry was in operation again—they have an office in most ports. But what lingers in my mind, after all these years, was going to check the plumbing and encountering a lady manspreading her legs, hoisting her dress and urinating in the men's room. There she was, relieving herself while standing, into a trough. I was astonished, not so much because she could do it well, but because she could do it at all, like a dog walking on its hind legs. Douala was acceptable, but still West Africa. If you look long enough at any town, you'll find something interesting to say. I remember little of the work since I hardly contributed. But by the time we departed I still thought I needed that long river passage, my Charles Marlow moment. We sailed south for our final destination.

The Portuguese named it Pointe-Noire when they found it in the mid-fifteenth century while seeking a route to the east. The usual responsibilities included watching the gang unloading the bundled donated clothing, which had been compressed by a mysterious machine in America. If you could break its constraints, the compacted clothing would detonate in a soft explosion of shirts, pullovers and pants. Once broken it was just a matter of time before every piece was somehow spirited away. Just when I thought her cities couldn't get any worse, the continent made a supreme effort and sank further. What despaired; the dingy life people have to live, the seediness of the infrastructure and the grubby industrial landscape. I felt that just over the hill it would be so much better, full of weird and wonderful lifeforms, as if I had been standing on the edge peeking through a dirty window. Nothing in Pointe-Noire seemed to matter.

We were ready to leave the continent, like in a movie when someone yells, "Let's get the hell outta here." I had seen enough grim port cities, and so had The Company. The coastal excursion had gone to schedule, as far as schedules go in West Africa, but I was now anticipating America. I felt overwrought by the bugs, the humidity and the poverty.

After a period, they all wear down on the visitor, like an incessant heavy veil. But then, as if in a remake no one wanted, an unforeseen telegram arrived stating, "Run like hell for Matadi. Must tender NOR[28] by 0600 tomorrow." The *Victoria U,* well past her sell-by date, struggled, but arrive we did, in a blaze of obscurity, off Banana, just after six in the morning, tendering the document a few minutes later. We were at the river, as Conrad's all-knowing narrator Marlow was, a hundred years earlier.

This was the Congo…

…a mighty big river, that you could see on the map, resembling an immense snake uncoiled, with its head in the sea, its body at rest curving afar over a vast country, and its tail lost in the depths of the land.[29]

I CAN'T hide the fact that the estuary of Africa's second-longest river intimidated us. The Congo is big, the giant blood vessel of Africa. Some incalculable volume spills from its hidden continental origin every second, resulting in a 175-fathom deep channel at Banana, while for a mile on either side lay shifting banks of mud, backed by a never-ending mangrove swamp. Approaching from seaward, both the north and south banks comprised dark rolling hills of dense vegetation, so impenetrable they merged into one living mass. Only the city of Soyo, through the binoculars, broke the monotony; whence the Banana pilot originated. We tried to locate Buoy "16" in the shifting mud banks on either side of the bottomless central channel. The pilot called us northbound, so we edged in that direction until the engine

---

28   The Notice of Readiness (NOR) is a document presented to the charterer indicating the ship is ready, in all respects, to load the cargo. It triggers time to begin for the charterer's account.

29   Joseph Conrad again: *Heart of Darkness.*

vibrations subtly changed and blooms of light brown mud stirred on either side. The captain, caught between making a decision and eating breakfast, as usual, procrastinated and ignored the shrill calls. He had arrived, somewhere near the pilot station, and tendered his Notice of Readiness—he wasn't going any further until someone joined him on the bridge, someone who, even if he didn't know our position, could at least accept the responsibility. But the Banana pilot knew where we were, and once having clambered onboard, headed the *Victoria U* in the correct direction—upriver—ordering, "Full ahead."

The scenery grew ever lusher and denser as though we were alone on the river. Our destination lay eighty miles upstream, along a line centered upon the breathtaking surge of muddy water flowing ever westward, separating Angola and Zaire. On and on we motored against the wet-season flow. By late afternoon the banks of the immense river had closed to half a mile, and the sides became darker and steeper, like a journey back in time to the beginning of man. The further we went, the further I wanted to go. As dusk approached, we arrived to the port itself, eighty-five feet higher than the Banana pilot station. Matadi, the furthest upriver oceangoing vessels can reach, lies on the south bank as the river bends northeast, entirely within Zaire. Three miles further the rapids begin, where not long ago the chart might have depicted mythological figures in bad perspective. We had reached the dark place of the river, and slid alongside the lengthy quay, full of general cargo vessels, our lines stressing to maneuver against the heady 5-knot current. We hung there as the water rushed between us and the dock.

I found all the beauty and ugliness of Africa in one day: the wild virgin forests, a vast, striking but tormented place that had turned into another depressing city of lethargic commerce. We had traveled so far and yet barely scratched the surface. Why the mad dash to Matadi? The

Company had fixed a consignment beyond our regular trade. With the ship half empty they agreed to lift a strange cargo, a two-hundred-piece portable oil rig for Colombia. The rig would arrive piece by piece to the dock during the following ten days.

It was December 1981, and I lived on a shabby, worn-out ship from a different age and commercial need, hanging onto a dock trying to repel us, picking up anonymous pieces of machinery and pipes—endless piping—stowing and lashing each deep inside the *Victoria U.* Almost all the work occurred in daylight. The nights were drawn out, boring and uneasy. I got to know the stevedore foreman, Mfumo, like you must when there's precious else to do. He hung around as if something might happen, but it never did. Incredibly, the night gang dressed more shabbily, the men thinner, propagating an aura of indigence. We had nothing in common, but I sympathized with their plight, and handed out quinine tablets to fight the malaria.

Hatch covers are essential kit for the general cargo vessel. They allow the ingress and egress of all that stuff. Each shipbuilder has its own preference for the design to install. The Company had purchased the vessel long after their input might be considered, but as luck would have it, they had the best, in stark contrast to all the other gear. An unsung hero of the maritime world, Robert MacGregor, born in 1873 near South Shields, became an accomplished engineer, and patented the single pull rolling steel hatch. The simple design comprised articulated leaves, linked by chains, that rolled on tracks along the hatch coaming and neatly stowed at the termination when unemployed. When closed they were clamped secure on a rubber seal. It became the standard, and the name MacGregor is synonymous with their ubiquity. Modern versions operate hydraulically, but our 1950s design ran wires to pull the covers driven by the derrick boom winches, which needed considerably more coordination than pressing a button.

As early dawn painted the sky one day, and I was feeling jaded and sleepy, ready for breakfast and my cockroach-ridden bed, it began drizzling. I peered into hatch No. 4 and saw what appeared to be the more expensive components of the oil rig. To resolve the dilemma, I chose what I believed to be the prudent path, and ordered the deck gang—two ABs as sleepy as me—to close the hatch. We picked up the half-inch wires lying beside the coaming, rigged them through the dedicated pulleys, switched on the electric motors and hauled. Anyone nearby stood aside as the first hatch leaf, perhaps 3 tonnes, shook itself loose of its confinement and clattered onto the coaming rail, reverberating through the ship, its chains tightening, pulling the following leaf with another thundering steel crash, and waking the sleepy, like heavy metal music does.

In all my fears and nightmares, standing to the side, I saw the first leaf's wheel lurch from the rail as it slid sideways, disconnecting from the following unbalanced sections, upending itself and plunging into the abyss, crashing to a cacophony of mangling, tearing steel below. The following leaves, leaderless, jammed. All was silence, like the heavy stillness following an explosion. The delicate rain ended and the chief mate and port captain stepped from the accommodation, coffees in hand. All eyes looked to me for explanation. I had no response, other than to hope we had insurance.

On Christmas Day we held a barbecue with convenient amnesia regarding the past three hundred years of empire. I couldn't envisage much celebration amongst the local populace. Feeling full, with ethics and logic providing little impediment, I strolled ashore through the damp, muddy, pockmarked dock path into the steep roads of the city, to see a rough-and-tumble town, all heat and dirt, the typical roar and rattle of hurrying throngs of people somehow absent that day. An uninvitingly mangy dog slunk past, tail between his legs, head lowered, teeth bared. There is a local saying that to live in Matadi, you must know the verbs "to go down," "to go up" and "to sweat." The few people seemed weary and defeated. How many did I pass who owned nothing but the clothes they wore? For so many, life was bleak. The main construction components were a hardened brick which turned into mud on the streets, and for the buildings, breeze block and rusty sheeting in abundance. Corrugated iron lean-tos covered sparse trestle tables holding unknown fruits and vegetables. Africa appeared to be made of corrugated iron, and yet I couldn't remember Conrad mentioning that. They muted all colors; even the rare car seemed to have forsaken the need for cleanliness—Matadi was a town where civic improvements went to die. In the sky hung the electric wires of the city, with the purpose of ostensibly diffusing electricity in abundance, as each household or mini-industry hooked up without fear of government utility obligation.

I sauntered down a dark and lonely road seeking signs of entertainment: neon, or perhaps fresh paint. Plastic containers and cola bottles lay where the greenery should have been. But hey! Let's forget the details and consider the giant embarrassing flaws staring us in the face. How could anyone govern such a disorganized mess as Matadi? I doubt anyone did. It seemed the city ran on the concept of inherent anarchy. My privileged life revealed the sensitivities through which I saw the world. The people gazed upon me with the bored acceptance of those who didn't care anymore. Who was I? Obviously not a tourist or the World Bank; maybe they accepted that foreigners emerged from ships and were not worth the bother. So, the people of Africa, with so much beauty and worthiness crushed from them, were where they always were. I had met their cousins in America; they were tall, broad-shouldered, often athletic, but here the people were small and wiry, characterized by their lack of decent food and suitable medicine. The violence would grow inside once the young learned what they didn't have.

The sun descended and I disliked walking those streets at night. I took another corner with the certainty I was lost, and it was growing dark, intensifying the moral and physical wretchedness of the city. The up and downs confused, but I turned towards where I believed the docks might be, down another steep street, and stumbled upon a small group gathered by an empty lot. I felt the darting looks, whispers and uncomfortable glances, the dreadful possibilities of life; the faceless face of Conrad's Africa. A body—a man—lay near them, lifeless in the casual attitude of death. I stopped and stared upon the sad scene with horrible fascination, holding my breath to hear the mournful sound of sorrow. The dead man's eyes unblinkingly followed me, like those in a portrait on the wall do. I froze, not knowing what to do as a useless impingement on their grief, or an easy scapegoat. Somehow, I resuscitated my mind, glanced away from the disfigured face as if it were contagious, and moved on with relief, escaping the vile slum. His name and life were unknown to me. Perhaps death was his freedom.

When Joseph Conrad described his journey much deeper into the Congo, he didn't really level with the reader about to just what darkness he was referring to. Was he suggesting that Africa represented something less civilized than the Europe he knew? I would be more comfortable discussing the horrific consequences of imperialism. They were poor because we were rich? Or am I being cynical again? Or maybe he saw the grubby, pathetic darkness in everyday life, just as I had seen it in that dingy Matadi street when the sun settled down.

I HAD limited my unwanted medical duties to a toothache, a head-ache, tetracycline for an uncomfortable discharge just where he didn't need it, and freeing up the hospital for two stowaways who rode from Tema to Douala. But for my principal business, I advised the Old Man we required charts for Colombia, fairly urgently—by hook or by crook. He, habitually, wasn't about to spend a hundred dollars on charts. So, we finally set to Colombia, sans the appropriate navigational aid. We had one sextant, one chronometer, one gyro compass and the smallest radar I'd ever seen. Everything I had felt comfortably provided with before was somehow now at a bare minimum.

Faced with a navigational challenge, I had an idea and, unusually, a good one; I was in my element. Once back upon the Atlantic, rested after a torrent of unsettling dreams, I set to creating a chart for Santa Marta, Colombia. Taking the best, old, out-of-date and unused chart, I flipped it over. The white reverse would now be my engineering draw-ing background. We had Admiralty Sailing Directions describing fea-tures of coastlines, ports, and harbors, so I digested the information and transcribed it on my clean canvas. The nautical chart is the bedrock of navigation, representing the maritime area and adjacent coastal regions at the edge. It symbolizes information for ease of understanding. I love charts for their accuracy, their sense of order and their completeness. Charts and maps grew up with me like an old school friendship, surviv-ing, along with beer, even the discovery of girls in magazines.

The Admiralty issue about thirty-five hundred charts, and the lack of suitable ones may well deem the vessel unseaworthy in terms of car-riage contracts—would you trust your valuable goods on a ship with no charts (the owners of the oil rig did)? They issue them in folios, but you can buy them individually to suit your purpose. I'm predis-posed, but I believe with some certainty the consensus that British charts are the finest. They seem more trustworthy; the detail is sharper, and they're made of better paper, but overall, they are superior because the British reconnoitered the world as they plundered, skirmished and sought control of huge swathes of the globe. I realized the entire world cannot be visited on slow-moving ships, but charts make it seem possible, so I dreamed of the places I scrutinized, like Valparaíso.

I had searched the Caribbean folio; it contained small-scale stuff, long out of date and uncorrected, but I supposed usable, since unexpected and inconvenient encounters deep-sea are rare. Surprisingly, though, an underwater mountain had been discovered accidentally only in 1973, when the cargo ship *Muirfield* struck an unknown object sailing in Indian Ocean waters charted at a depth of over sixteen thousand feet. It's now called the Muirfield Seamount. What worried me more were the approaches to our intended discharge port, Santa Marta.

The anxiety began approaching Trinidad and Tobago without a chart. They could have built a wall across the passage for all we knew, so we hoped they'd left the light on. Happily, we picked up the Toco Lighthouse at the extreme northeast end of Trinidad. We obtained good fixes from Aruba and eased past the Gulf of Venezuela, making landfall at the most northerly point of Colombia, Punta Gallinas. Santa Marta is a safe port to approach, but I drew the lines on my self-made chart comfortably clear of the beach. On my artistic rendering of the coastline I had gleaned some notable objects to use as points of reference: a small, steep-sided rocky island ("precipitous with fort ruins") less than a mile off the port, named Isla El Morro, with a spindly lighthouse flashing every 2.5 seconds. The anchorage lay to the southeast, with a bearing of the town's cathedral of 090°, and it was safe and deep. We had arrived and tendered our Notice of Readiness a mile from the port; perfect. Better still, the city, standing on the east side of the bay, surrounded by hills, looked deliciously inviting through the binoculars.

In January 1982, Santa Marta, hot and humid, but somehow in a fresher manner than Africa, was a tourist destination. Expectantly, we waited to step ashore. The oil rig owners had hired every truck near and far. A long line of disheveled, archaic, rusting cabs connected to and disconnected from trailers, like props from a 1950s ruthless trucking movie, lined up along the dock and out the gates, ready for the make-your-own-oil-rig kit. Guided by American roughnecks, the sections of equipment were hauled out and gently dropped to each waiting vehicle. Thievery and pilfering occurred, but nothing on the scale of Africa.

In the evenings we wandered ashore, through the liberally unsecured dock gates, along the Av. Rodrigo de Bastidas, a typically picturesque Latin America beachfront boulevard, drawing locals and visitors to the confluence of sea, beach, apartments and businesses. The scene promoted alfresco eating, music, walking and chatting with friends; about as good as life seemed to be. The sidewalks bustled with vendors proffering fruit, drinks and dainty, handmade trinkets. Somehow, I found the young, sweet-painted ladies who, either out of economic necessity or passion, seek the company of young foreign men out for a night of entertainment. Santa Marta was a tourist destination so congenial you'd think it wouldn't all be a cliché, but it was, and better for it. Yes, I worked, but it was mostly observational security stuff. The port was safe, the vessel didn't move and the excursions along the city front were well worth the visit. I never returned, and I have fond memories, like a postcard having slipped behind the sofa cushion of my memory. When, reluctantly, we departed this pleasant surprise, I picked up the weather forecast for New Orleans and informed everyone we were leaving 90°F for a freezing wintry Mississippi River covered in snow, less than five days away. The *Victoria U* headed home for winter.

MY PERIOD of employment had never been agreed upon, and although I had signed on articles, I considered myself through with this ship, and almost certainly with The Company. My newfound commercial sense, fueled by an all too obviously needed flag of convenience, prompted me to enjoin the captain in a rare conversation and, knowing he wouldn't take it well, I told him I wanted out. I would not revisit Africa on this ship. The bug situation had improved with the impending American winter, but the night before I found a mouse in my cabin. The *Victoria U* sailed to Sabine and stopped again in Houston, New Orleans and Baltimore, before reaching her final US port, Pier No. 1, Brooklyn. Waiting on the dock was my relief. I didn't know his qualifications or experience, but he was there, and I was going: to be free of the bug-spray smell native to the ship.

And what about God? On the night watches crossing the Atlantic, alone except for the thrumming, muted rhythm of the engine, I had time to consider the subject. Didn't we all yearn to know the answer? Didn't we all find God in that which we cannot comprehend? What I've since learned, but didn't understand at the time, was that growing up is not just a physical process, but a moral and intellectual one too. I very nearly wanted to open my mind and allow religion inside, become one of those well-read zealots who can quote convenient lines from the Bible for every semi-miracle they stumble upon. Try as I might, and I did try, I could not find it affecting; it seemed a lazy answer. So, I hesitated. I just wanted to know a little more before I could close my mind, discontinue my skeptic intellect and believe. Like so many before, for now the answer eluded me.

I STAYED overnight at the Seaman's Mission in lower Manhattan, near Union Square, where my mind found some distant, peaceful refuge in the stridency of the city that never sleeps. So, I headed for my—as yet only known—hedonistic center of the world: the junction of Forty-Second Street and Times Square. I left the *Victoria U* a better seaman, and an improved navigator, and experience—the more challenging type—builds character. Life onboard was expiation for me. I had served my time in the maritime trenches.

9

Just for One Day

1982

Our heroes are men who do things which we recognize, with regret, and sometimes with a secret shame, that we cannot do.

—Mark Twain

LIKE MANY young men I had spent my brief life venerating a few heroes, while witnessing all the faults and inadequacies in the mirror, somehow hoping one day I might do something worthy. Many English boys suffer the same inadequacy, growing up in a country gorged with bygone idols, usually because they killed countless people on the losing side. I still suffered these unfortunate tendencies, but I was actively aiming to amend my perspective. Beginning with sporting or popular entertainment types, I grew into adulthood understanding the importance of those who achieved significant progress for the common good in politics, literature, science and industry. One of my lesser-known favorites, Joseph Isherwood, worked in the obscure field of human endeavor called naval architecture, a discipline dealing with the engineering design of ships.

Before Isherwood, the building of ships had traced, resolutely, along lines prevailing from the earliest times. The hull of a ship is a long, square-sided tube, with the attendant benefit of being very strong when compressed at either end, but not so robust laterally. From the beginning, strength depended upon a series of closely spaced transverse frames and beams extending from the keel. Isherwood saw this as deficient. Ships built by the transverse method were weak in the longitudinal (forward to aft) direction, so he evolved a system which would provide all the desired longitudinal strength in the vast majority of ships built ever since.

Much like Clark Griswold designing a new crunch-enhancing chemical for cereals, this is essential stuff for us seafaring types. Isherwood ditched the ancient transverse framing method and replaced it with light, longitudinal members, closely spaced, running from aft to forward; longitudinal framing. The system had both lower weight (so ships could carry more cargo) and greater longitudinal strength for the development of larger and larger ships. It made possible all the advances in size ever since. When he died of pneumonia in 1937, his obituary proclaimed, "The name of Isherwood is known in practically every…shipyard in…the world…"

I HAD returned home from New York to a bleak and frigid English winter, unemployed again. I knew the future of expensive European officers did not lie with general cargo; the economics were amiss. I sought my third employer in six months in search of filthy lucre. Adrift on an ocean of unemployment, approaching my twenty-third birthday, I no longer feared being unable to swim. I nibbled at a few early offers as shipping lines dangled their hooks, but I knew crude oil would call me back. I wanted to resume the familiar, so I contacted the largest shipowner in the world, Sanko Line.

Created in 1934, by one-time candidate for prime minister, Toshio Komoto, Sanko had a volatile, successful and independent attitude toward the industry, but the 1973 oil shock and market collapse saddled the company with costly idle capacity. Rejecting subsidies offered by the Japanese government, they sought to build their way out of the economic depression and capitalize on low shipbuilding costs, ordering the construction of another 125 tankers primarily financed by foreign trading companies. In consequence, most of their ships were foreign owned and chartered long-term back to Sanko. This allowed cut-rate financing and hiring of foreign crews more competitive than their Japanese counterparts. A race to the bottom began, but for now I wanted to join the mighty Sanko Line.

The day they offered me employment, March 19, 1982, the television news showed a scrap metal dealer raising the Argentinian flag on the wet, remote island of South Georgia. The island, British since James Cook landed in 1775, was, in 1916, the center of a heroic story when Ernest Shackleton and five others sailed—incredibly—eight hundred storm-riven miles from Elephant Island in Antarctica in an open boat to find it. Many consider this the most remarkable accomplishment of navigation and endurance ever completed. Tensions between Britain and Argentina grew daily while governments dallied to diplomatically reconcile the future of the windswept archipelago predominantly inhabited by penguins. I flew out to Curaçao the same day the Royal Air Force bombed the Argentinian-manned airport at Port Stanley. The Falklands War had begun.

I had been there before and had low expectations, but was pleasantly surprised. This was finer, awaiting the MV *Arabian Addax*, lodging at an expansive holidaymaker establishment with the joining Yugoslav, second mate's wife, a pretty, somber, petite young lady from Split. Her name was Olga. Well, it wasn't, but I thought it should have been. Each day something drew me to Olga's slim, hour-glassed shape as a bear to honey, employing my finest, starry-eyed dialogue, as thin as the strap holding up her tiny bikini. Here I was, Jack Tar, living the lie of a girl in every port, enjoying paid-for meals and relishing the luxury of a full night's rest. I watched the evening news with growing disbelief whilst two nations plunged inexorably toward confrontation, as if both thought the other would admit the incongruity. No one else saw the conflict in such epic terms. Since I was returning to work, the day-to-day machinations of failed diplomacy and madcap combat would be mine to miss. Controversially, the same day I joined the *Arabian Addax,* the Argentinian cruiser *General Belgrano* became the only ship sunk by a nuclear-powered submarine in military history.

The agent drove us through the parched vegetation down to Bullen Baai, past a rusty blue anchor standing at the terminal gates. What startles when you first see a Sanko ship is the complete verdure of it. They painted the hull and deck entirely green, as if the company had purchased an abundance of leftover military camouflage. The accommodation house was buff, and the trademark green funnel had a thick white band with three concentric red circles, resembling a bull's-eye. It was distinctive and absolutely only Sanko. If you were in any doubt, behind the dark, thick streaks of rust, like an animal hiding in the bush, you would see painted in giant white italics on the ship's side the words *SANKO LINE.*

I sought, and acquired, the role of navigator. A Filipino third mate stood the eight-to-twelve, the Yugoslav second mate the four-to-eight (with his newly arrived Olga), and I the twelve-to-four. The Dutch chief mate had daywork; a concession to the frequency of port calls. The captain hailed from Ireland, the chief engineer from Northern

Ireland, the first engineer from South Africa, the electrician and second engineer from the Netherlands. The crew was Filipino. It was another cosmopolitan but eclectic ensemble, without the desperation and past-their-sell-by-date of the *Victoria U* castoffs. The sunny weather no longer matched my disposition, but I was glad of the cleanliness of the vessel and the sweet aroma of inert gas and crude oil; cockroaches, however hardy, don't appreciate hydrocarbons.

The Mexican oil conglomerate Pemex time-chartered the *Arabian Addax* to carry oil from two export terminals, both in the Bay of Campeche, a subsidiary of the Gulf of Mexico. I visited Coatzacoalcos only once. When finally called inside after days at anchor—all authoritarian panic as if it were a surprise to them, too—we motored towards the long, converging breakwaters. The deep blue sea of the southern Gulf transformed to muddy brown, then soft, chocolate still waters, as we entered the Laguna de Pajaritos amidst the flares of the four vast industrial complexes inside; Mexico's giant gas station.

Coatzacoalcos is twinned with North Tyneside in England, where my father was born. I didn't understand the association, but I wager he never imagined I would work there. We made fast at the newly constructed berth No. 8, still smelling of wet paint, and spent a day waiting for the president—of what I know not—who arrived for his cameo with a flamboyant entourage to ordain its opening. He didn't bother to come aboard, and upon his departure the cargo operation began.

Two hundred miles northeast of Coatzacoalcos lie three tiny sand cays, seemingly an unimportant fragment of the world. But Cayo Arcas is one of those anonymous spots that form an important cog in the domain of international commerce. It's a lonely and hot place, hiding from the world, comprising a chain of low, surf-encompassed islands about as close to the middle of nowhere as you might conceive it possible to be. The aggregate land area equates to fifty football pitches, formed from an extinct volcanic caldera where a lighthouse and a few tiny buildings stand. It's the sort of place that looks better on a *National Geographic* magazine cover. It's difficult to get to, and who would want to?

However, all this apparent nothingness is vital to the nation of Mexico. Three miles southwest lay their most important oil export terminal, appearing from the ocean like an abandoned, sub-Bondian movie set. From the platforms, they laid submarine pipelines to two SBMs. Nearby, a half dozen empty tankers awaited their fill. A few working boats sat lazily in the breeze, apparently without urgency or purpose. This could have been a grindingly hard trip, excepting that everyone waits in Mexico.

At night we lay anchored with the deck floodlights ablaze, swinging lazily in the warm, predictable breeze, while I occupied the routine of office work. All ships had amongst the radars, steering wheel, telegraph, knobs and buttons, perhaps buried in a corner, a box titled "radio direction finder" (RDF). The RDF, as its name suggests, is a device for finding the direction, or compass bearing, of a radio source. If, by twirling the appropriate knobs, you might obtain the direction from which a known radio source originates, then you have successfully obtained a line of position (LOP), just as I might have taken a compass bearing of a lighthouse, or a sight of the sun. What one gets from any single observation (manually or electronically) is not a position, but an LOP, upon which the observer must lie.

Our RDF was, like all the others, junk, at least as far as a modern navigator might be concerned. Using the bearings of two transmitters, I could theoretically determine the location of the ship, but I might use this method only when all others had been exhausted beyond viability.

A navigator relying on RDF might take time zigzagging to his destination, or perhaps miss it entirely, if it were not sufficiently large. No, the true usefulness of the electronic box was that it picked up land-based stations at very long distances, or "over the horizon." So, for anyone who doesn't put much faith in its efficacy, or if lying at anchor at a known location, then the RDF can pick up AM radio stations at long range, by far its most practical *raison d'être*.

I preferred American talk-radio stations, full of right-wing politics, crossing the Rubicon and conspiracies. On the night of July 6, amongst the background hiss and JFK assassination theories, I heard the announcer summon attention to an astronomical phenomenon I had not experienced. A syzygy, and resulting lunar eclipse, is an event of extraordinary natural beauty. The astronomical wonder happened right there before me, for one hour and forty-three minutes, as the moon passed through the center of the Earth's umbral shadow.

WE TRANSPORTED the oil to ports of similar character because they functioned with a similar purpose. South Riding Point in the Bahamas was a remote and boring place lying in timeless slumber, as if someone once had delusions of industrial grandeur, but ran short of money. The strange terminal appeared to float in the middle of nothing and nowhere; the steel island alongside which we berthed rested half a mile off the beach, where there sat nine fat, sandy-colored storage tanks. You could sense the port designer had run out of ideas early on. I saw an endless forest of spindly pine trees, uninterrupted except that a few miles away, like an astronaut waving from the moon, stood a radar station the Americans used to track rockets taking off from Cape Canaveral.

The terminal stands precariously on the edge of the Grand Bahama Canyon, the deepest in the world, falling three miles to the seafloor. It is so deep and precipitous that ships cannot anchor in the immediate vicinity, the terminal island structure being the last place that mankind can secure to the seafloor before it plunges down into nothingness. I presumed the Bahamas an agreeable place to visit, and one day I might do so and enjoy its first-class natural amenities, but the fragment I saw was an unforgivable blemish on the landscape of sand, cays and hidden depths. The crude oil we brought in would be exported again, to an American refinery.

THE HAYASHIKANE Dockyard in Nagasaki built the *Arabian Addax* in 1975. Being orthodox, the vessel had Joseph Isherwood's continuous longitudinal framing, resulting in strength and flexibility. She carried 83,000 deadweight tonnes of oil, so a quarter the size of the *Lampas*. She represented everything Sanko stood for, a design straight from the conveyor belt of conventionality. They made the vessel easy to operate, like my sister's Datsun Sunny. All the controls were light of touch, and everything mechanical worked as it should. The Japanese reputation for innovative simplicity and quality was all-pervasive. The accommodation was minimalism itself, clear and bare. And green. They spared every expense. It was as if in a rush to remove every nautical frivolity they forgot to keep some important elements; it didn't possess a bar, but beer was plentiful, and we met each evening in someone's cabin, like a rotating profanity-filled Tupperware party. The cabins themselves were functional, and it was all clean, and easy to keep orderly. I had a bed, a daybed, a desk and chair, and my own shower and facilities, as if I had condensed my life for four months down to these bare essentials. I never saw a bug. It all worked, and I liked it. The company kept out of the way with a pleasing lack of corporate nonsense or teleconferencing. A voyage order arrived and we did what we had to.

TWO OF my heroes' narratives collided in the Second World War. Joseph Isherwood was well-known to the maritime world, but as with many achievers, invincibility can become vulnerability. In the 1930s, believing he had one more significant contribution for the science of shipbuilding, Isherwood junked his own conventionality and produced a wine-cask shaped design called arcform, to improve fuel efficiency. It was revolutionary, but flawed, which explains why so few ships followed its design. One of that few, the *English Trader*, performed dutifully when war came, carrying cargoes to and from England. She lifted her final consignment in London, destined for Kenya, in October 1941.

Improbably, the dangers of the English Channel required circumventing Scotland to travel to East Africa. She formed up with others near Southend, ready to be guided north. The convoy set off, passing the Essex and Suffolk coasts. Early on the first day, however, the *English Trader* suffered engine trouble and slowly slipped astern. The next day turned tragic for the men of the fateful ship, but for another leading actor of this tale, it was both historic and virtually routine. Falling behind the convoy, the currents pressed her closer to the coast of Norfolk. Just after midnight on the twenty-seventh the vessel found the Hammond's Knoll and set aground, with a severe jolt and grinding of metal. She sat there, hard on the six-mile bank until daylight. As the sun rose, obscured by clouds, the weather deteriorated and the vicious wind grew to a gale.

Progress on the heeling[30] deck would be seriously impeded. At a wind speed of nearly 40 knots, waves might be twenty feet, and the

---

30 A vessel leans out of the upright due to list, the uneven distribution of weight within the vessel, or to heel, an angle imposed by an external force.

air wet and wild. This is weather you might rather watch in a movie; on a ship, as I had experienced, you hunker down, glad when the vessel shifts with the elements. But for a vessel firmly trapped, the waves crashed against the hull, taking with them parts whose loss might have been unimaginable the day before: the gangway, a lifeboat, and a derrick or two. Chains and lashings were no longer enough. I had seen vessels hogging and sagging in heavy seas, but the *English Trader* was fast on the sandbank, like a roller coaster trapped mid-run. Something had to give. Eventually her back broke. The one surviving lifeboat was un-launchable in the desperately heaving seas. The forty-seven men were now in serious danger.

TWENTY-TWO MILES west I can imagine the men running from their houses and places of employment, all flat caps and baggy trousers, like a black-and-white Pathé News broadcast, slipping round the tight corners of the small town of Cromer, hurtling down, always down, to the lifeboat station. Henry Blogg had first gone to sea aged twelve as a crab fisherman with his father, and when not at sea worked on the beach, hiring towels and changing rooms to tourists vacating London for the bracing air. At eighteen—amidst stiff competition—they elected Blogg a member of his father's lifeboat. His nephew described him as "stubborn" and "never conceding"; essential virtues for a lifeboatman, whose credo remains "Always go out," neglecting the concept of returning until later.

At eight a.m. on the twenty-seventh, Henry coxed the thirty-two-foot Cromer boat *HF Bailey* out into the turbulent waters of the North Sea, to seek the *English Trader*. Every time he went out, his pretty wife, Annie, dutifully awaited his return. He might not have been a church-goer, but he—like all the boatmen—had faith: faith in tradition, their boats, and themselves. He was the perfect lifeboatman: a rugged streak of independence, modest but proud, with an inner compulsion that others never understood, except perhaps Annie in their quiet moments together. He was a man you wanted on your side.

Incredibly, he had already taken the boat out a dozen times that year and saved over two hundred souls. By late morning Blogg arrived at the broken *English Trader*. She had by now lost three men overboard in the maelstrom, so the lifeboatmen attempted twice to connect a line by rockets, but without success. Blogg then tried to cox the lifeboat closer, and in the consequent heaving movement of the seas between the two vessels, swept five of the lifeboatmen into the water (including Blogg). In due course someone hauled them back from the raging seas, but one man perished from exposure. After an incredible seven hours of trying, the Cromer boat retired twenty miles to Great Yarmouth, its men exhausted and spent. "…It was nothing very much," claimed Blogg. "We all had hot drinks, some food, a hot bath each and some dry clothes and we were all right again." Some men talk like this. To those who knew him he was Mr. Average at home. For goodness' sake, his day job was running a deck chair and beach hut business. Where do men find their inner strength?

After breakfast and three hours of rest, the Cromer boat, and Blogg, set back to the *English Trader*. The weather now spent, and the seas reduced, the *HF Bailey* picked up the stranded forty-four remaining souls and took them ashore. The fortune of the ill-fated ship had run its course, so they left her to die on the Hammond Knoll.

Henry Blogg received another silver medal from the Royal National Lifeboat Institution for saving the forty-four men. During his tenure as a lifeboatman, until he retired at seventy-one, he saved 873 from death at sea, and proudly wore eleven medals, including three gold. He had launched in the lifeboat an incredible 387 times. The memorial on the cliff top at Cromer names him "One of the bravest men who ever lived." Could I do something vaguely similar? I doubted it.

So, what is bravery? Well, physical courage in the face of danger, I might suggest in this case. There are other categories of bravery, like the emotional kind endured by many people of reduced means, physically and economically, living every day not knowing how it will end. There are many brave military men and women of history who have committed incredible acts to save others, for which they were correctly awarded notice. I doubt if many had received eleven medals for bravery like Blogg. And Henry didn't commit his acts in a moment of adrenaline-inspired frenzy, like a soldier scaling a hill under enemy fire. No, he did what he did, time after time, for fifty-three years, never knowing which day he could remain on the beach, and which day he would ride the storm to another distressed vessel. He literally never knew which day he would die, and for sure he must have known one day he would, probably dashed against the side of a suffering vessel in the turbulent seas, just a few miles from his adoring Annie. The world doesn't make heroes like that anymore. But we had one thing in common; like me, Henry Blogg had never learned to swim.

IN ANOTHER world at another time, the Bazell family from New York decided upon a Caribbean vacation in the summer of 1982. Robert, his wife, Margot, and their children, Rebecca, fourteen, and Joshua, twelve, were enjoying the island of Grand Cayman. On Wednesday August 11, after a few days on the beach, they decided on an excursion offshore in a hired, 12hp, fourteen-foot, aluminum boat to try snorkeling. They brought no food, no oars or lifejackets. The weather was typical, Caribbean fine, warm and sunny, a balmy 85°F. It was a good day to spend some time in the water, if only to circumvent the heat.

As dusk approached, deciding to head back, they were confronted by one of those calamities that continue to assail the mariner throughout the age of motorized transport: they ran out of fuel. We can only imagine Robert's state of mind. Here he was, head of a young family, three miles from safety, with the most precious people in his life, surrounded by—from their perspective—an ocean of blue water. He made a decision, a heroic one. He told Margot to drop the anchor, slipped overboard, and began the immeasurable swim back to the distant lights of the dim beachfront.

With the adverse crosscurrent, it took three hours of arduous exertion, no doubt propelled by the contemplation of his family alone in a sea of nothingness. Upon struggling onto the Grand Cayman beach, he alerted the authorities and employed a police launch to search for his distressed family. "I almost drowned on my way in," the hero confessed. Meanwhile, Margot had followed his instructions and lowered the small anchor into the sun-setting, glistening sea to reach the bottom. It wasn't there at a hundred feet.

When the police launch arrived three miles offshore, the ocean was empty. We can only imagine a father's dread and anxiety. When you cannot view something within your two-dimensional plane, surely your mind drifts, however reluctantly, to the third dimension, the awful graveyard of the ocean. Perhaps he didn't realize the same flow he had so remorselessly struggled against had taken them further seaward in a westerly direction. It's called the Caribbean Current, and, sourced from the equatorial Atlantic, it transports large amounts of water northwestwards into the Gulf of Mexico, via the Yucatán Channel. To search further in the deadness of night was futile. Returning to shore, was the not-knowing more painful than the finality of death? Not yet. Robert knew he needed more eyes, so he contacted the US Coast Guard, who began an intensive search of the area from their Miami station. A cutter, along with military search planes and local boaters, participated in a search which spread over twelve thousand square miles. All without consequence.

For Margot, many miles away now, that fateful Wednesday night became Thursday morning, and with it the sense that something positive must be at hand, along with the rising sun, first warm and refreshing, but slowly becoming hot and intolerable for the three lonely boaters. We should note here some physical facts of trigonometry; sitting upright in a small boat, the visible horizon is two or three miles, perhaps four from the cutter. Coupled with this, the sun during the morning and later afternoon creates countless shimmering reflections on the small wavelets, rendering it impossible to view a small object across 180º of search. The possibility of seeing a small (and reflective) boat in the huge area south of Grand Cayman with a four-mile horizon is exceedingly small. The aircraft, too, were limited by fields of vision and the diminutive size of the target. Margot and the kids required some good fortune. As Thursday wore on, the water ran out. The depressing thought that their hero Robert may not have made it ashore grew inside them, although they curbed that discussion to support morale. Someone would see them soon—it had to be. Then it was Thursday night, and dark again. "We heard many motors and engines," declared Joshua, but they would need more than noise.

Friday morning slowly brightened their small—while at the same time—immense ocean world, and it matched the day before; blue beneath the searing crystalline sky, and unbroken monotony. Freshwater had condensed on the inner hull of the aluminum boat. "When we were desperate for water, we licked the metal." They kept a lookout, as best they could, for any passing traffic and discussed food, water and Joshua's upcoming birthday. Once your body has lost between 1 and 2 percent of its water, it will signal its needs by making you thirsty. By the time you are thirsty—I mean, really thirsty—you're already in the early stages of dehydration. Anything to combat the heat has to be attempted.

To resist the sun's assault, the three of them shared the small bottle of lotion. Then Margot had the cooling idea of taking turns slipping into the water. The water was as warm as the air, but the evaporation on clambering into the boat helped; her mind was operating now on survival mode. The deeper pelagic waters they had drifted into are known for tiger, hammerhead and whitetip sharks, but their brief immersions appeared to have attracted no interest. By Friday evening they were cold again, without sign of rescue. They had heard or seen four ships pass by, but without flares or mirrors, shouting and waving were of little use, other than for venting frustration. Darkness distorts perceptions; at night, the darting winds seem stronger, waves steeper, and it's difficult to judge if a light is two hundred yards or two miles distant.

The wide channel south and west of Grand Cayman is some two hundred miles distant to Honduras and about the same westerly to the Yucatán. The area is traveled, but not widely so. Most traffic heads north of Cuba for the Florida straits and the North Atlantic. Glance at the chart and Grand Cayman appears tiny, with the sun setting at about seven p.m. and rising again at six a.m. Without light, Margot and the children were essentially invisible to all traffic—including searchers—for half the time. During daylight, anyone who manned the bridge of a vessel would relax in the dearth of traffic and the fine summer conditions. It's a time to unwind and engage in reading or chart corrections, occasionally glancing forward to identify any modifications to the horizon. Navigational hazards rarely appear below it in good weather. A fourteen-foot aluminum boat would not register on the mind at that distance. The Bazells needed the hand of God.

Friday night, it rained, and they gathered a small quantity of water—perhaps ten ounces—in a plastic bailer they had brought aboard. "They drank it although they gagged on the hair that lined the bucket," the Gulf Coast News bureau later reported. It quenched their thirst for only a few minutes, but it may have been enough to save them. Friday night rolled on without a sign of other life. Then Saturday dawned, and Margot saw the children struggling. The lack of life-giving water and food, the incessant heat of the sun, and relentless rocking motion were taking their toll. She agonized inside; had Robert made it ashore? By the afternoon their heads were dropping. In their weakness it was difficult to remain awake and observant. She knew another night might prove impossible. The life was draining from their bodies; the younger ones first, naturally. Margot doubted she and the children would survive much longer. The terror and unpredictability of death gnawed inside.

They didn't know it, but their small, nameless boat was now forty miles from Grand Cayman and nowhere near land. But even here, hope refused to die. It flickered and wavered, a tiny flame in a sea of neglect. Then Margot heard the distant, deep thrum of an engine, unlike the other slighter, weightless noises of faraway aircraft and cutters. She lifted her aching head, turned and saw a lush wall of steel approaching beneath the falling sun. It strained her weary eyes to look, but she had to. She raised her children and forced them to see; this might be their final chance. The heavy ship pushed a wall of water in a white wave before it, the throb of the engine growing as it cleaved the seas, slowly approaching closer to pass two hundred yards away. By now the three of them were standing perilously in the rocking boat, waving and screaming "Help" from their dry, hoarse throats. Then they saw the mighty vessel eject a brief, dark cough of black smoke from the white funnel with a red bull's-eye upon it.

IN AUGUST 1982 the *Arabian Addax* had fulfilled its Pemex charter and sought new employment. We lifted our final cargo and sailed for Curaçao. Our weeklong satisfying voyage filled all aboard with a sense of relief; relief at moving on, earning a break, and escaping the delays, oppressive heat and workload. We were destined for the Persian Gulf after discharge. A time to relax, imbibe a few celebratory beers, clean the ship, run some maintenance routines, write a letter or two and generally let it all go.

On Saturday, August 14, halfway to Curaçao, we passed Cancun and entered the Caribbean, heading for a waypoint about fifteen miles off Grand Cayman. It was a bright, clear day, and no concern for the *Arabian Addax* pushing 80,000 tonnes through the water. As four p.m. came around, I completed my logbook, took a final glance about the horizon to find nothing of irregularity, and waited for the Yugoslav second mate to relieve me. The plan was as usual: go down two flights of steps, jump into the shower, back out and pop open a beer with the chief mate. Finest time of the day; right on schedule, at four twenty I cracked open the first cold can of Amstel.

Then, in my first blissful moments of respite, feeling the energy dissipate, the ship's horn sounded—a deep, booming, languid sound, like a close but brief rumbling storm—but it was a clear, bright day! Then the fire alarm jangled a few times. The mate and I glanced questioningly at each other. The bridge was calling attention to something untoward. He set down his beer and turned on a walkie-talkie, and the captain replied about someone in the water. Man overboard? We felt and heard the engine change its tone and a small dark puff of smoke drifted by the forward window. The *Arabian Addax* was maneuvering, and we didn't do that for fun.

Arriving on the bridge, the first sensation was the vessel turning. The captain, ordinarily a smug and risible, little man, was composed, relishing the unusual situation as he slotted the engine control lever into another position. The phone rang. Everyone onboard now knew we had a "situation." The story was breaking. My Yugoslav relief had spotted a small boat in the water, three souls onboard, waving for help. The captain had begun a maneuver to bring the ship back to the point it had previously passed through. A small group had gathered when I appeared. The ship was still swinging—a curious phenomenon rarely seen deep sea—as it cleared a huge area for itself. The Old Man, in danger of becoming a cliché, was the type who relished making decisions; now he had an excuse.

"Chief Mate"; no one knew why he was so formal. He chose words for their sound rather than their meaning, and he wore a white uniform for some reason. Nobody else did, and Sanko didn't require it. "You'll man the lifeboat winch. I need a safe launch and recovery." He was often wrong, but like many men in that position, never in doubt. Well, call me old-fashioned, but if the mate was to stand safely on the deck watching the proceedings, who was …?

"Third Mate, you'll cox the lifeboat," he finished, according to type.

I would say the command received a mixed press. I voiced something faintly nautical, like "Aye, aye," and pondered if any advice would come with the order. Apparently not. I retraced my steps down the three flights to the boat deck, as if slowly falling through a trapdoor opening beneath my feet. Through my mind ran his alternatives. The second mate—the Yugoslav—was on watch, and I supposed he didn't know where he had bought his Liberian license. The Filipino third mate he knew had purchased it in Manila. That left me, supposedly trained to understand situations and make decisions. He knew I had a British license; the same one he had obtained years earlier. He knew I had spent time rowing and coxing in a river somewhere. So, it was me. It was bad, all right, and I winced at the possibilities of it all going wrong. By the time I reached the boat deck the ship was coming to a halt, as the turn neared its completion. Just forward of the starboard beam we saw the small boat some ways off. We could see people onboard. What were they doing out here?

I had attended many lifeboat drills, but they were a consciously planned exercise rather than a plausible reality. Nevertheless, here was the chief mate directing ABs to rig a painter forward for the lifeboat. They released the gripes (they hold the boat tight against the davits while at sea) so she could freely hang and the falls take the weight.[31] The *Arabian Addax* was steady as the proverbial rock, but I knew the lifeboat was heavy, unpredictable and unwieldy. The falls always seemed excessively strained. I loathed lifeboats and their one-way mission design. They were not intended to return. I stood, buttoning my boilersuit and fixing my hard hat. Any escape hatches to avoid the situation were slowly bolted around me. The mate directed the bosun to ease the brake and the boat rocked and lumbered down, the rate smoothing out as the Filipino grasped the feel of its friction. The wires and pulleys all strained and screamed—I even hated the sound—as the bosun bought the boat to a swaying rest at embarkation.

The rescue party boarded: two ABs, the pumpman, the first engineer (a three-striper, so in theory he outranked everyone) and me.

---

31 They require no power to launch, the weight itself being sufficient to overcome the friction brake.

They lowered the boat and someone threw in a half dozen lifejackets, which defied sense, since there would be eight of us returning. A meter from the water, I gazed up and clenched my fist, signaling a halt to the descent. I told the First to start the engine (although he outranked me, I was the cox, officer in command, like John Chard at Rorke's Drift). I told everyone to secure their hard hats. The sea that seemed so glossy and calm from seventy-five feet above now appeared intimidating; the silky lee of the tanker became short pyramids of dark blue water about fifty yards out, and the swell I hadn't noticed from the bridge was very evident, lifting the Caribbean in a heaving, powerful, breathing motion.

Why the hard hats? Well, I opened my fist; the boat dropped the last meter and, once afloat, rose and fell in the swell, releasing the treacherous, heavy, non-toppling davit blocks[32] and freeing us from the wire, the penultimate connection to the *Arabian Addax*. I ordered the painter let go, and we were free. "Half astern." I needed to point the bow. "Half ahead," and I aimed the lifeboat somewhere just forward of the beam, avoiding those gruesome, heavily swinging blocks. We increased speed, rising and falling on the swell, and everyone settled in for our brief excursion, like young cubs leaving their mother's side. I glanced back at the green ship, so trustworthy and solid, as our lifeboat felt so small and vulnerable. They say drowning is a painless way to go, but I didn't believe them.

The tolerable ride turned to pitching and bouncing as we left mother's lee and chugged to within sight of the powerless craft, the men falling naturally into their parts, like a well-trained football team. As we closed in, I saw the young woman and two children, now sitting, looking exhausted but relieved. As we approached, I called "Stop" to

---

32   A design by which the traveling block (or pulley) remains upright when the weight is lifted, preventing fouling.

the engineer and swung the tiller, bringing the stern around to bounce against the helpless boat. The two craft leaped in tandem as if on independent seesaws, but were temporarily secured by the ABs and the castaways were gently transferred to the lifeboat. They were red with sunburn, tired and drawn. Their lips were broken and dry. They stumbled with exhaustion, but they smiled anyway, their dreary eyes now suddenly bright with relief. They were weak and dehydrated, but alive. Margot and the kids knew we had saved them; an unwanted sensation, but a moment to treasure.

We took the pleasure boat in tow but dropped it later while hoisting aboard. It wasn't ours anyway, so we allowed it to drift on its endless journey around the Columbia-Panama Gyre. I guided the lifeboat back into the tanker's lee, wishing right then that life had background music. We perilously re-hooked to the dangerously swinging davit falls. Up above they slipped on an air-driven winch and up we rode, slowly but surely, the wires and pulleys doing their irritating and frightening, screaming rendition as if they might not sustain the burden. Stopping at the embarkation deck, we all alighted, and with an allusion to tradition I felt it proper to be the last one stepping back aboard the mother ship.

The family were given a cabin to shower, and then joined us for a small steak dinner as the *Arabian Addax* motored the three hours to George Town on Grand Cayman. Before the light disappeared, an aircraft flew over and Robert Bazell saw his precious family waving up to him. Lieutenant Kelly of the Miami Coast Guard declared, "They were really very lucky," and he was right. Take even a cursory scan of maritime history and death is more than a statistic; Margot and the kids had beaten the odds. I enjoyed my beer of celebration and reflection that night, like the satisfying feeling of a hole-in-one. In my inner world I felt triumphant. I'd had little choice, but I did what I had to do, with seamanlike professionalism and fortitude. I was happy for the reunited family and their resolutely human-sized drama, but I had overcome my own fears, those emotions that withhold one's personal growth, like a childhood scar healing under the wrinkles of maturity. Compared to Henry Blogg, we looked like a gang who couldn't shoot straight. Heck! He had worse days untangling towels on the beach at Cromer. Would I have done the same in a gale? We'll never know. Actually, I do, but this had been a momentous day for me, hopefully a step in the direction of a more complete future.

THE *ARABIAN Addax* delivered her cargo. Then we were off on a lazy, transatlantic voyage to the Mediterranean, two dozen private lives interlocked like a clockwork mechanism with a human heartbeat, and we felt like a team. Somehow my fears had been assuaged and all that learning hadn't been in vain. I had time to contemplate God again, like a broken thought I couldn't repair. My heroes reflected the wisdom of secular learning, but loneliness and proximity to death concentrate the mind. The barely essential cabin now seemed stark and confined, as if something were locked inside of my thoughts and emotions by the steel bulkheads. Three things compound the seaman's mind on a long passage. First, the lack of intimacy frustrates, of course. Magazines were helpful, yes, but no substitute for the real thing. Women dwell in the chasm between frustration and fulfillment, and Olga met my perceived ideal of the opposite sex, like Marlène Jobert, although I was later to add the entire female population of Southeast Asia. Second, seafarers are supposed to be men of faith, but I'd seen no one praying, or even discussing the matter. I was no nearer solving that godly conundrum. And finally, when all other outlets were either blocked or proved too convoluted to fathom, my friend lay silently, cooling in the fridge.

IF THERE'S a special hell for seafarers, it's the Suez Canal. I knew to expect the expected. The remainder of the voyage now seemed so much an anticlimax. In the Canal we secured the bumboats amidships. The same band of old Arab men camped out on the lower companionway selling trinkets of local relevance: postcards, smoking pipes and mini pyramids, typically made in China to add an air of generally authentic bunkum. Whereas they might once have offered some notion of near-Eastern exoticism, by 1982 they were grubby, badgering visitors we didn't need. Whatever they were selling, I wasn't remotely close to being their target customer.

Completing the canal transit, I received notice to sign off in the Persian Gulf, along with the chief mate and the first engineer. They ordered us to wait at Khor Fakkan, just outside the Gulf, which seemed odd; tankers always used to wait inside. The mountains behind can be seen on radar from thirty or forty miles. Steaming full ahead in their direction, we acquired targets below the mountains. Increasingly we could no longer ignore the dozens of ships lying at anchor off the little-known port. But why?

Since I had last visited these politically charged waters, a major war had erupted between Iran and Iraq. Much had been threatened of tankers plying their trade, and whether it was justified made scant difference; the insurance companies were not about to cover the risk. If your vessel was heading into the Gulf, you now waited outside. So, we rode around the anchorage finding a place to swing. Right then I didn't think it mattered.

The next day we were off, with bags aplenty, and checked into a nearby luxury hotel whose name escapes me. The three of us sat in the restaurant drinking as our voyage-based friendship slowly dissipated with the lobster thermidor on Sanko's account. The conversation was hollow at the heart of the camaraderie—we sought a return to our friends, loved ones and familiarity. But we had one last toast to "the rescue," speculating if another ship might have chosen a different course of action. Who wants extra people and a deviation? We discussed the slippery nature of morality, as one does after a few drinks, and congratulated ourselves— no one else was going to—on doing the right thing in an increasingly ambiguous moral climate. The Falklands War had ended. I had missed the action, but the British kept it in the headlines for long afterwards. The Iran-Iraq War, however, having just begun, was to wearily drag on in horror for another six years.

And me? I had grown up a bit.

10

High and Dry

1982–1983

Of all sad words of tongue or pen, the saddest are these, 'It might have been.'

—John Greenleaf Whittier

THE BRITISH had won another far-flung war to be tallied with the others. It had lasted barely ten weeks and some nine hundred men had died; a scant debacle, compared to horrifying events in the Middle East. Returning home, I was drawn to the conflict's record, hungry for the daily propaganda as the newspapers dripped hate and lies. I had missed all the smugness, nationalism and trite military philosophizing. But I soon grew fatigued with the jingoistic press; *The Sun*, in its inimitable style, claimed "GOTCHA" after the British sank an Argentinian gunboat—about as journalistically impartial as a war recruitment poster.

Instinctively, I felt the strongest bond with men who had suffered at sea. I reflected on them working, perhaps deep below the waterline, and then the sudden, instant erasure of life as the weapon hit, doubtless many vanishing in the most terrible manner. I saw the pictures of seamen in life rafts adrift in the dark gray seas of the frigid Antarctic, sick and freezing. Fire happens at sea; it is the seafarer's utmost fear because there's nowhere to hide.

I spent two months on leave. My brother and sister, being older, had existed in social groups beyond mine while growing up. Since I'd begun this career, it was as if they had been waiting for me to mature. And growing up I was, and faster than acquaintances I had left behind. My siblings had both married, and since I drove supertankers, I now qualified for babysitting duties. But I also considered them adult friends, worthy of socializing with. They requested stories, whether out of curiosity or habit I wasn't sure, but they had no context. How could I explain? Neither had felt the vulnerability of crossing the stormy Atlantic, or rescued families off the Caymans. How many of my school friends had worked a shift of twenty-four hours, or scarred their hands raw with rust-encrusted valve wheels? It was tiring relating, so I didn't. I would describe my personal life as uninteresting, in that nothing was happening. I didn't mind living that way, quiet and alone, but societal pressure to settle down can be as cruel as loneliness. I understood the conundrum; if life was going to sea, where did it end? I concluded it too early to find out. My brother, my sister and a few friends had all, in effect, decided the final version of themselves: a house in England with a few kids. I didn't see how they could ever change that now.

Anyway, the calendar required another voyage to accrue sufficient sea time for a resumption of college. I set the philosophical babble aside for a future quiet night on a bridge wing, and called Sanko; better show up for work if they were paying me. On the spot they had a tanker in "Queen Anna, Australia," or that's what I heard him say. I couldn't find it in the atlas, but Australia was a place I had aspired to visit. Sanko overnighted an airline ticket to Perth, which is a longer flight than humans should suffer. The city, the most isolated in the world, from what I briefly glimpsed, looked agreeable; of moderate and walkable size, fine weather, affluent and very livable. I made a mental note to return. After the flight, exhausted and grubby, I needed, and was given, a pleasant night in a top-class hotel. A new captain, of pious disposition, joined with me; a tall South African who clearly spent time on his tan while squandering his few other positive attributes.

We rode with the agent the next day out into the Perth suburbs, to the town of Kwinana ("ah, now I get it"), where BP ran the only refinery in Western Australia. Waiting for us, alone and forlorn, as if the designers had missed the shipbuilding revolution, sat the unmistakable shape and color of a Sanko Line tanker, the MV *Manhattan Baron*. It was as if I had walked ashore from the last one and, while away, they had painted a new name on the side, leaving the bleeding rust streaks intact. I settled in, taking on the manner of an experienced, but still young professional. Show me my cabin, throw the bags in, take out some well-worn working clothes and I'm ready. My predecessor had drawn the routes for the next voyage—as one should with a good handover—so I stood my cargo watch until we were done with pumping oil. The *Manhattan Baron* contained nary a single original idea or surprise, but had a full world-folio of charts to be maintained. Fortunately, I was partial to the work; it perfectly melded with my cartographic inclination. Leaving the modern, colonial and faintly English Kwinana, we sailed north along the expansive Australian coast, heading for a break in the Indonesian island chain, into the Java Sea.

The Lombok Strait is of considerable scientific significance. More than just another pretty, deep-blue channel between the Indonesian islands, it represents the imaginary boundary known as the Wallace Line, a most significant faunal divide. It was named for the biologist Alfred Russel Wallace, who first highlighted the striking difference between the animals of Indo-Malaysia to the west from those of Australasia to the southeast. He saw the suddenness of the boundary and became a hero of mine, co-discoverer—yet barely recognized—of the greatest idea ever.

I'm not a biologist, but it troubled me, the conundrum posed by the Judeo-Christian God and evolution. The concept, published by Wallace in a joint presentation of papers in 1858, was elaborated the following year in *On the Origin of Species*. Darwin published the book, so attained the fame, describing the process of natural selection. I was supposing the God conundrum irreconcilable. Dig past the faithful topsoil and what do you have? I wanted facts, and religion appeared bereft of them. Fortunately, the ship operated in a theological vacuum and kept a well-stocked cold fridge from which I drew my daily supply.

Wherever we traveled, each voyage concluded at Kwinana. At night, gazing up at the dark ocean of space, I attained a first-rate inspection of that sublime cosmic spectacle, the Southern Cross. The stars boomed in like halogen bulbs; the constellations depicted as if on a giant 3-D IMAX screen. Kwinana was straightforward to locate, the weather subtropical and pleasant, appropriate to stand on the bridge wing and take in the vista. These were nights worth being at sea, far from home, but somehow at home.

I needed to see a doctor; ear trouble. On arrival the agent dropped me at the local clinic at the town center, and after a quick procedure involving a pretty nurse and a rubber tube, I strolled the suburban roads of Kwinana for half an hour. It seemed ordinary, quiet and familiar, much like the suburbia I knew on a peaceful weekday. The population had departed to work, the children in school. Only the skeleton of the English neighborhood remained. The weather perhaps—the sun-kissed luminescence—revealed the foreignness. I recognized that feeling again, of walking in the lives of others, pondering how ordinary their existences were in their bungalows with green lawns. I felt like an astronaut from another planet, having landed, and devoted thirty minutes studying this remote urban locale, and formed an opinion without ever meeting the creatures that inhabited it.

The *Manhattan Baron* needed oil to make money, and the place to acquire it was the Persian Gulf, which from Kwinana is two weeks' sailing across the Indian Ocean, the type of voyage I enjoy: good weather, little traffic, and time to hone my astronomical skills and settle in my new steel-boxed home with Madonna in her fishnets on the bulkhead. They supplied the bridge with two sextants. Henry, the Filipino third mate, took two morning sights of the sun. I took one, too, when up to it, and at noon, either alone or together, we agreed the height of the sun at its zenith, and we had our position. Some nights the sea transformed into a milky white as we motored through the bioluminescence of a trillion glowing things. It was a satisfying routine, following the same compass bearing for days at a time, as earlier mariners only wished they could.

ONE OF my earliest memories was sitting on the floor of my friend Punch's maisonette, about half a mile from our semi. We called him Punch because he had an older sister named Judy. In that time, children of eight were safe and free to wander suburb-wide, free from paranoia. We played with his impressive model armored-vehicle collection. I don't recall the strategic details, but I remember Punch's young mother sitting shoeless on the plush creamy carpet, dressed in her gossamer hose, legs to one side in her short black dress and white blouse. She had blonde, shoulder-length hair and feigned attention as her mind wandered elsewhere in an adult world; anywhere but the awful male obsession with war. Why do images remain in our minds for so long while I forget what happened yesterday?

Returning to Khor Fakkan after our sleepy two-week cruise, the *Manhattan Baron* joined the others waiting their turn to enter the high-insurance zone. With scant news, we gossiped and discussed the war, and the anxiety grew. For three months the carnage had endured. The Iranians, invoking the same God as all the other armies, called it the Holy Defense. The premise—which I declare without certitude—was to enlarge Iraq's petroleum reserves and render it the region's dominant economic power. 1982 persisted in its bloody, deathly manner, with an occasional cease-fire initiative that never materialized. It all made about as much sense as Punch and me playing with plastic tanks on his mother's living room carpet. I never saw her again.

As a key plot detail of this book, it is important to recognize that in a strict military sense, it had been primarily a land encounter. Compared with that bloody fighting, the Tanker War, as they later called it, became a mere sideshow, not yet drawing other nations into the conflict. We were cautious, but not nerve-racked. Wars and conflict were for the newsreels; they didn't happen to Sanko Line. It was just another Christmas at sea, an event I rarely relished. I found all the soppy nonsense so manipulative. On the twenty-fourth we sailed into the Gulf without military attendance. The seaman goes wherever the charter requires. He has no choice; it's the agreement he has endorsed. In trouble his only defense is the steel shell within which he lives and the state flag under which he sails. We took the southern route to avoid being in the wrong place, evading any military involvement that might occur on the Iranian coastline. It was an anxious time, hoping the reality of war would not intrude, like a man believing used-car advertising.

The port of Mina Ash Shuaybah (I'll call it Shuaybah; we all did) is in Kuwait, just south of Mina Al Ahmadi, close enough to be considered the same refining and manufacturing complex, acting as an immense export point for petrochemicals, sulfur, and petroleum coke. I saw only one terminal man, an Arab in green coveralls, no hat, but a thick mustache, as was the fashion in those parts. We signaled when ready to load and he rotated a giant valve, like a politician at a photo op, and in the oil gushed at whatever maximum rate we desired. He wanted to give us more, as if he were ready for dinner, but the *Manhattan Baron* was a minor player in these parts and we couldn't take the flow they offered.

Twelve hours later we were low in the tainted water and full to capacity. Shuaybah was uncommonly unattractive and as dry as a biscuit, the fuzzy burnt-yellow refinery to the west and hazy blue Gulf to the east, like sitting in an unreal nebulous gap in the middle. The city had no trees, no grass, just sand and scrub for a landscape. It was predictable, conservative, nationalistic and probably homophobic. The Americans had been friendly with Kuwait since 1951, so we felt safe, immune to the death barely a hundred miles away. They prohibited drinking, so there was no reason to linger. We took the southern route again, close to shallow waters, but the heightened tension was noticeable. Every other maritime object—ship, rig or boat—raised suspicion. We wanted to be free and deep-sea, back to our watery routine.

SAUDI ARABIA didn't sound like a merry place to stop, either, but we needed bunkers. It wasn't fun—it is a terrifying land that smacks of totalitarianism. Jeddah is the largest port on the Red Sea, and the principal gateway to Mecca. It's a large Islamic tourist destination, but what was there for me? Religion, scorching sunshine, covered women and all those wailing mosques? Nothing to envy here. While alongside we flew the Saudi flag twenty-four hours a day so as not to affront by hauling it down, a commission as difficult to understand as clapping with one hand. My only recollection was that the pilot accepted a bottle of Scotch on departure. The irrationality of it all baffled me. We set north to another continent, via the Suez Canal.

YOU CAN go east from Port Said, but few ships do. The *Manhattan Baron* headed west-northwest to skirt the Grecian coast and squeezed into the Adriatic Sea, heading for its northern limit. Venice, city, seaport, and capital of the province of Venezia, is an exotic destination which I never considered I might visit, but there we were—I suppose everyone needs crude oil. It's unique environmentally, architecturally, and historically. They once styled the city "the most serene," so it was quite a reputation to uphold, like a classic old movie showing at a modern Cineplex. It wasn't on my list of places to visit, like Valparaíso, but since the *Manhattan Baron* was going there, I gladly tagged along with an open mind. As commonly known, it lies in a lagoon of some two hundred square miles of mudflats, tidal shallows, salt marshes and some open, navigable water, where we anchored.

In the lagoon it was mid-January and suddenly much colder; a perfect example of the seafarer's meteorological lot. Wrapped in parkas, the hazy sun couldn't alleviate the wintry air mass and, in the mornings, steaming plumes of breath escaped our mouths. From the anchorage, we could see the jumbled low buildings of the island city dominated by the bell tower of St. Marks, but no one ventured a visit. It lacked romance in January, clutched by a deep freeze. I couldn't imagine a flamboyant cameo by Audrey Hepburn in a parka shivering in a gondola alongside the Rialto Bridge. The tiny Italian vessel *Caraibi* came along our port side, bizarrely, facing the wrong way, to lighter us. Plenty of arm waving and shouting from the Italians took place during the transfer, so we reciprocated, which they appreciated rather than protested.

Eventually we slipped into Porto Marghera, the beating industrial heart that supplied the more famous island. At dusk on the one available day, I walked ashore with the first engineer, a well-stuffed Norwegian fellow. We were not close, but he offered amiable company and spoke a few words of Italian. It was a cool, wintry evening with mist in the air. He found what I might describe as a working man's cafeteria, so close we could smell and taste the refinery. It was bare and cold inside, even with the kitchen's warmth. We had no trouble finding a seat. The customers—local working men—knew not who we were, and didn't care. We ordered something from a bear-sized man in an apron who might have been the chef, for all I knew. It was alien, it was unfamiliar, it was all the things I would never have considered a few years earlier. But the pasta was tasty and the bottle of economical wine plenty good enough for me. And that was all I saw of Venice, and I don't mind. I missed the touristy part, the canals and the gondolas, but I've seen them in the movies where they are probably better represented, and these few brief hours ashore in the industrial port have lingered in my mind. We loaded stores: food and Peroni beer. Well, it was better than grog, I suppose. The *Manhattan Baron* headed back to the warmth of Asia, back via the Canal.

A NEW chief mate joined, replacing a nice enough guy who, like me and others, enjoyed his drink. But the rule is you can't overindulge while others not of us are watching. I had learned early on you didn't drink while working crude oil in port with others who were without sympathy for our lifestyle, and he had broken the rule. With the new mate came the energizing news the *Manhattan Baron* had been stemmed for a dry-docking in mid-March. He took to organizing the preparations, a protracted affair. We all worked hard with a sense of anticipation. We'd been given a rough date but no destination. We didn't want the new giant facility in Dubai; we didn't want Portugal, or the UK. We wanted something exotic, somewhere worth visiting. I favored a few weeks in Japan. We'd been soaking up rumors one day during a routine discharge in Australia, when the news broke of the docking destination, and it disappointed no one: Singapore! Had there been a chandelier available…

Dry dock planning can take months, depending on the vessel's size and complexity. Fortunately, the *Manhattan Baron* was an example of one of the most common vessel types in the world, the standard Aframax[33] tanker. There were, and still are, many hundreds of them plying the world's oceans. They are the workhorses of the global energy trade. Their size and shape portend two things; first, their loaded draft allows them entry to most places where crude oil might be desired. Second, their size—about five hundred thousand barrels—is typically the volume that refiners buy and traders trade. All ships have a docking plan. It's not something anyone is going to concoct on short notice. The builder designs it during construction, effectively laying out how to dock the ship when the necessity arises every five years or so.

After all that planning, there we were, approaching Singapore from the south, furiously cleaning tanks, and I was filled with the curiosity not just of another port, but a big diamond of a port, one of a handful that stirred the wandering soul, like an appointment with a movie star. The *Manhattan Baron* motored into the mighty Western Anchorage.

---

33 A medium-sized tanker with a deadweight capacity between 80,000 and 120,000, deriving its name from AFRA, the Average Freight Rate Assessment, created in 1954 by Shell to standardize contract terms.

IN 1819, Sir Stamford Raffles established a trading post for the world's first corporate giant, the Honorable East India Company, when wars were about maps instead of religion, in what became Singapore. Sir Stamford was one of those dashing men that England produced plentifully in the late eighteenth century, but no hero of mine—too many like him were supremely confident of transforming the world in their own image. Raffles, as was the custom, negotiated the sale of the sparsely populated island settlement—with scant regard for the indigenous—to the corporation.

Singapore, the hinge of the East, is so close to Malaysia that it appears its international neighbor has scooped out a large semicircle for the island to fit within. To the south, the thousand broken-off fragments of islands comprising the Riau Archipelago crowd into the narrowing Strait of Malacca, causing one of the world's mightiest shipping bottlenecks, like Cairo traffic on an average day. Because the port is a major one—oil, containerization, shipbuilding, bunkering—there are so many vessels transiting and stopping that the waterway is further constrained by numerous designated anchorages. It all seems a mess, but somehow the Singaporeans have brought sense to it all, like solving an enormous jigsaw puzzle.

In operation from 1965, the multifaceted Jurong is an international, multipurpose port operator, part of the government's effort to develop the maritime and offshore industry as one of the key sectors of industrialization. A bewildering miscellany of goods passes through this model example of how to build a port for the world when you're blessed with geography. And it was to Jurong that the *Manhattan Baron* headed that hot, humid day in March 1983.

The dock master placed dozens of massive blocks along the floor to bear the weight of the ship. He used precision to ensure support for the keel while avoiding engine-room intakes, echo sounders, speed logs and other obstructions hidden below the waterline. We slipped into DD2, tugs pushing and lines pulling, with divers monitoring the placement. It's a long, slow process, but I didn't mind. I understood the millions of dollars' worth of engineering and refurbishment about to happen, and I knew that once secured, we would break watches. What was the point when we were no longer floating? Effectively, the *Manhattan Baron* would cease to be a ship for two weeks. I hankered for sleep, like a luxury I had avoided for months. Once in the correct setting, the dock caisson gate floated into position, sealing the entrance, and the pumping out began[34]. The engine room shut down and they connected a shore power supply. Final employment entailed removing each tank's bottom plugs. The *Manhattan Baron* was a ship, but for now no longer acting as one, high and dry, dripping industrial water onto the dark, dank concrete dock, like the proverbial beached whale. Alien people roamed about our home, but the mighty beast was somehow quiet in the unfamiliar environment, and I slept the sleep of the contented.

> *Singapore is what your city could become if everyone obeyed the rules, did their jobs diligently, and just shut up. When your city gets to be this paragon of efficiency and discipline would you still want to live there? Singapore is a model city, which is terrific if you happen to be a model human.*[35]

I'VE HEARD this common sentiment, but I feel it's disingenuous. I had to work, but also had two weeks to run free of my confinement. Singapore in 1983 was a different city than now, and I suspect it will be

34 In 1988 one of the dry dock gates sprung a leak and killed three men working on the dock floor.
35 Jessica Zafra.

different next year. It's a city on the move, recreating itself, but always in its own inimitable image: multiracial, modern, oriental, hot and humid, gateway to wherever anyone is going. It's unrealistic to discuss the city without mention of Lee Kuan Yew. He's rightly credited with hauling the tiny nation, not always enthusiastically, into the first world in one generation. He made Singapore, and it continues today, as a singularly idiosyncratic nation, something special, forever evolving.

During Lee's suspiciously long term as prime minister, he curbed unemployment, raised the standard of living and implemented a large-scale public housing program rationalized in rows of look-alike apartment blocks outside the central business area. Individualism may have dimmed, but he developed the country's economic infrastructure, eliminated racial tension and created an independent national defense. Others have tried to emulate the model, but it's a fortuitous mingling of geography, politics and his brilliant legal mind that would be tough to replicate in other, essentially larger states. Something made him for Singapore, and he made Singapore in his image. His government could be assertive; the "stop at two" policy and "the second can wait" policy snubbed the traditional Chinese family demanding more children. The government legalized abortion and sterilization. Irrespective of the people, Lee Kwan Yew did what he thought was right.

A more reputable crusade, perhaps, and renowned worldwide, was the "Keep Singapore Clean" campaign, to build a spotless, green nation, and enhance its appeal for foreign investment and tourism. They discouraged littering and spitting, and it really was a noticeably clean place. "Make courtesy our way of life" was a slogan, mostly for the tourists, but also a bid to build a caring, polite and civic-minded— read, guardedly, "utopian"—society. Its emblem, not surprisingly, was a happy, cartoonish lion, like an extra from *Top Cat*. Maybe you can understand the disconnect when I tell you that, contemporaneously, England suffered an economy out of control, industries weakened by layoffs, and corporate callousness. The government's main social initiative was reducing football hooliganism. Singapore was an altered state for me, like walking through an Asian Disneyland, freshly swept clean for the morning rush, an event masterpiece on the short list of why I went to sea.

The twists and turns I cannot recall, but from Jurong the tallest building of the Central Business District skyline was the Oversea-Chinese Bank. I could see it to the east, so I headed there. The public buses, double-decker, were non-air-conditioned, bumpy and cramped. But, heck, I was making real money those days, so I rode the yellow-topped black taxis, Toyota Crowns and Nissan Cedrics. Curiously, the most striking prospect in 1983 was the shopping, for two reasons. Foremost, the shopping centers were air-conditioned and Singapore was taxing for us dressed in our best going-ashore gear, unacclimated to the suffocating humidity and heat. Second, much like Japan, it was all glistening new electronics, bright lights, and this time with the added sales gift that the pretty shop assistants spoke English. And I could read the signs with the Chinese characters adding exotic decoration. Just about everyone wanted a new Casio watch, digital being the rage. And they were water-resistant and the battery might last seven years. Being contrary, I aimed slightly higher.

It didn't take long to discover the place to binge was People's Park at the foot of Pearl's Hill. It was an outstandingly unattractive building: the exposed raw concrete edifice of Brutalist style, somehow made turquoise and tan. The thirty-one-story building was the first shopping center of its kind in Asia and set the pattern for things to come, like nothing I had seen before, occupying a hectare in the heart of

Chinatown. It comprised offices and apartments above a podium shopping space, designed to revitalize a crowded enclave of post-independent Singapore, a city-state morphing from cheap low-rise to pricey high-rise. It was a transition from street-based food and vendors to an air-conditioned, Le Corbusier, high-rise nirvana, where streets in the sky were meant to encourage social interaction. The shopping center incorporated a large atrium with countless shops and kiosks, retaining the busy character of the original Chinatown, without the tinge and vice of poverty.

Moving inside, I shuddered, struck by the intense air-conditioning. Everywhere dense human traffic, with escalators rising seemingly in every direction and sales demonstrations of the latest fad. The place burst with life, an unusual mix of activity and, always, gorgeous Asian woman everywhere. The corridors were lined with travel agencies, reflexology shops, copy-music stores, Indian tailors and electronics, their goods spilling into the corridors, and the prestige Overseas Emporium anchoring it all. Walking around, the aromas of perfume shops, Chinese homeopathic spices and blaring pop music assaulted the senses. At the lower floor was a food court, another concept I had never imagined, serving a variety of alien tastes and palates for a consistently low price, and not a fly to be seen. People's Park was a game-changing eye-opener. I bought what everyone else wanted, mostly, pirated music tapes. I bought dozens, two for the America dollar, "cheap as cheese." It was the beginning of Cantopop, with an emphasis on appearance rather than music, which was fine since I couldn't understand the songs anyway, but Anita Mui soon replaced Madonna on the cabin bulkhead. It was time to buy a new music machine, and like everyone else who travels and finds space a precious commodity, I purchased the Walkman, and added speakers. Implausibly, I was shopping with enthusiasm.

SQUEAKY-CLEAN SINGAPORE delighted in being a mixed economy that worked; a sanitized Orwellian city-state, where making money was seen as more important than individual freedom, but I doubt Adam Smith would recognize it. It was regulated with strong laws concerning public toilet flushing, smoking and littering. But, thankfully, vices could be found in Singapore, the city's reputation ever sullied by the notorious Bugis Street in the heart of the Xiao Po district. The Sparky, a decent chap, public school, man-of-empire-type and I, headed out one night with my uncanny aptitude for gravitating towards the sleaziest part of town. Reputation—good or bad—is everything. We felt a need to find this refuge of immorality, or at least some shadow of it. The street was renowned from the 1950s to the 1980s for its nightly gathering of trans women, a spectacle which made it one of the city's top tourist destinations. Business boomed, and the area bustled with activity, celebrated for the hundreds of hawkers selling food, drink and trinkets along with its nightly parade of flamboyantly dressed Kai Tais,[36] and the hordes of gawkers astonished by the Asian queens in full regalia. With sufficient liquor, few found the concept suspicious. The whole lot was supposedly gangster controlled, but no doubt they were courteous. I considered the proposed visit hedonistic, but esoteric preparation for the body and soul, and alcohol sanctioned the simple acts of affirmation we English struggled with.

We failed to spot the legion of androgynous beauties, but, abandoning all sense of pride, Sparky and I tracked down the appropriate seedy locale where a few well-groomed, intrepid felines sashayed around in high heels gladdening the eyes. We were swiftly in the companionship of two ladies, one dressed in a sexy tight-fitting dress, the other in fashionable satin pants, as if Frankenstein's bride had escaped the laboratory. The usual questions I'd heard before: Where do you come

---

36 People who have a gender identity, or gender expression, that differs from their assigned sex.

from? What brings you to Singapore? Next thing, "Amy" was on my lap, which I considered cordial of her. Up close, the thick makeup, the too-narrow hips, and the slight height advantage over the average Asian female were not so easy to dismiss. Bewilderingly, in an exotic, far-off, steamy modern city, I felt obliged to try more than the special fried rice; I could get that in London. But let's be careful here. With Amy on my lap something was stirring, and not just my Singapore Sling. I was "excessively diverted," as Jane Austin might have written. As the cocktails poured down faster, either Sparky or I had an epiphany and discretion finally rose above my ardor; there could be no more willful disregard of the evidence. If the release of months of frustration was that important—and it typically was—there must be more traditional alternatives than Amy whispering in my ear. She could be more easily dismissed by the head than the heart before too many more drinks, and I couldn't allow passion to overawe my capacity for reason, so just in time, we departed the surreal encounter for more intuitive fare.

Though many locals accepted it as part of the culture, conservative Singaporeans believed it marred the newly minted image. The residents were humanely moved to the new housing estates with a predictably negative effect on tourism. A few years later the dirty back lanes, smelly drains and unhealthy sanitary conditions were cleaned up by Lee's beneficial juggernaut. Bugis Street was redeveloped into another retail complex of shopping malls, restaurants and nightspots mixed with regulated roadside vendors, marking the end of an era in Singapore's history. Most of the ladyboys departed for Bangkok, where so many had originated. All that remained was a glistening shell inhabited by ghosts, and a new subway station.

I'm sad that Bugis Street and the other places have gone. It was a shattering glimpse into a world so far removed from my own, and yet I wasn't running from it in fear. My final shopping trip was to the gleaming new Lucky Plaza, endearingly named in that innocent Chinese manner. Its main virtue was as a copy of People's Park, an air-conditioned, open vertical bazaar in the high-class tourist district of Orchard Road. It had electronics, cosmetics, perfumes, Filipino shops, a golden bubble elevator—everything, except zombies. Outside on the street I bought myself a new watch for twenty dollars. Why buy a genuine Casio when I could buy a counterfeit Rolex?

Well, eventually, my brief sojourn of Asian relaxation concluded, and I wouldn't have missed it for the world. Singapore is a small country that makes a big impression. I spent a lot of money, but then I had money to spend. We took on stores to replace the rapidly diminishing pile of Peroni with the tastier Tiger Beer. We had to work in dry dock, so I don't want to give the wrong impression, but honestly, eight-to-five is quite undemanding. The defining aspect of dry-docking is viewing the ship you thought you knew so well from such a singular standpoint, high and dry. Finally, we made sure all the tank bottom plugs were firmly replaced and the *Manhattan Baron*—all gleaming green paint and corporate logo, like a cartoon swoosh cloud—slid out of the fantastic port city in search of business. Like Hank Quinlan, I wanted to return one day. Leaving Singapore felt a bit like dying.

THERE'S NO better place or time for contemplation than when alone on the bridge wing of a tanker on a quiet, still night. The unceasing accompaniment of the engine pulse and the surge of the hull through thick black water acted like a hypnotist's swinging watch, encouraging my mind to drift, nothing but the dim horizon and the wondrous stars above. I had been the "man on the Clapham Omnibus," the "man in the Ford Cortina," reasonable and ordinary, but I sought a transformation.

The English are neither cosmopolitan nor philosophical, but being of an island nature, they understand each other. Communication between us is very subtle; you have to know the code. When traveling we have that annoying habit of congregating to recreate a little England of teatime, football and Marmite. I was a young man of pronounced opinions, especially when drinking, and I had changed during the previous two years. As an apprentice my brain and conscience, fresh out of school, absorbed everything, and everything I did was quintessentially John Bull, because the people I worked with were English. It was exhausting—the same old jokes told once too often, the same remote political stances I might have heard in London.

I continued drinking deep from the Shell fountainhead, but Ching was the impetus. He had exposed me to a universe of cultures, languages and traditions alien to my native land and I wanted to see, breathe and live so much more. For two years now, I had sailed with Dutch, Yugoslav, South African, Filipino and others; all citizens of Earth, just like me. I hadn't talked of cricket, Benny Hill, nor used the word *bollocks* with someone who understood it. There had been no English beer, no Yorkshire pudding or *News of the World*. Now it was *nasi goreng* and Anchor beer and the Voice of America, and I liked it. On this ship we were all the same, with a strange decency and politeness bestowed upon us as our own national identities slipped away, going about our business, socializing and effectively working. I was proud to be British, but increasingly I wanted to be a man—a citizen— of the world. I longed to depart a ship when my time was done, but I didn't always want to return to England.

WE FOUND oil in nearby Dumai, Indonesia, and headed west for the Land of Milk and Honey, which regrettably meant transiting the Suez Canal. It was the same as last time.

It was a comfortable, luxurious crossing, the ship's white wake running along the lead-gray lines I had drawn on the chart. Drinking? Yes, but the rotating cabin system of socialization tempered any excess. The weather was good, which made the ride comfortable, safe and relaxed. The routine of deep sea bestowed little stress on the ship or me. The news came through for my journey's end, as usual, by Morse code one day in a routine dispatch from the head office. The company was drifting into financial difficulties again and I had already booked a return to college, so I sensed my time with the mighty Sanko Line might be approaching its conclusion.

The *Manhattan Baron* arrived at the Delaware Bay and the fragrant smell of land, sliding between Cape May and Cape Henlopen, chugged upriver and pulled into the Crown Eagle Point refinery in the borough of Westville, which rather pretentiously names itself "The Gateway to New Jersey." For me, it was. I had little interest in the tangled web of pipes and black towers; the agent sat in his car to greet me on arrival. And, since I was in Philadelphia, I decided on a three-day vacation in New York. My earlier stopover had imbued me with a sense of wonder unfulfilled.

I arrived at the Taft Hotel in midtown, just above Times Square. In the early '80s this area lay deep in an era of tawdry theater, drugs and pornographic bookstores north of Father Duffy Square. It might have affected the tourist potential, but I didn't mind; in fact, it added to the allure. I had lost the innocence of youth long ago. I walked from Fifty-First Street to Wall Street in the beautiful spring weather. I rode the elevators up the Empire State Building and I zigzagged back and forth across Central Park. I ate good steak in comfortable restaurants, drained the sea from my body and considered my place in life. I complained so much I must have been a socialist, and my earlier revolutionary enthusiasm for Thatcher had dissipated. I didn't want to change people's lives; I just hoped they could be better.

I HAD come to a fork in the road and Sanko, sadly, were not on it. After a month at home I drove down to Plymouth, a five-hour drive along some entertaining roads in my newly purchased, used Audi. I believed it might be a more enticing choice than South Shields. It was. Another student and I lived with a family in the suburb of Plympton—a suburb of a suburb, if you will—some fifteen minutes from the college. It was like transferring from my family in the London suburbs to another in Devon. The work was hard and compressed. We sat the maritime license: Class II Deck Officer (or what used to be called the Chief Mate's Ticket). As always, and not with any reflection of my talent, I passed the examinations. The college class that semester contained a few people from Canadian Pacific, the giant North American conglomerate, whose British subsidiary, CP Ships, operated out of London. After college, fresh license in hand, I called them.

11

The Atlantics

1984

The voice of the sea speaks to the soul. The touch of the sea is sensuous, enfolding the body in its soft, close embrace.

—Kate Chopin

THIS VOYAGE transpired in my Anglo-American-centric home, the Atlantic Ocean. It separates the Old and New Worlds, the two forever joined by its oft-traveled enormity, the slate-gray sea's epic narrative formulating the intellectual evolution of civilization, or at least the fragment whence my forebears came. I sought travel, to learn of other cultures and customs, but from the beginning all I knew were the English-speaking values of my recent childhood. Going to sea was changing that, evolving another man. The Atlantic—a metaphor for life—was both a barrier and bridge. For centuries the only way to traverse it had been on ships, and then came the telegraph and the wireless. Now, in a matter of hours, the almost indefinably vast divide could be crossed by commercial airline, as I had done to arrive at one of its illustrious cities, New York.

A transient night in a noisy freeway hotel with too much time to ponder, then a return to work, as if being woken by the jailor at dawn.

A third engineer and I rode the famous Miller's Launch from next to where the ferries leave Staten Island, out to the Stapleton Anchorage, just north of the Verrazano-Narrows. There we boarded the pocket-sized tanker MV *Fort Kipp*. Alongside her lay one of those boxy black Bouchard barges that ply their trade about the harbor, lightering the oceangoing ships. The magnificent vista of the Manhattan skyscrapers seemed as good a place as any for our arrest. I should explain.

She had arrived the day before and was already pumping gasoline. I settled in as the work went on; my fourth employer in three years. I was dangerously on the cusp of becoming a journeyman. As expected, the work was challenging and sleep-depriving, but nothing untoward. I was rather disposed to set to sea and establish myself, but a day later, still lying at anchor, a radio message arrived from the head office with instructions to suspend cargo transfer with 5,000 tonnes remaining. The captain's first allegiance is to the owner who employs him, then the charterer. The next morning, surrealistically, a uniformed US Marshall boarded, gun in holster, as is the custom of that place, and arrested the vessel on behalf of the charterer who had issued a writ in rem[37], i.e., on the property. Since the property in question—the undelivered oil—was in New York, then the claim established jurisdiction there. The Marshall, an old, rumpled fellow who wore his uniform rather more casually than he perhaps should have, introduced himself, and attached a Notice of Arrest to the steering wheel with Scotch Tape we proffered him, ordering us—on pain of contempt—not to depart with the remaining cargo. Satisfied of his jurisdiction, he retired to the pilot's cabin for a nap.

The following day, the shipowner and cargo owner, having reached an amicable solution, instructed us to deliver the remaining cargo, and

---

37 The power a court exercises over large items of immovable property within its jurisdiction.

all was well with the legal world.[38] The Marshall removed the warrant and bade us safe passage. It was all anticlimactic. Free at last, like an escaping prisoner, we slipped away in the night. Seafarers rarely dwell on unfortunate situations; the predicament lay elsewhere. We set to our next business three thousand miles distant, and I unpacked.

THE ATLANTIC is immense: tens of millions of square miles covering 20 percent of the Earth's surface. When you are standing at the beach, or eyeing from the deck of an oceangoing tanker, this watery world of ours seems so immensely lost to the horizon it is convenient to suppose it a constant; an immutable expanse of salt water, always changing but always the same. In reality, though, the world balances on its surface five enormous, slowly spinning vortexes of water, called gyres. They are central to the global system of water flow and weather. Two such colossal spinning circles exist in the Atlantic, one north, one south. The two half oceans are distinct, primarily due to the equator and the Earth's Coriolis effect. The gyres rotate in opposite directions. The weather is kinder in the south, until one reaches the higher latitudes, but tankers rarely journey there.

Eastbound, we crossed the leaden waters of the northern ocean, and it was on its best behavior; cloudy, for sure, but unusually temperate, the waves gentle and lazy. The surface circulation is dominated by four well-known, interconnected currents. The Gulf Stream flows northeast from the American coast at Cape Hatteras; the North Atlantic Drift streams north and eastward from the Grand Banks; the Canary Current broadly flows south from Europe to Africa; and the North Equatorial Current, just above that line, runs west to the Americas, completing the circle of the mighty vortex. These are the core movers

---

38   Canadian Pacific (Bermuda) Ltd. v. Lagon Maritime Overseas (The "*Fort Kipp*") before Justice Bingham in the Queen's Bench Division, April 2, 1985.

of water in the north, and for a long time, of ships too. Departing New York for Europe, every vessel hitches a ride on the immense North Atlantic Drift, as a massive quantity of balmy water is pushed towards Europe at up to two knots. Characterized by warm temperatures and high salinity, the Drift is often buried by a succession of low pressures trundling off the North American continent, headed for the Old World, like giant, stormy unwanted Frisbees. But it mixes with polar water to produce excellent fishing grounds along the northwest coast of the continent and maintains the mild, wet climate of England, with which I was so familiar.

The two largest European Atlantic ports are Rotterdam and Hamburg, lying at the culmination of the North Atlantic Drift, where it butts into Europe and splits into lesser flows. Pernis was an arduous time, but I liked Rotterdam. I just felt right there, like James Bond does in Monte Carlo. Hamburg was a one-day, frenzied passage away. Each hour blended into the next, working cargo, mooring operations, demanding navigation and a fleeting nap when possible. In 1984 no restrictions were imposed on working time; every day was "on." We just appeared, aching, hour after hour when needed, or until the work was done. It was busy, but broadly satisfying; it was why they paid me.

The grind continued, hectic, tiring and challenging, clambering over and around deck piping, up and down the pump room, swinging valves; the little clean-oil tanker continually busy loading, discharging or tank cleaning. The soft lingering of New York lay far behind. We carried only three mates, so six hours on, six hours off, plus overtime, became the standard. A new captain joined who we soon named "Boomer," since he noisily blundered around, bumbling from one significant decision to another. I liked him because I could see myself being him; he seemed happy to be ignorant of events, so his only job—responsibility—could be rationed until needed. We took the short trip south to France and the navigation watches were chaotic, strenuous and exciting. The Channel, this time, was stormy and vision-restricted, but Boomer left us to it, available if needed, keeping low unless required. He saw things in big, sweeping actions and avoided subtly, like a man unsure of his character. The ship was nimble and accurate to place in a turn when needed, so we plowed south at full speed through the fishing boats and yacht races. The darkness and the stormy weather muffled anything that might have happened.

The Bay of Biscay is notorious for its storms and wonderful seaside resorts. La Rochelle became a favorite, mostly because it was French. The whole region is a popular tourist attraction, and rightly so. The wide vistas of aquamarine water and light blue skies dotted with colorful yachts where they meet, endow the observer with a tranquil frame of mind. There's a straightforward, deep-water approach and an unchallenging brief pilotage. Naturally the tanker berths were the outermost, as if held at a two-kilometer arm's length from society, but it was a casual Citroen ride from the fringe of the city's fringe at La Pallice, into La Rochelle for those craving distraction and Gallic revitalization.

We settled into La Rochelle where a delightful small-boat harbor nestled at the heart of the Plantagenet city. We sat amongst the beautiful people consuming snails, crusty bread and cheap house wine at an open café on the Quai Duperre. Picturesque waterscapes rarely come finer; if we rubbed our eyes, it afforded a vision Monet might evoke. In the late afternoon sunshine, overlooking the crowded harbor with an ancient fort as a background, we sat and took in the afternoon promenade and allowed the world of petroleum to recede, if only for a few hours. La Rochelle was one of those brief excursions that linger in the mind and refresh the body, captivating and all too pretty to leave.

The next day we set back out to sea and headed south for the Pillars of Hercules.

PASSING GIBRALTAR has been a rite of seafaring since antiquity, an experience few others witness. The name derives from the Arabic Jebel Tariq (Tariq's mountain). The seven-mile-wide strait united the Atlantic to the Mediterranean and separated Gibraltar (a British Overseas Territory) and Spain, from Morocco and Ceuta (an autonomous Spanish exclave) in Africa. It once marked the limit of the known world, a myth cultivated by the Greeks and Phoenicians when the universe wasn't much more than they could see, although I knew it as the spot where Peter Brown called to say John and Yoko could marry. Approaching from the west, the narrows appear too snug for safe passage, the illusion created by the tips of Africa and Europe approaching steeply from each side, so solid and immutable. I assumed the watch at midday as we closed in on the narrow waterway. At least the day was clear, made brighter by Boomer staying below after lunch, where he belonged. I knew it was "his ship" and all that that entailed, but I preferred captains to stay out of sight until I needed them, which didn't happen anymore.

Traffic negotiating the Strait abided by a separation scheme, although some obeyed their own impulses. Additionally, ceaseless streams of ferries traversed, like negotiating a busy street. The mind-boggling scale of modern shipping is fueled, in part, by the world's insatiable desire for stuff, with container vessels carrying all that material we're so addicted to, making their way from Suez into the Atlantic. The scheme separates east and westbound vessels in two-mile-wide corridors with only a half-mile separation zone. Plotting my position and tracking a dozen other vessels was hectic work. On the *Fort Kipp*, amongst all the congestion, I relished the opportunity for some maneuvering. I directed the lookout to the wheel and nimbly choreographed a maritime ballet of stress and entertainment, like a video game you have to win. By then, Boomer had sensed the subtle changes in vibration and, as was his manner, boisterously lurched to the bridge to assuage his concern. But the *Fort Kipp* was like my sister's Datsun Sunny, light of touch, nimbly altering course and never getting away from me.

Twenty minutes later, looming through the clouds abeam, there it was, the immense monolithic limestone promontory, a sublime and unique majesty rising to fourteen hundred feet. And what is it, this enigmatic wedge of land at the tip of Spain that isn't Spanish? It keeps Spanish time and they drive on the right. Its total area is only two and a half square miles, it has no natural resources, and the Queen is the head of state. It has good weather and grand views. It's so small the road in closes when planes land. It's a wealthy eccentricity of a bygone empire, but well worth seeing. Then, by four p.m., I was through. The watch had been busy and interesting, a notion I could accept now and again.

The Mediterranean is voluminous enough to suffer its own weather and currents, but improbably has less than 1 percent of the world's watery surface. To put it in context, it contains about 30 percent of the world's shipping traffic, so it's busy, constrained at its limits by the Strait and the Suez Canal. Our minor detour from Atlantic travails took us to the satisfying city of Tarragona in the Spanish autonomous community of Catalonia, where my all-time literary hero George Orwell served with the Workers' Party during the civil war, trying to save democracy from fascism. I would recommend it for the tourist; and for us, once ashore, a stroll along the gloriously wide beach road and a brief pause for cervezas was enough to reenergize the weary seafarer, while the weather was as good as you might imagine.

REGRETTABLY, I was through with Sanko Line, a good employer. They created a sense of maritime worth, of contributing, of being left alone to do what they had trained me for without corporate interference. I had a Class II license now. The learning and examination had been a worthy accomplishment, much like riding a bicycle, sitting through the solemn slog of classes contributing little but attention. Whilst in college, the Tanker War finally flared up in the Persian Gulf. We paid it no heed, what with drinking, occasionally and forlornly chasing females, and some academic activity. Having made contact, Canadian Pacific (CP), invited me to their London office in Finsbury Square, between Moorgate and Liverpool Street; prime real estate near the Barbican. Their building was an anonymous silver-gray concrete-and-glass affair, by which they define the modern city. But they were nice people and, implausibly, they liked me. They offered me the job on the spot, starting pay £11,736 per annum for a second mate/navigator with a Class II license. It was what I wanted to do; my dreams replaced with hard cash. They liked me because I had experienced "foreign flag," so open to avoiding all that tax, just as they were. By now we knew the industry was spiraling down to the lowest common denominator. I felt no compulsion to fight the inevitable. My union dues were now my only connection to maritime England.

She was a Handysize tanker; an apt name expressing their usefulness to the world of trade. They are ideal for ports of any size and, hence, the most common oceangoing vessel. Transporting finished petroleum products and small bulk cargoes are their prime function. This one was built in 1975 and could haul 31,000 tonnes of oil. CP registered her in Bermuda; British, but foreign, like the rest of us. She had been built in the Netherlands for $15,900,000. For this, they gained a squat, muscular vessel with a black hull, the usual green deck and a boxy white accommodation block. The view from the bridge was dominated by two large Samson posts which few were heroic enough to venture aloft, and a funnel emblem in dark and light green, and white, resembling—absurdly—a Pac-Man, that annoyingly addictive arcade game that swept the world in the eighties. The crew was Filipino and the officers British; back to the floating land of irony. All the elements of the traditional British Merchant Navy were there, but with welcome moderation. The accommodation house comprised five stories of rooms and I settled into the assigned, comfortable cabin on the starboard side, all carpet, wood furniture and the usual Formica paneling. The décor was predictably clean and barren, but I posted Anita in prime position on the bulkhead.

The alcoholism that had taken a brief respite during the Sanko trips was now back in full stride. In the officers' lounge, where someone had installed a Commodore 64 computer—none of us thought electronic Ping-Pong would change the world—drinking was a nightly or daily routine; sometimes it was hard to discern which. The company required an informal system of uniform attire; much less the fake service ethos of Shell, but it was still there. I was battling hard to be contrary, but in the end, one has to conform to endure.

WEST AFRICA passed in a haze of drudgery. The oil trade hardly disposed the seafarer to the nicer parts of town, and the continent had few to begin with. It was more of the same West African dilapidated petroleum infrastructure; if anything, perhaps less of the same, so we did our work in each place as quickly as we could, day after day. We cut our losses and moved on. This trip wasn't the proper manner in which to appreciate Africa, and perhaps the seafarer confined to the docks never will. I had been to great places, and not so great; all of West

Africa was in the second category. I, like the ship, needed the fresh, salty scent of the ocean.

Free from land, we set to washing down—freshwater if you've got it, and we did. Traffic was absent heading west, where few traveled across a veritable marine desert, so I adhered to the familiar routine of shooting the sun and establishing noon. I liked the feeling of knowing where we were, while anyone staring out the window doesn't. Some overtime and socializing whiled away the other hours. It's strange how a few half-complete characters avoiding society can sustain regular conversations with hardly any knowledge of the outside world, where small things become epic.

Few nights in the bar spring to mind, but it was the manner of voyage we needed and I relished. New stuff is exciting, but doing the same is comforting, those endless conversations about mundane things. When the cold beer poured down my neck, I felt a little freer. Drinking is where you lose yourself and find yourself, a vague, half-defined spiritual questing. I got on well with my twelve-to-four counterpart, the third engineer, who I'll call Eric, a hairy, Sasquatchesque, man with tiny spectacles, the sort of man who kept an Allen key collection on his belt, just in case. He could drink—I'm not blaming him, but we once made it from four thirty in the morning to the seven bells lunch. That was a long afternoon coffee watch!

Tank cleaning endured for a while, naturally, but that didn't dispel the agreeable nature of the ride. In and out of multiple ports is fine for the commercial people of the industry, but West Africa now lacked interest for me. I'd done that, but Brazil had eluded me, so whatever happened, I was determined to walk ashore upon arrival. Traveling slowly allows one, unlike jet travel, to contemplate the event. The orders were to load a full cargo of gasoline—30,000 tonnes—at Santos and Salvador, then convey it to New York. The voyage rested me, and surprisingly, we arrived sober. It had been a three-and-a-half-thousand-mile passage, but trifling for the *Fort Kipp,* in the refreshingly mild seas of the South Atlantic.

Santos functions as the port for the growing megacity of Sao Paulo, some fifty miles away. In the nineteenth century it was considered the "port of death" due to yellow fever. We anchored a mile offshore and beheld the wonderful vista of the wide, three-mile-long beach that fronted the city, backed by a densely urbanized array of medium-sized apartment buildings. After too long at sea, on the beach we imagined the thong-clad parade of mermaids and the beach bars just beyond the capacity of our binoculars: a winning and all too rare combination. I had to get ashore. We entered the narrow channel, perhaps a thousand feet wide, with an eclectic fleet of international merchant ships secured on either side.

Despite the prospect of sleep deprivation, it is a mistake not to take advantage of a chance opportunity. The very young third mate and I were ashore, seeking refreshment and relaxation. The taxi driver, accustomed to soliciting rides from a certain type of foreigner in the port, with no recognizable conversation, took us to the Porto Paqueta area, past the warehouses and businesses barricading for the night, and found his sure-felt, familiar way to the infamous Love Story Bar and Restaurant, with a sign outside saying "We Never Close." We were enticed inside by the pulsating sound of generic mid-Atlantic pop music, and facing the paradox of simultaneously being insiders and outsiders. It was warm and humid, the overhead fans spun and our suburban-English eyes feasted upon an irresistible vista of young, golden-skinned, curvy ladies in thin-strapped halternecks and shorts, drinking watered-down caipirinhas below the strobe lights and cigarette haze. We came, we saw…and, rather predictably, succumbed. A man enjoys sex more when it means less. My young companion looked like he'd fallen from a tall building into a vat of ice cream. We knew we were being manipulated, but we didn't care; it was a pleasure to see how well it was done. Two of the world's oldest professions met as they had done a million times before and forever will. Neither the girls nor we had an option, both reconciled to our fate at too early an age.

SANTOS WAS fun, but all too fleeting. The following week they berthed us at Salvador, three days north in this sizable nation. More accurately, the *Fort Kipp* found the backwaters of the city, where eight miles inland lay the pint-sized port of Madre de Deus, a sort of forgotten little community surrounded by oil tanks. The municipality appeared worn-out and half-finished at the same time. Too many buildings brandished incomplete breeze-block exteriors, but others were starkly painted in red, green or blue. It had a short beach and palm trees, the same warm, humid but not uncomfortable weather in the early Brazilian spring, where young boys played soccer barefoot. It was devoid of tourists and, therefore, more honest. Big Eric, reminding me of Paul Bunyan with his ample physique and beard, and I took the early evening opportunity for a few quiet beers, intending to return early to grab at least two hours' sleep before the midnight watch.

Sauntering down the streets of an unfamiliar town, hypnotized by whirring cicadas, ought to instill caution. It's one of those notions that looks good on paper but, where Jack Tar is concerned, typically stays there. We had visited suspicious areas of the world and believed ourselves seasoned enough. No, we were safe, walking the tranquil streets of Madre de Deus, secure, that is, until in a waking dream of operatic dimensions, the most unexpected confrontation—*mugging* might be more germane—befell us. Not the swarthy, leather-clad archetype of fiction for us, but the world's most frightening demographic: the young female teenager. Ten girls approached, all innocent and joyous, whom we neither feared nor felt intimidated by, until they boisterously crowded around, their hands all asunder, experienced despite their age. We pushed and brushed them aside as they jumped joyously about, their hands sliding in and out of pockets with malicious finesse. Then, just as they appeared in a girlish giggling of female criminal action, like Keyser Söze, they were gone. We stood, dismayed, and inspected ourselves. Eric had lost forty dollars and his Seaman's Book to the hucksters of easy profit, but happily, we had secured the majority of our valuables inside our shoes, so enough remained for cocktails and garrulous contemplation of the early evening's encounter.

We arrived back alive that night, chastened perhaps, but almost giddy from the encounter. The Filipino chief steward returned later, accompanied by a friend holding a lit cigarette on the deck. The next day, we completed loading the *Fort Kipp*, minus a chief steward, down to her marks with gasoline, ready for New York. It might seem self-evident when a vessel is full, but like many other issues of the maritime world, it's not so simple; tankers can be full by volume or weight.

Restrictions concerning weight are common to all ships, and indeed, to anything that floats. There is a limit to just how much can be placed into or onto a floating object before it becomes unsafe. Adding to the problem, it must be safe not just in situ, but for the whole intended voyage. The overloading of ships reached its dreadful zenith in the nineteenth century with the loading of "coffin ships" for profit and fraud, until the subject finally found common sense in the guise of the Bristol member of Parliament, Samuel Plimsoll. Upon his motion they appointed a royal commission, and eventually the idea of a load line was accepted, forever after known as the Plimsoll line.

Puzzlingly, the concept is sometimes misunderstood to represent a maximum draft to which a vessel can safely be loaded ("her marks"). In reality, the load line—a circle with a line through it—is determined by the amount of "reserve buoyancy," represented as freeboard, *above* the waterline. To complicate matters, the oceans are divided into areas based on the expected weather in different seasons. Recognizing this, load lines display discrete marks for diverse water densities and expected weather.

The safe weight that can be loaded will lower the appropriate mark until it touches the water. The position of the marks is determined by a classification society, who issue the relevant certificates for the different zones: tropical, winter North Atlantic, etc. A vessel without the certificate will be unable to obtain insurance, and hence, unable to find employment. One more consideration: tankers can be full volumetrically before the weight sinks the appropriate mark to the waterline. Generally, they load to 98 or 99 percent, allowing room for expansion. The inconvenience of load line law is that it applies everywhere, so a vessel—under pain of serious legal consequences—must never sink the appropriate load line on any portion of the voyage. We sailed from Brazil, loaded to our summer marks.

TOWARD THE end of September, after fighting the Brazil Current (the western section of the Southern Atlantic anticlockwise gyre), then picking up a thrust from the Guiana Current that runs along the northeast edge of South America, catching our old friend, the Gulf Stream, we arrived back to New York, completing our circumnavigation of the Atlantics. You're familiar with the place: Stapleton Anchorage, the

Upper Bay, the Kill Van Kull and the Exxon Bayway refinery that straddles the interstate in New Jersey. The ten-mile meandering Arthur Kill, connecting Newark Bay in the north and Raritan Bay to the south, was the essence of industrial decimation in 1984, the sewage of civilization, sustaining scarce life due to decades of pollution. Once known as the Chemical Coast on the Jersey side, across the channel on the Staten Island swampland sat the giant twenty-two-hundred-acre Fresh Kills Landfill, a lush decrepitude of a compost heap, once the largest man-made structure in the world. Garbage scows arrived every day to deposit the trash of the city's ten million inhabitants. Its name derives from the Anglicization of the seventeenth-century Dutch term *achter kill*, meaning "back channel," which seemed wholly appropriate.

New York was New York, but I had lived on the *Fort Kipp* for four months and I required some respite. Fortunately, Canadian Pacific agreed and told me to pack. We sailed down to Panama, heading for the Pacific Ocean, which I might have wanted to stay and experience, but no seaman ever says they want to stay. One early October night, we slipped between the breakwaters of Cristóbal, the Atlantic terminus of the canal that links the two oceans, and dropped anchor. I enjoyed the *Fort Kipp*; well, bits and pieces along the way. It had been another opportunity to see a world far wider and more exotic than the rainy suburbs of London. But, at journey's end, I was fatigued and required a break. Boomer and I took the agent's launch ashore, stopping to drop a package on an ammonia carrier anchored nearby, whose eye-wateringly bitter reek of a botched chemistry experiment contented me with my lot in the petroleum trade. We entered the night of Panama at the Avenue del Frente. Cristóbal, even in the dark, appeared tired and uninviting; the sort of place one didn't linger, like an old lady of the ocean's back streets. We saw few people other than the desperate and disenfranchised viewing us from dark entryways, shrouding the city in weary fatalism. We were not offered the opportunity to stay, nor did we seek it, taking the long, dark, two-hour drive to the Panama City airport on the Pacific coast through the isthmus jungle. In the black early hours of the next morning we flew out to London.

WEEKS EARLIER, while sitting alone for a few moments in the Love Story, drowning in that cliff-falling sensation of drained deflation, I had felt an emptiness that kept returning on quiet nights, and pondered where my career might lead, or what indeed was the point to all of this. Don't we all wonder, now and again, what is the purpose? My only conciliation was that traveling—when sufficiently stimulating—might just find a better way for me. I believed that the work, the accumulation of every new license and experience, and the money were only foundations of something momentous I couldn't see. Like a slipping clutch, I grabbed at an answer, but decided I may just have to live without one. My career seemed like a never-ending deep hole. As so often before, I took the comfortable route, going with the flow, hoping it might improve, or something might just come along.

And what was there in Blighty for me? With early adulthood and a new worldview, it hardly seemed the storied promise of a green and pleasant land anymore. I faced the unpleasant fact that the England of the country pub had met the football hooligan, while the IRA tried to assassinate Thatcher's cabinet. The larger picture was even grimmer: Solidarity in Poland, famine in Ethiopia and the assassination of Indira Gandhi. And then, in a Kafkaesque political upset, the good people of the United States elected an aged Hollywood ham as president.

In the end it was the girls of Santos who lingered on the mind.

12

So Close to Heaven

1984–1985

When young Galileo...noticed one day...a chandelier swinging backwards and forwards, and convinced himself, by counting his pulse, that the duration of the oscillations was independent of the arc through which it moved, who could know that this discovery would eventually put it in our power, by means of the pendulum, to attain an accuracy in the measurement of time till then deemed impossible, and would enable the storm-tossed seaman in the most distant oceans to determine in what degree of longitude he was sailing?

—Hermann von Helmholtz

THE ECONOMIC and social changes of 1950s England must have seemed so threatening to my parents. I believe they lived a modest life, but it's almost courageous to have been so down-to-earth. They married, bought a house and had children. That's what good people did in the austerity, rationing and gloom of postwar Britain. If their marriage was traditional, that had helped them raise the three of us through noticeably hard times. I felt dejected the corporation had somehow made my father—one of millions of national war heroes—a lesser man by letting him go at a most inopportune moment. I have very little sense of family before I was about five. My brother and sister were already in early high school by then, and I hardly knew them. But now I discovered we generally shared political, moral and social views. We had the same deep English humor and I followed the same football team.

By now, I hardly maintained relationships with school friends anymore, but that isn't at all uncommon. The same would have occurred if I had moved to, say, Canada. It takes two parties to socialize, and they were no longer seeking me either, so it was agreeable to encounter my siblings at last.

In my experience there's seldom sufficient time to achieve nothing when paid to do so, but I'd lingered two months at home and accomplished exactly that. I didn't own a car, so I just rented and journeyed to weddings and parties of the people in my new maritime life; I could relate to them on some level.

I pondered buying a house now that I had financial standing. I no longer relied on others monetarily; I was independent. I was also rather fond of this new employer who had an eclectic selection of ships manned out of London: product tankers, container ships, bulk carriers (geared and gearless), and even a few crude oil tankers, to which I set my mind to avoid, being keen to broaden my perspective. Life was on hold, except for the faint sound of ticking. One day, on schedule, the shrill phone rang like a tornado warning, as I knew it would.

"Hello John, we have a ship for you, the [SS] *Port Hawkesbury*," she declared.

My brain engaged its first gear in eight weeks and I answered, as unenthusiastically as possible, with the most fundamental question, "Great, what is it?"

"It's a VLCC and we thought…" Her voice drifted away as I discontinued listening, concentrating instead on the wallpaper, where I was instantly taken by its repetitiveness. Could I survive another four months on a supertanker? Here I was extolling the benefits of this diverse fleet and the seafaring potential it offered, when they proposed another dreary supertanker voyage. My prior benevolence slipped away before she completed her pitch. But work is work, both a four-letter word and an inevitability. Her soft but resolute voice explained the ship lay off Aruba on a six-month long-term storage contract, so I said I'd go. Besides, I shunned Christmas at home—I had an aversion to shopping in England and craved to be back in Singapore or Japan. I packed.

I flew to Aruba with a rejoining radio officer, Irish and agreeable, who clarified the circumstances onboard. She had a permanent rotating staff, familiar with her idiosyncrasies and systems, and I was filling in for the regular second mate on leave. The climate had changed from dull, overcast, shivering England to the pleasingly starry-clear night of a warm Caribbean island. The intense transformation of humidity and ambience characterized my career choice; the fear was that it might be the highlight of the trip. We drank a quiet night in one of those sun-drenched and balmy resorts that are so appealing if you're not paying for them, The Manchebo Beach. I felt the customary anxiety prior joining, like a soon-to-be-dead man contemplating his last supper, imagining my new floating home, the expected clique of in-jokes and strange routines, but I was a well-qualified professional now, no longer the untested adolescent sent for a "long weight," and quite prepared to stand by my own acumen. The next morning, when we rode out on the choppy Caribbean seas, I stood with a determined resolve, ready for anything this trip could impart; frankly, I imagined it might be dull.

The tug needed to be full-sized, and was. The waves were sharp and precipitous, consistent with the predictable Northeast trades. Of the three large targets ahead, I identified the low black hull of the *Port*

Hawkesbury, not from the CP Ships logo—mostly obscured by seeping rust—but from the familiar green-and-white Pac-Man on the funnel. She looked old and worn, like a discount store going out of business. The seas were too short and steep to come alongside, so the tug bumped into the flat stern of the supertanker and we ascended by way of a pilot ladder onto the poop deck. I shook a few hands, then signed articles before Captain R., one of the best, too obviously well-tanned, who had that trick of making demanding situations seem effortless. I was ready to work, but there was nothing to do.

The tanker had lain idle off Aruba for three months, never swinging in the fresh and predictable breeze. The floating storage daily rate of $17,000 almost mirrored my annual income, but supertankers cost serious money to operate, and that was what the market would bear. Surprisingly, the Indian crew stood the bridge anchor watch, not the staff. Otherwise the Old Man was happy to leave the ship to its own cognizance, so sure he was of those ten immutable shackles[39] of cast steel cable laid out ahead between the anchor and hawse pipe. Nothing else anchored in swinging or dragging distance; the other two ships—in the same employment—were miles away.

What to do while anchored off Aruba with two million barrels of crude oil? Well, the cargo, securely sealed inside the tanks, required intermittent attention. Now and again we ran the inert gas system to re-pressurize, but the warm weather held the oil snug and still, like a bomb whose fuse had flamed out in the breeze. The whole system operated with pressure-vacuum valves maintaining a slight positive pressure to avoid ingress of air. Supplementing the valves was a deck water seal, a twelve-foot-tall cylindrical affair, preventing hydrocarbon-saturated inert gas from leaking back to where the fires lay below. If all else failed,

---

39   A unit (ninety feet) used for measuring the length of anchor chains. Ships typically have twelve to fifteen shackles on each anchor.

there was a glycol pressure breaker on deck, with a column of liquid from which vapor would burst forth if the system ever got away from us. Crude oil is a commodity that everyone needs, but nobody wants to see or touch.

When the mail arrived, I busied myself with chart corrections; cartography being a favorite pastime, perusing the rarely visited corners of the world, like a hobby financed by someone else. Then, an encounter with a shipboard computer, almost exclusively for making lists, in between playing Tetris and Battlezone from a 5¼-inch floppy disc. Apart from these, the routine revolved around general maintenance, faintly plausible deck tennis on green steel, re-watching the same dozen movies, and generally mucking around for wholly implausible reasons, the company simply paying for months of outdoor entertainment. The officers' lounge was lively, noisy and, as always, in some rotten manifestation of colonialism, separate and distinct from the Indian mess room. I enjoyed the slow, sunny predictability of it all and gradually the regulars accepted me. Christmas dinner was an occasion without the responsibility of giving. About the time the bad language started someone deluged us with cheap champagne and fruitcake, as a seasonal cassette played on an endless loop. The captain exhibited a smiling sense of affable cultural superiority when sober, and without batting an eye, veered toward outrageousness while imbibing, but he held it all together as if teeing us up. As things fell apart, the bellowing and exposition of testosterone-filled idiocy deteriorated into painful memories unearthed and loyalties tested, until our behavior escalated to an inexcusable level whilst wearing a uniform.

Every two weeks a tug took those who sought to journey ashore for the opportunity to spend money. My ears were blocked again, and I yearned for a walk to moderate the frustration of observing the bikini-populated golden beaches of Oranjestad every day. The fourth engineer, eyes wide with energy, fair-haired, smoker and all-round Jack the lad, accompanied me to the hospital because it was a free ride, and a bad ride is always better than a good walk. He fed on attention, but lacked the verbal ability to sustain the act in polite society, or in shore employment, perhaps. Eccentrics were acceptable at sea, because of the difficulty of replacing them. With my hearing fixed, we made our way to San Nicolas, with a duel mission of intent.

Aruba is a fairly flat, river-less island in the Leeward Antilles, famous for white sandy beaches. It's sheltered from the relentless trade winds blowing from Africa on its southwest side, while the northern and eastern coasts, lacking this protection, are pummeled by the sea and have been left largely unaffected by humans. Along with Bonaire and Curaçao, it forms the ABC islands, surely the first geography lesson for young Dutch schoolchildren. Unlike many Caribbean delights, Aruba is neither green nor humid, but dry and riven with cacti, thorny shrubs and aloe vera, all leaning towards the west in the unremitting breeze.

San Nicolas, a melancholy town with a heroic past, twelve miles east of the capital, Oranjestad, like the rest of the island is dusty yellow, with clean, narrow streets. It's named after a Mr. Nicolas van der Biest (1808–1873), who owned a tract of the land there, and it's called the "Sunrise City" because those in the capital look east to see it. The houses were neat and tidy, green, orange and white, although a little threadbare. However, unlike their Dutch ascendants, they were backed with vivid blue skies and the ever-present fair-weather cumulus, like one of Van Gogh's better days. Then, like a silver-grey eyesore, the refinery, which dissipated smoke westward on the ardent trades. For the seafarer, the town of San Nicolas has two enticements. Like the tourists, we visited Charlie's Bar & Restaurant, famous since the 1940s, when scuba divers hung their underwater discoveries upon the walls. It has become an institution in the decades since, with a colorful reputation as a hangout for boisterous sailors and oil refinery workers, rightly famous for the variety of bric-a-brac, old photos, business cards, license plates, sports shirts and various miscellanea adorning the walls and ceiling, much like a teenager's bedroom.

The fourth and I strolled in late morning and found it quiet, but that didn't bother us. At sea the conventional social drinking constraints never applied, as we lived in an all-day-happy-hour at fifteen cents. It had been a hot morning, our faces already feeling the sizzling Caribbean heat, and we needed one or two of those famous Dutch lagers with the foamy head that needs scraping. The barman poured the pilsners and dropped them on the counter, allowing the foam to cascade to the stained wooden bar, adding to the ambience. We sat on bar stools and downed the first ones easily. As we ordered a follow-up, a man, weathered face and white-whiskered, bringing to mind the old man of the sea, appeared and began a fund of anecdote, without invite. When he uncovered our involvement with oil, he volunteered to relate the gratifying historic fable of black gold in Aruba. He was an affable fellow, so we listened. It was one of those tales you didn't really need, but as he droned on, and the beers tumbled down, it stirred more interest.

Aruba, being sunny, but lacking freshwater and greenery, had, auspiciously for the Arubans, little agriculture, so the Europeans who dominated in earlier centuries—primarily the Dutch—found no use for sugar production or other agriculture endemic to the region. Some gold and phosphate extraction took place, but the island had nothing else to recommend it, limiting the customary scar of slavery. Its fortunes changed in 1914 with the discovery of a vast sea of oil under

Lake Maracaibo in nearby Venezuela. The Royal Dutch Shell group developed a transshipment port and, eventually, refinery at Willemstad in Curaçao, since Maracaibo was too shallow for larger export vessels. Their competitor, the American-controlled Lago Petroleum, sought around for an alternative and, quite naturally, settled on next-door Aruba, where an excellent harbor existed at the tiny community of San Nicolas, long disused since the end of phosphate exploitation.

As activity progressed, the hamlet grew from a few huts to a decent village, with buildings and sheds for the oil business and houses for the employees. They made enormous investments, refining began, and then Lago divulged ownership to the Standard Oil Company of New Jersey; since then the name Esso has been forever associated with eastern Aruba. San Nicolas emerged as a melting pot of cultures and languages, and at the commencement of the Second World War, with American isolationism preventing the supply of aviation gas to the British, the Lago refinery filled the gap and continued until the conclusion of hostilities.

They were satisfying hours listening to the old man, a kismet event we hadn't planned, completing another jigsaw piece of the industry I existed in. Some of the best stories are left half-untold, so we expressed our farewells and journeyed in search of more pressing matters at the highly recommended Roxy Bar, two blocks away on Jan Steenstraat, which, like the way evening overtakes the late afternoon, was the second reason for visiting San Nicolas; the Dutch openness of sex for sale, unburdened by anxious pretense.

EARLY EVENING, everyone rode the tug offshore, regaling with the stories of the long day done, which seems an opportune moment to enlighten you regarding my new home. Everyone knew her as the

"Black Pig," because she was black and a pig to operate, with a good-enough-for-government-work feel about her. She was the earliest interpretation of the Second generation VLCC—this year's muddle, if you will—built in 1970 of 253,000 tonnes deadweight, so things had improved by the time the *Lampas* arrived. The large white accommodation block that wrapped around the engine room was commodious enough, although worn and lived-in, if I were being generous. Too much of the equipment was out of date, shabby and lacked hydraulic power. Everything was going to be hard on the *Port Hawkesbury* if we ever had to move, but I settled into the relaxed life of drinking and deck tennis.

On a later trip ashore, lost in the unfamiliar territory of thought, I mulled over revisiting the old man. But I dutifully did the rounds of the tourist trinket shops in the pretty capital of Oranjestad, whose overwhelming sensation is the scent of sunscreen lotion. It was diverting to move among the normal people for an hour or two. They were the same as us, other than the fact that they had an expensive resort for the evening and we had the Black Pig, so, feeling superior, I cabbed to San Nicolas. It saddened me that the old man didn't recognize me after two weeks, but with the purchase of some white rum he related another Aruba story of strangely alien events.

With his eyes occasionally yielding tears, the old man rehashed that part of his life with pride, candor and sadness, reciting the story of a Second World War incident that, surprisingly, occurred in this Caribbean backwater, whilst Europe erupted in flames. With Lago producing a sizable quantity of aviation fuel for the Allied effort, perhaps unsurprisingly with hindsight, the Kriegsmarine acquired an interest, dispatching the underwater demon *U-156*, armed with torpedoes and a deck gun. She spent a while reconnoitering the area before beginning the attack on February 16, 1942.

An hour after midnight the *U*-boat surfaced a mile off San Nicolas and fired torpedoes at two tankers lying in the harbor. The *Pedernales* burst into flames, killing many of the crew, while the *Oranjestad,* striving to depart the harbor in a frantic dash for survival, suffered a hit and sank. Two hours later, *U-156* struck the Texaco tanker *Arkansas* near Oranjestad, partially sinking her. The *U*-boat then set back to San Nicolas utilizing the deck gun to fire on the oil installation itself. I saw, from his intimate details, the old man had firsthand knowledge of the events.

In dread of belittling a marine war casualty number too large to comprehend, let me concentrate on the fate of five men in this incident, who, like a plot twist in a Lewis Carroll story, typified the incongruity and squander of war. First, the absurd fatality of a leading seaman, who died in an explosion on the deck of the *U*-boat because they had failed to remove the cap (or tampion) of the deck gun muzzle before firing. Second, the attack near Oranjestad left a misspent torpedo lying prone and exposed on the beach. The following day, in the calm aftermath of excitement, four Dutch Marines unknown to history, died when it detonated as they examined it.

I left the old man with the dignity of his memories, sensing they were more personal than historic. I came away with the robust opinion that war was capricious, and I wanted nothing to do with it.

ON JANUARY 17, 1985, after many agreeable weeks of sunny, alcoholic fun, and long stretches of pointlessness reposing in an alternate maritime world, and wondering how much we should be enjoying ourselves, the unthinkable came about. A message arrived from the charterers, as if someone in an unknown corporate office leaned in to move a piece on a Monopoly board, triggering their seventy-two-hour option to have the vessel deliver the cargo. Well, that was news we didn't need, and a state of disbelief and panic infused the Black Pig. I giggled to myself—this enormous thing is full of crude oil and I haven't seen it yet. The engine necessitated heating through, stores and food had to be taken aboard, cargo pumps tested, and we resumed watch-keeping; a standard I had been happy to shun. Two days later, with the mighty steam engine coughing black smoke, we spent hours heaving the anchor cable like a starting gate that wouldn't open. Predictably, the windlass power proved insufficient, so we steamed ahead to ease the strain; the maritime equivalent of a kick in the pants. Finally, the 20-tonne anchor broke out from the sand and rocky depths, and we heaved it home.

Bullen Baai, Curaçao, welcomed us the next day. Having put behind us the sensation of hard work, we suffered now in the relentless, never-ending cargo watches, standbys and sleeplessness, as we crude oil washed and delivered the cargo. Following instructions, we cleaned the *Port Hawkesbury* sufficiently for a prospective dockyard, and when we were finally departing, both men and ship drained, they advised us of its happy location. Cape Town.

CELESTIAL NAVIGATION — an ageless science—has been improving over time, with the noble intention of enabling a navigator to sail the oceans independent of the vulnerable concept of dead reckoning, our last resort, just before the dreamy realm of speculation. I found it irresistible. I didn't care where we were, as long as I knew where we were; I took a professional pride in the combination of hand-eye coordination, perfect timing and mathematics.

We used a sextant, naturally, and the chronometer. Longitude is tricky, no matter how good the chronometer, but the sextant is so virtuous because it annuls comparative motions, maintaining the angle between the observer, the object and the horizon, without requiring a completely steady aim; it measures the relative angle, while feeling just right in the hand.

You may have read that if you know the time of noon at two places—one typically being Greenwich (which the chronometer displays)—then the difference between the two is the longitude. So it is! The problem remains that the moment of this glorious occurrence is not readily apparent: the sun rising, then lingering in your eye on the horizon, then slipping below. What we needed every day—and you may be ahead of me on this—were two lines of position, one of which could conveniently be the noon latitude. The observer is somewhere on that line. To determine the position, he requires another line. Two or three would be beneficial. Once he has determined the position, then that can be reflected as latitude and longitude.

Put aside the Copernican theory of the universe and believe, just for a moment, the Earth is the center of all those heavenly bodies revolving around us, which is what we thought for a long time anyway. The sun (and every celestial body) has a geographical position (GP), a place on the Earth above which it appears to be. Consider now that we are on a circle with the GP at its center. Naturally, it's a very large circle, but it's not a huge leap of the imagination to consider a direct proportionality between the body's altitude, as measured by the observer, and the distance of its GP from the observer; the lower the altitude, the farther away the GP. When we measure a body's altitude, we are obtaining an indirect measure of the distance we are from the body's position directly above the Earth. With some inspired mathematics we can draw a straight line representing a very small portion of that very large circle.

These observations were generally taken during the morning eight-to-twelve and transposed to 12:00 p.m., ship's time, where they crossed with the transposed noon latitude to give us the noon position: latitude and longitude. Glorious stuff. Once weighing the individual character of a sextant after a few days, a kind of operative confidence ensues, allowing the observer to know if a sight is good. Confidence in the correct angle obtained, a crisp horizon and the exact time, combined with mathematics made simple by premade tables, allowed us to draw the line on a chart. There's no point in adding a line without confidence. Celestial navigation wonderfully discards the delusion of good or bad, right or wrong; we were insignificant for nature on such a scale to care.

SURPRISINGLY, CAPE Town is not the southernmost point of the continent; that's Cape Agulhas. But it is a spectacularly fine harbor, protected by the Table Mountain National Park from the south and westerly weather. I recall we entered the port from just east of north, having completed tank cleaning and gas freeing the day before. We were exhausted and ready for the dockyard, habitation of the landlubber, where a man could disappear with a clipboard for a whole afternoon, and the nights were free. With celestial navigation (both sun and stars), we plotted our positions crossing the South Atlantic, and we picked up Africa on radar comfortably from forty miles, like seeing it as a preparation for seeing it. It wasn't a surprise we arrived at the correct location, the Pilot Book confirming the vista, "…probably the best-known panoramic view in South Africa."

AND THERE was Table Mountain, like a flashing neon "You Are Here" sign in the mall. Low on bunkers, we took the pilot, carrying minimal ballast, the propeller churning around and slapping the opaque water, struggling ahead. We entered the buoyed channel, and I can't remember why they allocated me the bow mooring station. The *Port Hawkesbury* was a quarter mile in length; Cape Town wasn't really prepared for us. I radioed from forward as we drew near, but with all that momentum and size, with little propulsive control, all I could do was relay the countdown as we ran over the last red port-hand buoy before entering the breakwaters. It didn't bode well.

We left the mortally injured, suddenly free buoy adrift. The four tugs held on and assisted with turning the leviathan, XXL, clunky and ponderous, as we edged forward in a splashing of gray-blue coastal ocean into the famous Duncan Dock. At the conclusion of an eighty-degree turn to port, a slight katabatic wind freshened and bumped the mighty black tanker up against the mole, digging a twenty-foot gash into the side of the engine room. The tugs straightened us up, edged us onward inside, and finally held us tightly alongside berths one and two, as we ran out our wires. The last line sent out forward was a too-steep headline of little use. The *Port Hawkesbury*, aged and weary, finally gave up when the port winch—a coughing, stuttering steam affair—jettisoned a relief door with a sharp detonation into the air, and just kept spooling the giant wire through the Panama lead into the placid water below. The forward gang and I had abruptly departed the fo'c's'le upon the explosion, standing twenty yards back, watching the steam screaming into the air, the winch drum spinning at an ever-increasing speed in a billowing cloud of dust and rust. As the wire trended towards its bitter end, a fearless AB found the courage to climb back and shut the steam valve with two turns remaining on the drum. Everyone had good reasons for feeling pretty embarrassed about the inward passage, but the Black Pig had arrived, like a slow-motion train wreck. They welded a cumbrous accommodation ladder to her port side for the leading members of dockyard personnel, and I doubted Cape Town would have a happy ending.

CAPE TOWN'S setting ranks as one of the most distinctive in the world, nestled at the southern tip of the vast African continent; the city unfolds before the three-thousand-foot, flat-topped Table Mountain and sparkling blue ocean. It goes without saying it looked gorgeous. From the Duncan Dock the city seemed small; sure, a long walk, but an easy drive from the surprisingly open port facilities. The second evening alongside we saw for ourselves, but with some uncertainty and foreboding of the political arrangement of enforced separation and pass laws, staggeringly at variance with the scenic ambiance. Apartheid, the system of institutionalized racial segregation initiated in 1948, was, regrettably, still embraced as a policy in 1985, so we found our moral justification in our service to the nameless, faceless corporation.

Like a political parody of the ugly intolerance, we accepted a ride from two heavyset black gentlemen in a Rover. They deposited us in the smart, urbane city of the twentieth century, somewhere around Long and Strand Streets. February being the hottest month, the evening was warm, but comfortably so. Like most cities, the nature of Cape Town transforms significantly once darkness comes, and we understood its high crime rate, but we thought the benevolence of our two carriage guests boded well. The dreary mists of time and my old age have lost forever the name of the establishment we finally entered after too many tributes to South Africa's national beer, Castle Lager, but I sense it was enjoyable. We went with the best intentions, so it was bound to end badly.

I awoke the next morning, surprisingly no worse for wear. At least the surroundings were familiar. Opening my cabin door, I came across the chief mate, who, for some unknown reason, they called Cat. He was youngish, and enthusiastic when he had to be, but a good drinker and all-round party guy when the work didn't interfere. It was a dockyard, and the mate was the leading liaison with their people, who believed he understood everything of the ship. He didn't, but he knew more than most. He stepped through the adjacent cabin door.

"Er, Cat, slight problem 'ere," I admitted sleepily in reply to his greeting.

"What? It's eight o'clock, let's go," he replied, like a man chasing the bus.

Apologetically, I countered, "I've got a girl in my room."

He gave me that face a man does when he knows you've broken the rules but maintained the faith. "Well, send her ashore, there's work to do."

"Erm, she's black, like." At least I didn't say "blick."

"Oh, fucking hell," he breathed, while eyeing around conspiratorially. We tried to imagine the legal ramifications. I understood the workings of a ship and our ambassadorial status in a foreign land. We stood silent while Cat's mind whirred around and a solution popped out: "Keep low until the ten o'clock safety meeting when they'll all be in the conference room. Take her ashore then."

So, let's set logic aside and give me the benefit of doubt. And you know what? We all survived; Western civilization endured, and Bridget (I think), who had a lovely looking voice, and had been commendably uninhibited about removing her clothes, made it safely ashore. The daily routine of the dockyard endured. With the shoddiness of day-workers sweating over their evening beer, we lost another wire when the dockyard men dismantled a winch brake with the wire under tension tied to the dock; people do silly things. Another day one of the black workers fell down a lightering hole in the cavernous forepeak and, sadly, died. I expected to see his body crushed into fragments of warm flesh when he was clumsily hoisted out, but I considered nothing other than staring, suspecting his fate revealed the poverty into which he was born. Regrettably, people do silly things. The work continued, hectic while lacking fulfillment, thus paradoxically ending up both irritating and boring at the same time. We donned our half-and-half uniforms one evening and gate-crashed the Royal Cape Yacht Club, and they liked us. We arranged a party and invited dozens of people—mostly through the agent and some nurses someone had unearthed—with the tagline after people asked for directions, "Just head for the harbor, you'll see us." The Black Pig, on berths one and two, was the largest object in view. Well, second after Table Mountain.

The party was one for the ages, like an unscripted English farce, but then the guys on the *Port Hawkesbury* had plenty of practice long before I joined. The admittedly large officers' lounge was busy, but with just enough space for dancing. As the night wore on, someone designated me to take a small group of interested visitors to the bridge to show them the view and one of the radar screens. It was while reciting my sermon on the advantage of ten-centimeter over three-centimeter electromagnetic waves, and tracking a car moving past the harbor, when I gazed up and saw reflected in the eerie green glow of the screen the most delightful female face, all full-eyed wonder, and bangs. Her concentration drew my attention, but then her diminutive beauty, perfect complexion and long, dark brown hair, like a life-size representation of one of those porcelain models by Ladró.

Completing the bridge tour, we had nothing else to reveal. The control room, being too disheveled, and the engine room too sweaty, grungy and terribly loud, were not for innocent civilians. What else was there to see? Rooms? Back in the lounge, with pop music playing, she wiggled her way further into my consciousness, and I stepped to the brink of the abyss that few men have the courage to go to, and actually asked the gorgeous creature for a dance. Why women like dancing is one of the unsolved mysteries of life, but I knew why men avoid it at all costs; I had to admire my own gallantry as I engaged her in the opening notes of the ageless sonata of life: "Come here often?"

I enjoyed schmoozing with Annette; it was like a real relationship, or at least the opening gambit. I met her boyfriend, a giant South African, who gave the impression he wrestled the larger categories of wildlife at weekends, the kind of man who looks good in shorts on the veldt. But it didn't matter; all the inconveniences of him and the short six weeks of the *Port Hawkesbury*'s planned visit were just irrelevances when compared to the thought of knowing this beauty. Completely misunderstanding my intentions, she gave me her telephone number at the evening's conclusion.

My faith in humanity restored, I called the following day, like you do, doubting if she remembered my name. But she did! So, we arranged to meet that coming Sunday, March 3, for a trip to the summit of Table Mountain where I might entertain an angel. What could be better for my dull, romantic yearnings than playing tourist for the afternoon with a local guide who just happened to be the prettiest girl in town? Sometimes you have to throw your arms in the air, scream out loud and ride the roller coaster.

On the Thursday we received a message advising of the regular second mate's return and my transfer to another vessel on Saturday, March

2. I felt like I had just robbed a bank and locked the keys in the car. Love is dangerous when rationed and starved. I knew happiness needs to be more than a very brief burst of emotion, and this, in a non-crowded field, was my standout relationship disappointment so far.

13

A Surrogate Trade

1985

Travel makes one modest. You see what a tiny place you occupy in the world.

—Gustave Flaubert

I ARRIVED in Krung Thep, the "City of Angels," in the early evening after a long flight from Cape Town, via an overnight stop in an agreeable hotel too plush for the purpose in Colombo, Sri Lanka. Following the *Port Hawkesbury*, it was odd not to journey home, but Canadian Pacific sought me for additional employment. The confused crowds of foreign visitors mingled amongst the indigenous Asians, the females of which gave my eye-rolling muscles a hectic workout, like the dazzling jewels of their gender. The humorless officials caught the eye, too, along with the strange signage, as if English words had wilted in the heat and humidity. It was stiflingly hot when stepping from the airport air-conditioning, but there he was, the agent, holding a sign to greet me. He appeared to have brought the family, so I put myself in their hands, relieved and expectant.

The car lurched into the Bangkok night, the hot air striking like a blast furnace before he rolled up the window and turned on the air-conditioning. I took my first ride into a new city at night, dodging cars, motorbikes, buses and the three-wheeled scooters (*tuk-tuks*, they call them). He spoke broken English with that melodious, welcoming accent of Siam, his two kids bouncing on the front seat and staring back at the occidental with the strange blond hair, beaming excitedly like wind-up dolls, full of infant energy, smoothing the social terrain between us. I was lost in the glaring lights and sounds of the metropolis. Thailand's capital may be the world's supremely inscrutable city, a head-on clash between tradition and modernity. The unexpected concrete canyons and ultramodern, billboard-covered skyscrapers surprised, as we arrived at a hotel, the business-executive Impala, just off the main thoroughfare, Sukhumvit Road. Stepping from the Toyota and its freezing air-conditioning, we ascended through ten yards of heavy, sauna-like air into the marble-floored icebox of the hotel lobby. Finally, elegantly uniformed women, click-clacking effortlessly about on heels, delivered serenity. The agent wished me well. The passionately cheerful, petite dolls (not sure of the sex) bounced three or four more times and disappeared.

The people had been illusory until I saw them, like they never existed, but I could not deny the effervescent welcome. When an opportunity of such magnitude arises, it is imprudent not to grasp it, so after a shower I headed into the early night, when Bangkok awakes, with the one prospect I needed to forget Cape Town: Patpong, the beginning and the end of imagination, all at the same time. How long can you live in the memory of something that's gone? Twenty minutes of stop-start traffic later, alighting from the taxi and leaving my disbelief at the door, I took a strange detour into what-the-fuck land, accosted with invitations to shows: ladyboys, lesbians or the creative use of Ping-Pong balls. Conventional naked women were considered too humdrum for the hedonistic center of the world. With the usual Thai openness, the words *solicitation* and *discreet* never met in the same sentence. Pushing aside the pimping fraternity and forcefully taking a few paces, I brushed shoulders with the multitudes on the street in the suffocating humidity, my eyeballs monopolized left and right by the view of young ladies in the uniform of the Patpong street, one-piece, skin-tight micro-minis and heels. I found my way into my first show, ostensibly for the air-conditioning, and quickly found my way out again, having the sensation I was never to extract the entrance fee value from the experience.

Patpong is only one of Bangkok's red-light districts, comprising a maze of small streets (*sois*, they call them), deriving its name from the Patpongpanich family of Chinese immigrants who bought the land in 1946. Ever since the late sixties when the nightclubs were frequented by American servicemen on R & R from Vietnam, the area has expanded into nearby streets. Crowded together were Thais selling paraphernalia, Europeans, Americans, Japanese, couples holding hands, single men, groups of men, all seemingly meandering with no purpose other than to soak in the atmosphere outside the indelicately named clubs: The Electric Blue, The Super Pussy and The Bada Bing. Tasteful eroticism suddenly seemed taboo.

Thai people, I've since found, are quite enchanting, but their grip on my language can be shaky at best. They accosted me from all sides with short, too-explicit invitations to come inside—"come, come," "bang, bang," "fucky-fucky"—but I received no animosity, at least in English, if I kept walking. Inside, the uniforms changed; all kinds of girls, young, not so young and indeterminate age, swayed to music in bikinis, wearing numbers for the audience's convenience, all to make money; capitalism run amok, like an homage to Ayn Rand. At some point, I was offered a trip to heaven and back by a lady named, incongruously, Meow, lips heavy with gloss, eyes coated in blue eye shadow, and I saw no point in negotiating. She won me over despite myself and enticed me to her lair. I would lose my pocketful of dollars somehow this evening and her business and mine were both work that mandated a reward, while I considered her occupation a noble one, selling her body and mind, just like me. I wished we both didn't have to do it, but that was the way it was.

Ten yards from Patpong, traditional Thai culture is everywhere—an urban cornucopia of smells, tastes, sounds and sights that draw the visitor in deeper. There were street-side shacks selling food so spicy it burned my tongue, like tiny, glowing, red chili embers, drinks to soothe the pain, T-shirts, copy-watches, handbags and costume jewelry at throwaway prices because they're all fake. I strolled past restaurants of varying sizes and cozy hotels. Music resounded from wavering directions, principally from the clubs and bars that lined the streets. Neon lights flickered and danced and when my senses and body were tired, I stopped for a massage and walked again. Hanging over everything were sagging lines of lights, strings of bunting, and the smell of sweat, sewers, stale beer and cheap perfume.

It's an extra-large city where the rational rarely wins. Some love it and others can't wait to escape the heat. For me, Bangkok is one of the world's most effervescent and stimulating places. As a youngish, liberal and well-traveled man, it was an entertaining and slightly depraved evening, especially when the Singha beers numbed my senses. How could I ever rationalize the sensation to people in suburban England? Some say Patpong is seedy and lacks culture—perhaps—but no one said it wasn't unique. I considered it a guilty pleasure favorite, perhaps not somewhere to visit regularly—unless, without self-pity, you're supporting a family, like Meow—but for a once-in-a-lifetime sojourn in vice, it was brash, bracing and provocative. Bangkok was a healing. I never revisited Cape Town, and life has been better for it.

THE FOLLOWING day, dazed and drained from the long flight and even longer night, I was picked up by the agent, fortunately after noon. I joined the MV *R. A. Emerson,* while she lay alongside the brown, muddy waters of the Chao Phraya River, the mother river of Siam, its drainage basin encompassing the entire country north of Bangkok. The off-signing second mate furnished a decent handover, wished me well, and set off home. After dinner, I found the Old Man, the inimitable Boomer again, so I spent a few hours drinking and catching up before turning in far too late. They said they called me three times at midnight, but it wasn't until one thirty in the morning I stumbled down to the small cargo control room, my brains in a tumble-drier, to face an understandably irate third mate. Being late for watch is a serious transgression of maritime amity, but I eluded the ramifications, it being my first night. The next day, sober and chastened, I set to work proper. I didn't realize the following three weeks were to be the hardest of my working life thus far.

The *R. A. Emerson* was a tanker engaged in a business other than petroleum, so on deck I was confronted with the unfamiliar sight of black rubber hoses hung directly into open deck hatches lashed with rope. Instead of the familiar reek of gasoline or diesel, she had the sweet, sickly aroma of molasses arising and enveloping everything. It is a thick, syrupy by-product of sugarcane processing, used by liqueur distilleries, MSG and yeast production, organic chemicals and animal feed. It's dark brown, and of viscous necessity, very hot when transported, so we heated the thick gooey liquid until it bubbled with a sickly layer of foam on its surface. Malaysia and Indonesia account for some sixty percent of the global seaborne exports of plant-based materials, so we were the right ship in the right place for this surrogate trade.

We lay alongside the lazy river for a few more days, inundated with a smorgasbord of golden-skinned, smiling bundles of sexual energy, the type of ladies who spent their days in the shade and their nights working. They cheered everyone up; they made what little spare time we had ever sparer. They prompted you to make sure you locked your cabin door, because, as nice as they were, they were not of us. I was out of cash anyway.

FAR FROM such satisfying diversions, the Iran-Iraq War continued to rage in 1985. January saw Saddam launching a major offensive, only to be rebutted by a vast army of Iranian conscript cannon fodder, ready to die for their God. One hundred sixty thousand troops were thrown into the melee against the Basra-Baghdad highway in the sort of military hell impractical to portray in a believable movie. Just when everyone—those inured to the carnage anyway—thought it couldn't get any worse, Saddam responded by launching chemical attacks. Ominously for my ilk, in February the tanker *Neptunia* suffered a strike by an Iraqi Exocet missile and sank, the first to perish in the new Tanker War.

The tanker, no matter its trade, makes money by moving. The 560-feet-long *R. A. Emerson* was, effectively, a sister ship of the *Fort Kipp*, built at the Van der Giessen yard in Holland, in 1973. Categorized as an edible oil tanker, she could carry 31,000 deadweight tonnes; thoroughly Handysize, but scuffed, perhaps, like a good suit fraying at the seams. We sailed into the South China Sea, where, two days south, lay the brand-new Kuantan Port, what they were to call multipurpose, lacking specialty. We loaded three or four cargoes of palm oil, each with its own shipper and consignee in Europe. This was our trade, loading twenty separate parcels of vegetable oils. And why not? Palm oil is a miraculous vegetable product and a major source of income for the farmers of Southeast Asia. What makes palm so wonderful is its ability to produce up to ten times more oil per acre than the equivalent of, say, soybeans, or rapeseed. The shortsightedness of man to make a profit has, unfortunately, changed the geography and diversity of the region, but on a personal scale, in the scant free hours available, I spent my time plotting the courses for subsequent destinations, clustered around the world's most congested waterway.

You might visualize it as a giant reverse check mark lying between Indonesia, Malaysia and Singapore, congested like the English Channel, but without the comforting names of home. Here we were, heading towards twenty days of tumultuous traffic congestion at the epicenter of the maritime trading world. The three countries have been petulantly debating their sea boundaries for a long time, but in 1981, the now established traffic separation scheme came into force imposing some order all the way from the Horsburgh Lighthouse, just east of Singapore, to the infamous One Fathom Bank adjacent to Kuala Lumpur, 230 miles to the northwest. The resultant narrow lines portrayed on the sea, liberally sprinkled with sandbanks, wrecks and crossing areas, are a watchkeeper's nightmare.

This unavoidable concentration of shipping, together with treacherous, restricted shallows and numerous islands, inlets and rivers in which to hide, have made it the confluence of trade, commerce, fishing and piracy for generations. For traffic transiting from China, Japan and all points east, to India, the Persian Gulf and all points west, this happy geographical accident has endowed Singapore, where it all comes together, with an abundance of wealth.

OVER NINETY thousand vessels transit annually, carrying about a quarter of the world's trade. When approaching from the east, the entry beacon is the Horsburgh Lighthouse, resembling a miniature Alcatraz, typically visible from twenty miles. Better still, it had a racon, booming into our radar screens, pulsing like a giant glowworm, even in the frequent showers. I liked the sophistication and organization of cartography. I liked being responsible, leading the way. I enjoyed the predictability and thoroughness of it. We might not exactly follow the lines I drew on the chart, but that was everyone's goal at the commencement of a watch. They trusted me, and were guided by my slender pencil lines. The Singapore Strait is not a place one wanders into by mistake or traverses on a whim, but without alternative, we sought more vegetable oil.

ONE HECTIC day south of Kuantan, we were amongst the dizzyingly overcrowded waters. Passing Horsburgh, I edged the *R. A. Emerson* to starboard and spliced myself into the traffic flow, gasping, wow, it's busy! There's no specific bad area; it's all bad, and nerve-racking stuff. The sheer volume astonishes: three ships a minute, twenty-four hours a day, passing through. The intensity continues before and after the Keppel pilot, where I headed. There's no watery place like it. Tankers, bulkers, box-boats, barges, tugs and fishing vessels transiting at all angles between the shipping lanes and the island. Furthermore, hundreds of ships lay at the vast Singapore anchorages. During the approach I monitored a crushing number of targets, concentrating on the perceived perilous few. The Old Man had been called (at his pencil mark) and should really have been there. Once I had the pilots on the chattering VHF, I called Boomer again.

Unexpectantly, a heavy, thunderous squall materialized, shooting down from the leaden skies. When I looked forward, Keppel had disappeared. The sun vanished and, one by one, the traffic hid in the rain, as the world grayed out, accompanied by booming cracks of lightning and thunder. Radars are better than good for tracking solid objects, but regrettably, rain meets that definition, reflecting and obscuring everything in its path, hiding fishing boats in the clutter. Unlike every movie you might have seen, radars don't bleep as they paint a target; the screen just glows brighter where the echo was until it sweeps again. Radar, like viewing from a balloon, became my blurry eyes. It's less effective in the rain but it identified the larger objects. Where was the Old Man? Then the clouds lightened, and the rain diminished, allowing the sun to shine through. Boomer, perhaps once an athletic man, finally appeared—in uniform for goodness' sake—like a man wearing a hazmat suit.

"Where's the doo-dah pilot, John?" He asked, with his usual tactlessness.

"Keppel?"

"Yeah, where the fuck are we?" He wasn't subtle, either. "Is the engine…?"

"Yes, they're on standby", I explained; "Two miles out, time to…", but with his usual bold and spirited approach, he threw the telegraph into 'Half Ahead' without me completing my pitch. I stood, open mouthed and wide-eyed as the speed dropped away and all my plans dissipated with the rain. I warned of the situation close astern, but Boomer, with his heavy and self-assured touch, had the helmsman turn to starboard across the traffic, like a learner-driver with no mirrors. In a blaze of impulsive engine movements and extreme helm orders we slid into the Keppel pilot station. It is a truism of the sea, that the captain's always right, even when he isn't. He was also lucky.

Keppel then isn't what it is today, a giant container terminal edged with high-class condos; that day it looked like a wet weekend. The harbor the British found for the white man was a stretch of protected water between Singapore and Sentosa at the tip of the Malay Peninsula. Its deep, naturally sheltered waters were ideal for colonists attempting to establish a Far East maritime colony, and thereby setting the stage for the eventual formation of Singapore as a successful independent state. We loaded some palm olein and palm kernel oil[40] through the usual black hoses with nary a human being in sight. I longed for some diversion, but a run ashore proved impossible. Hard work occurred day after day.

One day north of Singapore, still in the Strait, laid the port of Belawan, on the Deli River. The berth was ringed by a lush canvas of verdant riverbank, much as it might have been before the palm oil trade. It was hot, like Singapore was hot, like Bangkok was hot. The air-conditioning struggled. Like all tankers, petroleum or otherwise, they had not built the *R. A. Emerson* for open windows and airflow; without air-conditioning, life would be intolerable. But it labored along, as did we, grimacing through the pain of sleep deprivation. The uniform of cargo watches became shorts and T-shirts. With the crushing humidity, all movement was like walking in a sauna. The temperature lingered at 95°F and it rained, and it rained, until life became soggy. We loaded top-of-the-line refined, bleached and deodorized palm oil. Precious stuff if you can get it.

Palm fruit is reddish, about the size of a large plum, and grows in bunches. Each fruit comprises an oily, fleshy outer layer with a single seed (the kernel). They extract oil from the fruit and the nut. I can't

---

40   Olein is the liquid fraction after processing.

imagine how many fruits had to be picked, crushed, milled, refined, fractionated and degummed to fill a few tanks of the *R. A. Emerson*. She was small, but enter any single tank and one is struck by how cavernous it feels. Our tanks were clean—they had to be—and were inspected (and not just by us) with white gloves, before loading edible oils.

One day across the Strait sat Butterworth. By the twentieth century, it had become an industrialized, moderately sized port of wharfs and warehouses. I spent too much time working from twelve to six, either on deck, or on the bridge in heavy traffic, at the same time both frantic and static. On top of that, I had to plot courses to the next port, and I undertook my daily chores: washing and drying gear, standbys and eating. Boomer was perceptive enough to forego the weekly fire and lifeboat drills, but when all was done, I slept two hours in the morning and three before midnight, if fortunate. It was an age when physical suffering was acceptable.

Two watches south lay Port Klang. In 1985 it still had that rotting colonial air, where the old buildings, without a mass of poor to upkeep, were overcome with decay, far from the grandiose achievements of the nearby capital, Kuala Lumpur. The tourists didn't go to Port Klang. We lay alongside another barren, dirty dock with a warehouse twenty yards beyond. Time had not favored this part of town. It felt curiously dated, like a city lost from yesteryear. There's evidence, from one or two scant photos—my visual footsteps of the voyage—that I managed an excursion ashore, but I have little memory of the outing; not due to the usual spiritous haze, but because people just don't reminisce about the area. They once named it after Sir Frank Swettenham, Britain's Renaissance man in Kuala Lumpur for years, in that strange place called the past. He was famous for organizing the railway from there to Klang because he felt the horse-drawn wagon journey was "rather long and boring."

He was a man of his times: white suit and empire-building mustache, ignoring the sweaty masses. By the time we'd had our fill of another grade of palm oil, we had few tanks remaining. Klang is now another super TEU container port.

In an irrational disregard for natural rotation, the charterers had the *R. A. Emerson* motor back through the Strait of Malacca, circumvent Singapore, and load the final two parcels in Pasir Gadang, across the Johor Strait. As each cargo completed splashing inside, we cared less and less. The whole sub-trip back was devoid of any appeal that wasn't centered on boarding the outbound pilot. Southeast Asia had fleeting moments of beauty, and, dare I say it, poignancy. I knew I wanted to spend more time there, to learn of their customs and traditions, but this endless, almost sleepless exertion was not a suitable approach. Everyone was grateful to finally be on our way.

A DAY north of the One Fathom Bank, its light now distant and miniature, we aimed left, north of Sumatra, and headed west for the tip of Sri Lanka. Everyone felt they needed the fresh breeze. Finally, a chance to relax, clean the ship and catch up with the routines we had avoided the previous three weeks. The voyage was nearly five thousand miles, or two weeks. Not without incident, or traffic, and with a few challenges, but nothing like the Strait of Malacca. This was time to be left alone on the bridge without interference. We followed the bread-crumb trail of oncoming traffic toward Suez, avoiding the awkward puzzle of how we would discharge all this edible oil bubbling inside our tanks upon arriving in Europe.

Also, time to philosophize, especially on those quiet nights. Was there an alternative to the career I had chosen? Once there it seemed easier to continue—without an economic or personal diversion—than to quit, seek a new career, and pay taxes. I either didn't know why I went to sea, or I feared to admit reality. There were many ordinary people at sea, so ordinary they took their wives, as if in some British Rail Awayday vacation to Margate. The ship's company comprised a fair share of oddities, those who found it hard to fit into the normality of society, or lacked the basic social skills, or had progressed so far, they cherished the hype of authority they had long since lost ashore. And some—me perhaps? —like the character John Flory, the tortured soul of Orwell's *Burmese Days*, who found society challenging to tolerate. Going to sea had made it easier to escape the restrictions of England, of peer and family pressure. If I didn't free myself from those burdens, then I would stand on square one forever. I had become stronger than my parents and I hadn't seen them growing older. Every man must eventually ask: Am I for real? What is my life worth? The longer it went on, the less I felt a need to return; my mind had already pointed to living another life and going to sea was a stepping stone to something larger. I didn't know what it was, but I had already peeked over the fence in a few places—I knew the world was big and I aspired to keep exploring and discover what I needed. I needed serendipity.

WE ARRIVED at Suez with assembly-line familiarity. It was an attractive passage…if your eyes didn't work! They confirmed the delivery port for all the vegetable oil. With a narcotic surge of nostalgia, nine days later, we docked at Vlaardingen, a mass of cylindrical tanks by the Nieuwe Maas River, and a suburb of my old friend, Rotterdam. Like a salmon, the *R. A. Emerson* was returning home. I wanted out by now. I needed a rest and the company had promised me relief at the following port, wherever it was.

The problem had arrived, like an ill-mannered visitor from three weeks before: the daunting reality of how to discharge the cargo. We had carried twenty parcels of vegetable oil, all heated and segregated, each with its own bill of lading and consignee waiting to take delivery. A mass of inspectors and receivers came aboard, all wanting their individual cargo first. We couldn't use the ship's fixed pumping system, contaminated long ago. No, we had two portable hydraulic pumps, each a sort of six-foot, cumbersome steel cylinder connected to thick, heavy, rubber hoses and all powered by a screaming, hydraulic pressure system using more hoses, while sounding like an out-of-tune, high-pitched orchestra warming up forever. We worked six hours on, six hours off, leading a gang of five men to haul the entire ensemble around. A leader should know what he's doing, and we didn't know what we were doing. We could have done with some help on this one.

Like one of those dreams come true, somebody hired a couple of Verwey portable pump experts to assist, so that we could pump four cargoes simultaneously. They had their own gear, much lighter and more portable than ours, so as we required the six of us to drag each section of heavy hose and then wrench them together with nuts and bolts, the Verwey men just threw out another lightweight plastic tube and clipped it to the next one. They were up and running, pumping the next cargo of hot, heavy palm oil while we searched for the right spanner. It took four days to deliver the twenty cargoes into shore pipelines and barges. Our fumbling seemed out of place in a port that belabored its efficiency. The vegetable oils spilled everywhere each time we disconnected a hose, but it didn't matter; we just power washed it into the river. At night, as a spring chill suffused the place, the spills solidified on deck and everyone, as if walking on soap, slipped and upended themselves on the stuff.

We used gangs of Dutch labor—goodness knows what they cost— to sweep the tanks, entering as the liquid level reached the heating coils, where they frantically brushed and squeegeed the remaining oil towards the pump suction. The stuff was so valuable the receivers wanted every barrel, every gallon and didn't appreciate the physics of hot oil solidifying on the cold steel bottom. Fortunately, it's easy to clean once back at sea, but the consignees with their bills of lading seethed at their losses. Vlaardingen wasn't as bad as I feared, but it wasn't good either.

Two weeks later, exhausted, I finally headed home. I had a night in Sicily, after taking the agent's launch ashore through the breakwaters of Augusta, but I remember not one minute. After five and a half months it's as if my memory banks had overflowed with the *Port Hawkesbury* and the *R. A. Emerson*. I was fit, tanned and slim, but I desperately required a rest. It had been a middling voyage all-round, neither pleasant nor terrible, efficient but unexciting, like an action ride for which I didn't want a ticket. Meow, something real, urgent and human, lingered on the mind longer. There are things you can't tell your friends and family. In England, I encountered the familiarity of seeing a few ex-friends again and I understood their point of view. The bond that held us together through school, sport, music and underage drinking could not be maintained in the light of our new divergent lifestyles. How many had got married because they had to? How many had taken the safe route due to peer and family pressure? Naturally, they were growing into young adult men—some with families—with their own troubles and worries. Although I felt my own life beginning to drift without meaning, I still didn't envy them.

14

Where the Flying Fishes Play

1985

If you really want to escape the things that harass you, what you're needing is not to be in a different place but to be a different person.

—Lucius Annaeus Seneca

SCRAP METAL. It summoned up images of shady characters and nefarious business in the grimmer part of town, like the death of Mr. Solo in *Goldfinger*. Since I had no metal to scrap, I thought it unlikely I would cross paths with such colorful rogues. But here I stood beside an immense, elongated mound of the stuff; more than I could imagine, in the Sint-Laurenshaven cut-out, across from the Botlek refinery, just west of Rotterdam. I exited the car beside the glistening silver-gray mountain, and looked up to the black hull lying alongside.

I went back to work after two months of glorious late spring in England watching cricket, a wonderful way to pass long, lazy days. The day after arriving home from the *R. A. Emerson*, the British Antarctic Survey announced the discovery of a hole in the ozone layer; few understood or cared what they were saying. A tropical cyclone had hammered Bangladesh, and we had to uncomfortably view the TV images of muddy dead bodies.

The ship beside me was smallish, but loomed above us with the familiar corporate color scheme and logo. As I climbed the accommodation ladder, two grabs noisily spilled their vast loads of scrap metal—cast iron, tin, turnings, milling waste, copper, brass and nickel—into the open hatches of the MV *Fort Hamilton*, my home for the next four months. It was undeniably a hard hat area. The ship was modern and conventional, but with five white stationary cranes thrust motionless into the air, as if paying respect to a bygone era. Once inside, I was confronted with the familiarity of CP Ships, functional but congenial. I unpacked and set to work.

Two days later we set out with 20,000 tonnes of scrap, passed Gibraltar, and as predictable as the falling leaves of autumn, we heading for my nemesis, the Suez Canal. I suggest my choice of employer and the disparity of vessels they owned fairly represented the worldwide trade of goods, and I believe you can judge from this noticeably flawed statistic that a lot of ships transit this homage to drudgery. The passage through Egypt, as always, was slow-moving, torpid and about as welcome as a dust storm. We were going east, and I related to Rudyard Kipling's evocation:

Ship me somewheres east of Suez, where the best is like the worst,
Where there aren't no Ten Commandments an' a man can raise
a thirst;
For the temple-bells are callin', an' it's there that I would be—

Escaping the Canal, we raced down the Red Sea—there's nowhere else to go—and I have always found this an agreeably simple voyage segment, with clement weather, temperate seas and little traffic to cause anxiety. We drank again once the bond opened, but with restraint until clearing the southern terminus, the strait of Bab-el-Mandeb, ("The Gate of Tears") between Arabia and Abyssinia. I had settled quickly into the comfortably familiar life at sea with an amiable contingent of fellow travelers. We pointed into the Gulf of Aden and from there, the wide Arabian Sea.

I slipped back into the comfortable world of navigation, but I was unacquainted with the geared dry bulk cargo equipment. I learned the theory at school, but never set my hand to it. A fundamental aspect of the business is stowage factors, as in volume per weight. You can enclose a metric tonne of water within a cubic meter, but, as you can imagine, some cargoes are self-evidently heavy, like scrap metal. Quite obviously the weight will linger lower in the hold. Scrap has a stowage factor of about 0.6 (only 0.6 M^3 weighs a tonne), which produces a "stiff ship," since the weight, below the center of gravity, instigates a rapid return to upright when heeled. The unnatural roll period was jerky and uncomfortable. The southwestern monsoon had the anemometer touching 40 knots passing Socotra, and the ocean had evolved markedly, increasing sea and swell heights, as we headed somewheres east of Suez, for Bombay.

There are several monsoons regularly shaping the world, but the most economically and socially influential is, doubtless, the southwest monsoon, affecting as it does the entire Indian subcontinent. It's expected, but annually unpredictable. Our stiff ship rapidly commenced rolling from the long swell tilting into our starboard quarter, like an irate parent injudiciously rocking a baby stroller. It was a vicious movement I had not experienced. Everyone feels the violence of it: the continuous hanging on, bending a knee into the sway, bearing the pressure back and forth, strangely running upstairs and struggling down, chasing cutlery on the dinner table and pencils around the chart room. In my cabin of peace and solitude, scarce time was spent trying to remain upright in the slippery shower, securing all those items one thought might never move, and struggling to attain a wedged position for sleep. It was all so exhausting. On our happy little island in a sea of storms the thoughtful amongst us realized our insignificance.

Despite the never-ending, intense motion, in the communal center of social life, the bar (named "The Gypsy's Tent"), a consensus evolved to host a fancy-dress evening on arrival off Bombay. Sociologists have a complex theory concerning the strength of weak ties which lends credence to happenings in the confined, semi-militaristic, forced association that transpires on a ship with limited companionship. With privacy restricted to one's closed-door cabin there are few, if any, larger spaces where someone could find isolation, which is why it was so emotionally satisfying to sit alone on the bow of the *Lampas*, with only the rush of clamorous water as accompaniment.

The *Fort Hamilton* had nowhere to escape. Almost every day the same individuals congregated in the same confined bar between just before dinner and late into the evening. We knew we would connect for only a few months and perhaps never meet again, but a bond, a tie, had been formed between us; those few other lonely souls were my only human contact for months on end. Every feeling, every physical pain, every mistake is played out before the others. This was a good bar, and it had to be. With no alternative, it was incumbent upon all who attended to play by some unwritten rules. They say that sailors' minds stay at home, but our home was where we were. So, we traveled to foreign places, met a few people, and hours later concluded our expectations, being content returning to the warm familiarity of the bar with good beer and the free use of spiritous liquors.

I had the party to prepare for, ship reeling or not. I approached it with the same fervor as I would Morris dancing, i.e., with dire anticipation. I hated performing. I had no guilt about drinking excessively as a refuge for embarrassment, but since everyone seemed to take the invite seriously, I finally set my mind to creating a costume with the limited resources available. I took a brand-new orange boilersuit, cut advertisements from the scant pile of glossy magazines onboard, and glued them on. Wedged into the gap between my daybed and table, I created a full-face headdress from a fire locker helmet and old charts in the happy delirium of the ship's movement. I covered it in cling film and paint, donned the commercial-covered boilersuit and jammed my pant legs into my socks.

The vessel's relentless motion in the uncomfortably heavy seas made existing difficult, but after a demoralizing and exhausting six days we arrived off Bombay and anchored. The racing white clouds of the sea gradually evolved into a cadaverous dark blanket covering the coast as the monsoon reached the mountains of the Indian hinterland and burst forth in that drenching rain so specific to the phenomenon. The fancy-dress party arrived. I appeared on the allotted night as a Formula One driver. Quite imaginative, I thought.

The night was a wild success, and I was proud, not just of my costume, but of the inventiveness of my peers. True, some outfits suggested the supermarket discount bin, but what can you expect? The first person I had met upon joining was the chief mate, Brian, the manager of the ship, an ample, cheerful man with thinning hair and the same estuary London accent as me, our stamp of lowly origin. Competitive and well-read, he had that sarcastic trait so endemic of the age and place, but he knew far more than I about bulk cargo. He was rendered of soft material, but his sardonic humor cut through any weakness in performance and he filled the room with his personality. He came dressed as an Arabian sheik, although I believe he lacked sufficient facial hair. His wife, Bo, an Essex girl through and through, like Sueperman's Big Sister[41] with long, wavy hair, was a credit to her gender. She nightly sat at the bar, and we all appreciated her smiling feminine charm and unsullied demeanor, subduing the usual misogynist nonsense. Like all shipboard wives she exhibited a good suntan and was interested in the lives of others, which made a pleasing change. Ironically, she appeared as Boy George.

Mike, the third (engineer), was tall and angular, as if he'd grown out of his clothes, with black, thick-lens glasses that matched the color of his hair. He was a quiet man who evolved as the evening wore on, a combination of introvert and extrovert, who drank so rapidly we never saw his glass half-full. He was the sort of man you imaged would be kind to old ladies. He came as a monk, simple but effective. The second (engineer) became a good friend: Larry Ball, a regular-irregular, and a man every good bar craves, like a slightly rounder version of Jack Nicholson, with the same receding hairstyle, but without the risky edge. Like an escapee from a cheap fashion shoot he dressed as a mad chef, which was too obvious. I thought I might win the prize, but then Peter Parker, the too-happy third mate, like someone who'd eaten a box of chocolates, appeared as a man riding an ostrich, which was imaginative, and a lot of work. He was young and eccentric enough to pull off the charade and deservedly won the prize. Most nights the same people somehow unearthed something singular, or the same, to discuss and debate, which was no mean feat. The bar lived with the sound and personality each character bought, with the anthem of Live Aid tapes as its background. The atmosphere oscillated between the white man's club and the asylum, but this was the noblest bar since the *Opalia* and

---

41 Ian Dury deliberately misspelled "Superman" with an extra *e* to avoid copyright issues.

encompassed the incredible strength of weak ties. I still had a family at home, but my world was here in this steel box. How could we drink that much without using up the ocean?

Bombay, the "City of Dreams" (now Mumbai), seemed limitless, surprisingly much larger now than then. A long time ago it comprised seven swampy islands, dangerous and unhealthy, but in 1985 had a population of nine million and was already cosmopolitan and multi-cultural. The first Europeans to arrive, the Portuguese, came up with the name of Bom Bahia, a good little bay. After a week at anchor, we rode into the harbor, drained of color as it was by the overcast skies, making a long, slow turn around the red-and-white-banded Prong's Lighthouse at the southernmost point of the city.

Unlike tankers, banished to the edge of town, we berthed at the southern tip of the Bombay peninsula, where the city began all those years ago. The gated Indira Dock had a quayage of some four thousand yards. The entrance was narrow, but suitable enough for the *Fort Hamilton*. Inside, the twenty-one berths were part of the Carnac Bunder section of the city, three hundred feet from passing traffic, and only a mile from the Gateway to India. Clearly nothing was going to happen hastily in Bombay, so we broke watches. They were devoid of dock cranes, but provided magnets, which we attached to ours and hoisted the 20,000 tonnes of scrap, one lift at a time, day after day after day. I considered this civilized.

Unlike the tourist beach hotels, we sat at the center of life, amid the swelling slums as millions arrived every year in search of a better future. The hard-working chaos passed us every morning as the thousands of small businesses that keep the industrial giant of Bombay turning began work. The city is all anyone could have imagined of India. I pictured it a true reflection of the mighty subcontinent: insistently modern, yet verging on medieval; fashionable, yet rough-edged; dazzlingly multinational, yet essentially, always Indian. Almost everything seemed unique: Standard Time was, bizarrely, five and a half hours ahead of Greenwich; scruffy, tiny shops sorted used bottle caps and we found a dentist practicing on the sidewalk. Earplugs would help on the street, due to the incessant horns, and cows wandered in their own world, while the humans just lived in it. Few places depict so easily, yet so meticulously, the historical sense of a world bent out of joint.

I am a competent driver, but I would not tempt fate and attempt the task in Bombay. It seemed an altered-state exercise with buses, trucks, cars, and mopeds crowding the street with scant regard for the drive-on-the-left rule; I presumed there was one. Buses were not a viable option since I never saw one without a plethora of men hanging on the outside. The taxis, bewilderingly outdated, were Hindustan Ambassadors, black with yellow roofs, heavily festooned with religious ornamentation—an essential accoutrement for anyone driving on or near the roads. Walking was no easier; broken pavements, open manholes, dirt, debris and people sleeping were just some of the common issues. The noise and the vibe were pure India, and with wealthy residents living adjacent to the poorest, the contrasts of modern Bombay became ever more apparent, but what you cannot miss was the poverty. How could anyone of modest wealth live here and just hope that the poor, like the disabled, might go away?

Seemingly, one-half of the population lived in corrugated slums or were homeless, in tenements and huts, on pavements, under bridges and in open spaces. Their lives appeared pointless and interminable under the terrible conditions of squalor and deprivation. But from this adversity emerged every day a remarkably industrious labor force, shockingly all ages and sexes. The four million slum dwellers of Bombay were an all-round, astonishing array of industrial laborers, potters, embroiderers, construction workers, and thousands of one-room recyclers and domestic servants, denied utilities like electricity, sanitation, and water. The attire of the modest and poor was inimitable; the women, with their long, flowing black hair, wore silk saris of purple, green, blue or red, which appeared cumbersome, but utterly feminine. The men wore an ankle-length dhoti round the waist, usually off-white, which looked comfortable, but would be a tad risqué in London. Children stood at intersections selling single flowers, mopeds passed with the family onboard, and the old men with leathery skins sat and stared amongst the smell of heat, rotting everything and exhaust fumes. Yet in all this, nearly everyone was curious and friendly, while preparing for the annual Hindu festival of Ganesha—that's the one with the elephant head on a four-armed human body.

It is with some regret I have to report we visited the Kamathipura area of Falkland Street, to see the appalling red-light district, like a Hammer horror show as a prelude to dinner, passing the groups of men staring at and choosing the most abandoned of abandoned women; young and old on display in barred little rooms, like dim, dingy cages. The whole place was suffused with a quiet hopelessness, like Whitechapel a hundred years before. The pimps and madams promoted the girls in sexual and economic exploitation as if selling vegetables in a market, while the helpless and subdued expressions of the prostitutes screamed an unethical, disturbing and sad objectification that was difficult to watch. The only improvement I could imagine for the area would involve a match and an accelerant. They suffered no moral consequence. They had their gods, but it was a challenge to see where the perceived eroticism lay, so I walked away in my awful shame.

To seek more traditional fare, it would have been wise to hire a guide, but of course, we didn't. Anxious to avoid lengthy outings with the ubiquitous, threatening stormy skies, we set to nearby landmarks. The Gateway to India is a colossal structure seemingly without purpose: eighty-five feet of basalt at the tip of Apollo Bunder where it faces east, fronting the harbor, built to commemorate George V's visit of 1911. Across the street is the five-star landmark, the Taj Mahal Palace hotel, rising to seven gloriously ornate stories, famous for accommodating maharajas, dignitaries and celebrities. Built in the late nineteenth century on a hectare of land, the massive building incorporates Indo-Saracenic architecture, with Victorian, Gothic and Romanesque details, and a large courtyard and central dome of Moorish and Florentine styles on a grand scale. It would all be too much anywhere else, but somehow fitting for Bombay, a kind of muse to what man had in him to accomplish. We dined in the grand restaurant on *pakoras, vada pav, jalebi* and spicy curry all washed down with Kingfisher beer. Some suffered gastric revenge the next day, but I loved it, and have grown fonder over the years.

But after two weeks a distinct feeling of getting nowhere suffused the ship, every day peering deep into the hatches, never seeing the floor. Then one day, there they were, one by one revealed, scratched and shiny. Bombay made England seem drab, although much did not appeal. In the end, my most disaffecting memory of the city was of the young barefoot children who lived in a Darwinian nightmare around the docks, handpicking the tiny scraps of copper and brass that fell from the magnets, to keep their families alive.

THE *FORT Hamilton* plied the tramping trade, and I liked trips that didn't settle into a well-worn groove. We had no long-planned route, but someone in the office found another cargo surprisingly close: Karachi. Well, not exactly, but five hundred miles north of Bombay is the deep-water Port Qasim, the outer harbor of Karachi. Qasim was new, still under construction, twenty miles east of the capital, built to relieve the congestion. It lay on an old channel of the mighty Indus, the river that defines Pakistan, among a hundred miles of mangrove coastline. The giant industrial port seemed empty, as if plastered with "keep out" signs. It was so new, nothing was moving; a giant empty concrete expanse, like an inert cure for insomnia. We were there for rice, thousands of bags, which took a week to stow. With time on our hands, we held a soccer match, rather obviously, and sadly, us against them, the British staff against the Chinese crew. We had some fun, then sailed with 20,000 tons of rice for Malaysia, where we might eat some spicy garlic food.

The Sanoyasu Dockyard built the ship in Osaka, in 1978. She could carry 22,170 deadweight tonnes, driven by a large six-cylinder engine, like an oversized truck. She had five holds without tween decks, so purposefully built for bulk. Instead of derricks maneuvered by a gang of men, she had five hydraulic cranes dominating the view. Predictably the hull was black, the deck green, with a white swedged, or corrugated, accommodation block, quite obviously built in another part of the yard and simply lifted onto the hull at the opportune moment, like a giant Meccano set. The vertical corrugation allowed the elimination of conventional stiffening, thereby saving weight, maintaining rigidity and looking ugly. Behind the living quarters sat that tall, square smokestack adorned with the corporate Pac-Man. My cabin was pleasant enough and even more so when I pinned Kate Bush to the Formica paneling, no pun intended. The crew hailed from the People's Republic of China, in a bid to cut costs; red through and through in their ill-fitting coveralls and bad haircuts, the lowest rung of the multibillion-dollar shipping industry. I was leaning red myself, but for the democratic style.

We set further east, as I always wanted, to deliver the rice.

If you've 'eard the East a-callin', you won't never 'eed naught else.
No! you won't 'eed nothin' else
But them spicy garlic smells,
An' the sunshine an' the palm-trees an' the tinkly temple-bells...[42]

I had for some time been drawn to the Orient, independent of the charterer's orders, my urge borne of an irredeemable need to expand my horizons and associate with people, I admit mostly female, alien to my homeland and becoming to the eye. It meant the headache of transiting the teeming Strait of Malacca again, but I had learned; as always it is experience, good and bad, that makes the man. Passing Singapore, we entered the South China Sea and headed northeast towards the little-known and off the beaten track. As always, the navigation enthralled me with the drawing of lines on those multicolored, thick folios kept nicely stowed in canvas covers on the bridge. I was blissfully busy breaking out unseen plans and plotting the safe tracks to some new, distant destination. I cannot imagine navigation without paper charts, 2B pencils, parallel rulers and Staedtler erasers. They were like ancient books written by heroes of old, talking to me across the ages as the centuries between us evaporated.

They define the South China Sea at its eastern edge by the Philippines and Borneo. Where they meet is a small, dangerous passage rarely negotiated, like a hidden door leading to a lost, secret world. The Balabac Strait seems fine, deep and inviting at first glance, but closer

---

42   Rudyard Kipling.

inspection reveals the navigable breadth is only a mile or two because of the shoals, banks and islands concealed within. We left the brightly colored tan-and-blue modern charts and slipped back in time to the old gray ones that had yet to be resurveyed. Though the charts were older, they were still reliable, and the sophisticated endeavor of navigating proved successful with the lights and radar to guide us.

We took the bagged rice to Sabah state, where the Sulu meets the Celebes Sea; the sort of place where you'd expect to find scantily clad bathing beauties diving for pearls, and a Jules Verne-approved giant squid, as only celluloid might offer. I had never heard of Sandakan. Despite the location it lacked a picturesque aspect, and had suffered more than its fair share of bloody conflict over the years, due to no fault of the natives. During the nineteenth century, the usual players had plundered and built statues of the guilty: the Dutch, the Italians, the Germans, and, of course, the British, who brought trade and the Chinese diaspora, which helped contribute to the cosmopolitan ethnic diversity, whether or not the locals wanted it. The violence and coercion were lost amid the grand adventures of people like William Pryer, the first British Resident, who in 1879, it is said, established law and order with remarkable tact and courage as the "new-caught, sullen people"[43] cowed before Royal Navy guns. It all sounds so familiar because I grew up with the lies of the victors.

Today many of Sandakan's speedily constructed buildings hardly merit a glance, but what the town lacks in photogenic charisma, it makes up for with a diverse, friendly citizenry and vibrant streets oozing pungent aromas and old-world charm. The streets near the docks were safe enough, unpopulated by greasy, grimy types, but filled with commercial buildings, hotels, shops, and apartments, all with signs in a confusing mix of Malay, Chinese and English. It was hot and humid,

---

43   "The White Man's Burden," Rudyard Kipling.

but the atmosphere of the street just felt fresher than the familiarity of the ship. The cars were small and Japanese, because the people were generally small and content. It was strange to reflect such a place existed on the other side of the world, unbeknownst to me, or anyone I knew. I can't say I wanted to live there, but it was a likable town, civilized and satisfyingly unfamiliar. There were notable tourist attractions, but insufficient time. I leant my hand to the cranes. There's a lot of power in hydraulics. Subtlety is everything, but the capacity at one's fingertips quickly becomes boredom watching men load bags of rice onto a pallet, as interesting as watching the draft change.

I mention Sandakan, and other unspoken places, because in their subtle and slight ways they educated me regarding the world more than a book or television documentary ever could. Any place has something to add to your experience, and some large percentage of it is absorbed on the first visit. Returning to the South China Sea a day away, I was back amongst the tan-and-light-blue charts of the well-traveled water, and we sought the capital of Sabah state, entering Teluk Gaya, the large, well-sheltered bay that protects Kota Kinabalu. The Old Man set us down in the well-charted anchorage.

Anchoring is its own discrete exercise. It had a maritime history, once employing gangs of men singing uplifting songs. Now it was just me and the bosun. The technique is to lay the chain out on a long reach; it's the chain's friction on the seafloor that holds the ship, allowing it to swing in the tide and wind. It works like this: stop the vessel, then reverse slowly until she begins to creep backwards. There's a lag in all this, but experience solves everything, and the Old Man had it in abundance. On the fo'c's'le, the bosun and I lifted the guillotine, a hefty, hinged lump of steel that checks the chain. Disengage the windlass and the friction brake now held the anchor's weight. Release that grip and the anchor will run, dragging with it tens of tonnes of chain in a storm of rust, debris and sound. It's so deafening you can't hear the enormous splash of frothy water as the anchor disappears at a threatening speed. A good bosun will learn the "feel" of the brake, so I signaled him to run the anchor out in a sensational splash. Then we acted in coordination, the captain on the radio, me leaning over the rail watching the chain's direction and weight, while the bosun operated the brake to stem the inevitable runaway mass of steel. We laid out six shackles (540 feet), braking and releasing to prevent the chain piling upon itself, and waited till it lay broadly ahead, tightened the brake and reapplied the guillotine; safely at anchor. On a small ship like the *Fort Hamilton* it might have taken an hour. Or two.

Fittingly, we had nowhere to go. A week of tranquil days, hot, clammy and sultry, with no breeze to lighten the mugginess, waiting for the call. With the bridge doors open, the air clung like a second skin, feeling unwashed as soon as you took the watch. Boredom set in, which is better than panic, but time slowed until I sensed the voyage was getting nowhere. Then abruptly, they summoned us in. We tied up, port side to, at the far reaches of town, where plenty happened within walking distance.

Larry and I set to strolling ashore. The population fused a colorful mix of Chinese, indigenous Kadazan and Malays, with a sprinkling of Australians. They mostly spoke Malay, though everyone knew some English, even the Australians. This working section of the city was colorful and vigorous, an antidote to boredom. The street attire demonstrated the city's diversity; a few women in hijabs walked alongside Westerners and locals in miniskirts. The same white, anonymous Japanese cars joined the streets choked with mopeds. We strolled past restaurants, shops and bars causing an olfactory overload. The scent of spices, herbal medicines, curative flowers and fried food included beef rending, *char kuey teow,* and *wonton mee* and chilies. Larry and I stepped off the edge and ordered the special fried rice and ice-cold local beer. Malaysia is a secular state with relaxed Islam as the official religion, if that makes any sense. Kota Kinabalu didn't overwhelm with its beauty, and I might have dug deeper earlier in the voyage, but I have no complaints. It wasn't ready yet, but it was the future of Malaysia. In 1985 it was the sort of place where you could find a quiet beer, sit outside and view the horse we rode in on in the near distance. I would probably never return, but my friends and family hardly knew it existed.

The *Fort Hamilton* was an agreeable ship, easy to operate, and the crew were keen enough. The language barrier and lack of historical or cultural association hampered any friendly rapport. And that was the end of rice for this voyage. This happy trip continued, though I sensed I was running low on fuel. I was growing tired after three and a half months of overindulgence in the Gypsy's Tent. The conviviality of the bar continued to buzz, when time and work allowed, but some of the fancy-dress gang slowly drifted home.

Three days southwest we closed the distance on the Musi River Delta of Sumatra and headed upriver to load a cargo even stranger than scrap—timber. It's an extensive river, and we journeyed fifty miles upstream to find the city of Palembang, which straddles it. Famous for the export of rubber and petroleum in an earlier time, the river drains a substantial portion of South Sumatra and flows muddy brown, winding its leisurely way to the sea.

Recollection is a strange function that does its best and fails, then shines brightly into our conscience. We lay alongside the right bank near the island of Pulau Banjar. The moonless night glowed dim with bright, shimmering stars, the pitiless lights barely opening the world of darkness concealed beyond. Dawn came up, like it does, a sodden morning without rain, and burned the thick mist off the fertile green fields, revealing a lush, dark, emerald farmland, fresh and moist. I still recall the soft breeze, the taste in the air of eucalyptus and jasmine, a fragrant memory like a pressed flower in a journal. Walking on deck, we crunched on the flying insects that infested the ship and viewed the wooden shanties at the chocolate water's edge with residents sitting on their decking, washing clothes and dishes in the river, and hanging laundry, while the children played and jumped and swam.

Timber is a valuable business for Southeast Asia, and let's be frank, sometimes lacking a moral element. We were in the legal business though, here to fill the *Fort Hamilton* with hardwood like it had never been filled before. Timber is an exotic material, which I hardly understood, but I knew from school it came with benefits and detriments. The advantage—for the shipowner and the charterer—is that the traditional load lines can be augmented by timber load lines higher on the ship's side, allowing the vessel to load deeper in the water. The reasoning goes as follows: timber, stacked tightly together in bundles and strongly secured, adds buoyancy, and protects the hatches from seawater ingress and damage. The wood is lashed securely so it won't move in the worst-predicted seas, up to a predetermined height. But there's a downside. It's hygroscopic: it absorbs water, lifting the center of gravity in bad seas and affecting the stability, like a man standing in a rowboat. The *Fort Hamilton*, with timber on deck, would become "tender," the opposite of stiff.

I HAD a solitary, contemplative childhood and was what I might consider a slow developer, socially. My later semi-addiction to alcohol had prevented me from ever really getting at the pain and self-doubt that had swirled around all those years. For some time now, I had thought to broaden my relationships, seek something more meaningful, since those I had seemed ephemeral or illusory. Life is problematic without aim, and pressures were capable of pushing me in one direction or another. Strangely, I was not wholly against the prospect one day of a long-term relationship, but one of life's lessons was not to make hasty decisions. I had spent so much of my short life being against things and now I could consider the prospect in a relaxed and thoughtful manner. I had become the mirror of what I had thought once I wanted to be. I knew plenty of people who had married young—teenagers really—and those lives seemed so dismally wasted. The more I found nothing, the surer I was I'd find something; I just needed some good fortune.

The word "serendipity" was invented by the son of the first British prime minister, Horace Walpole, after he had read the fairy tale "The Three Princes of Serendip," an English translation of an Italian story based on Persian fairy tales concerning the country of Serendippo (believed to be modern Sri Lanka). Walpole clearly explained the princes in the story were "always making discoveries, by accidents and sagacity, of things which they were not in quest of," which implies a random event. *The New Oxford Dictionary*, however, narrows the meaning, suggesting that discoveries or innovations are made by people able to see the benefit of a chance event, as opposed to the flaws it might portend, based on the perception of a noteworthy connection. A chance is the event; serendipity is the capacity to exploit it. So, famously, Alexander Fleming's development of penicillin depended not only on the happy chance of a petri dish containing *Staphylococcus* being mistakenly left open, and then becoming contaminated by mold.

Fleming concluded that the mold released a substance that repressed the growth of bacteria; that was the difference.

I wasn't planning anything at all, other than putting one foot in front of the other. If my life was to evolve further, I had better expand my social horizons, but not in England; I'd given up there. I would undertake correspondence with a cornucopia of characters around the world. To narrow the endeavor, I would concentrate on only fifty percent of the population.

FEMALE FAMILY and acquaintances inquired about the girl in every port, as if to assuage their emotions concerning their drab lives, they initially had been so adamant should come to pass. But these girls didn't exist. And the captain didn't steer the ship. We didn't anchor at night and switch on the lights. Sodomy was unheard of, and mostly the work was numbingly boring, like any other employment. The "five percent" was delivered intermittently.

> I am sick o' wastin' leather on these gritty pavin'-stones,
> An' the blasted Henglish drizzle wakes the fever in my bones;
> Tho' I walks with fifty 'ousemaids outer Chelsea to the Strand,
> An' they talks a lot o' lovin', but wot do they understand?

It was four and a half months for me and I was flat and tired, like yesterday's Christmas balloon. Early one evening we crept into Padang, West Sumatra. It was raining lightly. The few people who visited were sheltering under the overhang of the dock warehouse as we came alongside. We were a large foreign ship, so some came just for the spectacle, but I saw the agent's car, and I saw the white man in the back seat. He was my relief, and I was going home. The *Fort Hamilton*, sadly, like a long love affair, just petered out. It had been a voyage of companionship, loneliness and, tentatively, a realization of a new beginning.

15

Chasing Elcano

1986

How vast those Orbs must be, and how inconsiderable this Earth, the Theatre upon which all our mighty Designs, all our Navigations, and all our Wars are transacted, is when compared to them. A very fit consideration, and matter of Reflection, for those Kings and Princes who sacrifice the Lives of so many People, only to flatter their Ambition in being Masters of some pitiful corner of this small Spot.

—Christiaan Huygens

I THOUGHT Ferdinand Magellan was the first person to circumnavigate the globe, but I had it all wrong. Juan Sebastián Elcano, a Castilian explorer, had set sail with Magellan from Spain, along with 240 other men on five ships. After crossing the Atlantic and subsequently discovering a passage at the tip of South America, they sailed through into the Pacific. After years at sea enduring storms, mutiny and local tribal wars, the fleet had dwindled to one remaining vessel, the *Victoria*, commanded by Elcano. They continued westward, crossing the Indian and Atlantic Oceans, and reached Spain in September 1522, having sailed fifty thousand miles. Magellan had died in the Philippines sixteen months earlier, so it wasn't him after all. Charles

I awarded Elcano a coat of arms with the motto *Primus circumded-isti me* ("You went around me first"). One might consider the return voyage as a long, serendipitous moment, especially since Elcano had participated in the earlier mutiny.

In 1986 it was time to take stock. I had begun this career in some amorphous desire to find maturity and independence. I lacked a plan, or even an idea of how one might be achieved, but leaving the security and familiarity of domestic life in England was the determining factor. I was twenty-six and had matured. I worked hard, harder than anyone I knew in England, but not like a poverty-stricken eight-year-old in Bombay. How to measure success? Well, not materialistically; that couldn't be the answer. I was doing fine anyway, but would never be rich working for the corporation, even avoiding income tax. I was unattached, but is that the measure of a man? I had a penchant for alcohol, but I attributed that to my employment; drug users always find an excuse. I had acquired wisdom. People had changed over time. My parents had grown older, while surprisingly, my siblings had become closer. Old friends, clones of the robot army, were even more distant. When I returned to work, that emotional bond with home had weakened considerably. Impulsively, I decided to buy a house and entered the first one I found on the back page of the local newspaper, declaring, "I'll buy it!"

I relished my navigational work, but realized it had no long-term future, as the British-manned fleet continued to shrink. I didn't see how Canadian Pacific could make the economics work; the ships seemed to be run for the fun of it. Gaining promotion to keep my career afloat would require a Master Mariner's license, but they didn't give them away. I needed something else I was heedless of: the missing piece of the puzzle. I felt, intuitively, that just traveling would enable the next stage. I, like Juan Sebastián Elcano, had to seize it when it came.

I had been to Australia before and liked what I saw. It was English but roomier, with better weather. I flew out with five others (including the audacious Larry Ball from the *Fort Hamilton*) to Perth for the MV *Fort Providence*, another dry bulk carrier; larger and gearless, which for the uninitiated, seemed to proffer less stimulation. I was open-minded though. The day after the late-night arrival, yawning and stretching, we stepped out from the hotel into the glorious Australian summer and took the agent's launch to the ship lying at anchor offshore, between Perth and Rottnest Island. The *Fort Providence* lay peacefully empty between the blue waters and the cloudless sky, lazing in the splendid climate and rippling sea. I had a comfortable handover and settled in, cleaned the cabin, as had become my routine, rummaging through the charts and bridge gear to make sure all was in order, and generally found my way around. The early evening bar scene was most enjoyable, with two young wives filling out the busy lounge, decorated in a dutifully uninspired fashion. The ship gave off a welcoming, happy vibe, especially with the bustling newsworthy joiners.

Three days later we entered the Swan River, serving as the harbor of Perth. The port is named after Captain Charles Fremantle, a British naval officer who hoisted the Union Flag, and in the narcissistic manner of his time and nationality, casually declared possessory rights "of the whole of the West Coast" in the name of the King. Once a penal colony, now it's one of the loveliest places in the world to live. The regular sea breeze, known as the Fremantle Doctor, gives it a Mediterranean feel and cooling relief from the afternoon summer heat.

Preparation to load a cargo of grain in nearby Kwinana required unionized shore labor. Fremantle had notoriously robust unions who dictated that only Australians worked, and only in daylight, and only if it wasn't too hot. It being the southern summer, it was too hot by lunchtime on the vast, open concrete expanse of the giant hot plate of a dock. The work took five days, of which, perhaps, one was spent cleaning. I sympathized with my comrades; we were enclosed in the port, no weather, no seas, so we broke watches and managed a few runs ashore.

Larry, a family man, came from somewhere in the north of England. An intelligent fellow, he could easily perform the buffoonish role when work didn't interfere. We already had a fun and mischievous relationship, so we joined others on a run into the neatly laid-out historic streets of Fremantle, as welcoming as a place could be. The evening began around South Terrace and Market Street, with three others, including the new Old Man, Captain M., who promisingly relaxed his mandate for the evening. As usual, we overdid it, but that's the way of Jack Tar ashore in a foreign land. The evening had proceeded well, and just within acceptable bounds, when we agreed to move on. With no cabs in sight, impulsively, Larry and I jumped into the front seats of an open-topped Jeep parked outside the bar. The other three, joining in the entertainment, made to climb in the back, until I saw the key in the ignition and gunned the engine into life. Larry, for some reason wearing an eye patch, like Spuds Mackenzie, glanced at me with one of those roguish, wide, one-eyed smiles, while the other three, caught in the legal horror of the moment, alighted in trepidation. Knowing we were sitting ducks for a fist from some panting-mad Australian rugby player, I notched the gear lever forward and exited the lot with Larry holding onto the window frame shouting, "Woo-hoo, kemosabe!"

I took two corners. "Are we really doing this?" shouted Larry. The alcohol imbued us with the bravery and energy of a child. "Shouldn't we put the lights on?"

We took off across the Swan River towards the harbor, where I voiced the idea of parking beside the ship's accommodation ladder, but Larry pointed out the absurdity of being caught with our hand in the till, so we abandoned the ride prior to the dock gates, jumped out and, like two wayward schoolboys skipping class, exhaled with the adrenaline. We hailed the elusive taxi, whose absence earlier was really responsible, and headed back to drink the evening dry in liberation.

I kept a low profile for a few days. When an inspector considered the holds sufficiently clean, we moved down the Cockburn Sound to Kwinana, where the BP refinery lay. Just south, fronted by golden beaches, proudly stood an enormous blue elevator, through which ships half of Western Australia's grain. The substantial, reinforced silo's capacity is over a million tonnes; the dramatic blue and white colors of the concrete, combined with its size and remote location, endow the impressive complex with a sense of otherworldliness. Its concrete jetty stretched 750 yards into the sparkling electric-blue water with a capability far outweighing ours; we could feel the *Fort Providence* sinking by the hour as the grain accumulated in a vast fog of eye-irritating dust. The Old Man, an almost Jack the Lad in Fremantle, metamorphosed into Edward Hyde once we set sail. He didn't socialize, but simmered and plotted in his lofty apartment, which suited us. We mostly wanted our few hours of human interaction, an exercise made so much easier with alcohol. The bar was a good one. Larry and I led the way, naturally, but it held a congenial congregation of the less-stressed sort rarely found on tankers. By arrival in Egyptian waters three weeks later, I had settled into my routine, both at work and at play.

The Suez Canal could have been worse, but not much, like a lackluster tray of leftovers served by a sleepy lunch lady. We departed Port Said having paid our twenty-carton fee, the bar reopened and, like winter follows autumn, we resumed the social routine. The majority of traffic leaving Suez heads for Gibraltar, but we headed northwest for the Greek islands and the Aegean. I was, shall we say, over the legal limit, when I took the watch at midnight, beer-pickled, content we would find negligible traffic in that direction. The third mate, displaying scant suspicion, handed over the usual rote markers: true, gyro and magnetic, weather (fine), a few distant non-worrying lights. My type of watch: open waters, one course for the next four hours. In a soft Amstel haze, I glanced around at the lights and indicators of the wheelhouse, leaned on the chart, tentatively viewed the blurred line I had drawn days before, picked up a pencil on my third attempt, and then forgot why I needed it. The lookout lingered on the starboard wing, so I sat down to rest my weary body, the buzz of drinking dissipating and becoming lethargy. Nothing, not even coffee, could halt the relentless disintegration, like a slide down a garbage chute. Then the yawning began.

I heard him, unconcernedly, "Sec', light to starboard. Crossing light, Second." I arose awkwardly from my temporary slumber and noticed the dim clock: 1:45 a.m. Strange, must have dozed off. I widened my eyes and peered to starboard, seeing the light, or rather murky collection of white and red—a ship crossing. I sat down again and lined up the lights and window frame to monitor the bearing, my experience distilling into overconfidence as I rested my heavy head on hand and elbow.

The Indian lookout again, shriller and urgent: "Second Mate! Crossing ship still there!"

I stirred from my torpor and saw again. Oh, my God! The crossing ship was closer, filling windows, and his port sidelight glowed clear and bright. Fucking hell! I tumbled from the pilot's chair and stepped briskly to the radar: less than two miles. Fuck! I was awake now, as if standing on the edge of a tall building. Skin crawling, I strode purposely to each wing—nothing behind. The lookout, blissfully without responsibility, frowned back at me and then the other ship, perhaps waiting for an order to man the helm. Fuck, this is bad! He was so close I knew I wouldn't make it astern of him, even with full helm. Ingrained in every watchkeeper's mind, rule 15:

> When two…vessels are crossing so as to involve risk of collision, the vessel which has the other on her own starboard side [i.e., me!] shall keep out of the way…

I groaned inside. I had three imperatives: I would not shift the telegraph (the inquisition would have consumed days, and I wasn't sufficiently lucid to conjure a blameless tale), I would not call the Old Man, and lastly, and irrefutably, I had to do something. Fuck!

I stepped to the wheel, snapped it into manual and set her to port, twenty degrees. As the *Fort Providence* slowly turned, the other ship began fading astern. Damn! I nearly forgot the off-course alarm! I stumbled to the chart room and flicked the switch before it woke the dead. I heard the gyro repeater clicking faster as we spun, more and more, the head went in a long, dizzying turn. I eased the helm. I had to accomplish this while waking no one with the subtle change of vibration; seafarers notice it, even when asleep. The other ship was astern and fading clear, riding on his contented way. He had done his duty— no flashing lights, no angry VHF call, no blaring horn. I was the other guy. Our turn progressed like a slow-motion skid in the dark, down an icy blacktop.

After much anxious dragging of time, I returned the *Fort Providence* to her original course, and slipped her back into automatic. I had wasted much time of our passage and the evidence lay writ large on the course recorder. Chastened, I remained wide awake for the remainder of the watch. It may not have been a full-blown disaster, but it came close. Was it a crime if unwitnessed? If there were justice, the Board of Trade should have been knocking at my door to take my license away.

THE DARDANELLES, like Katmandu or Shangri-La, is one of those mythical names that linger in history, whether or not we value the stories. It's one of those places we can forget, until the next time. It was, along with the Bosphorus, the only southern route to the Soviet Union—230 miles, narrow and congested at each end—between the Balkans and Afghanistan, in that unreal expanse of choking, geographic confusion, where so many tragedies have arisen and stalled.

ONE DAY north sat the famous Soviet naval base at Odessa. A child of the Cold War, here I was, slipping behind the Iron Curtain, like passing Checkpoint Charlie. I remember being called aft for standby just after breakfast, clammy and cold, waking from my slumber. Outside, the sun was running late, the sky gray with the vast suffocating bleakness of fog. It was strangely disorienting; our breath smoked in the cold, the atmosphere eerily cloaking us. The top three inches of the ocean were ice. The sea, placid and spooky, was solid. We tied up alongside the elevators where once, perhaps, the Soviet Union had exported grain. Now they were importing it from Australia. Close by stood the passenger terminal, a monolithic glass and gray, fake-marble edifice with that strange Russian calligraphy atop, like bafflingly reading words in a mirror. Nearby were a collection of dark military vessels, guns and other menacing protrusions, but few appeared recently seaworthy. They warned us not to take pictures. A pallid, steely mist overhung the port, blending into the topography of the city.

It took three days to unload the grain, one slow grab at a time. For security, they stationed an armed soldier at the foot of the accommodation ladder and mooring lines, not to constrain us, but to prevent anyone from stowing away. So, this was it, the Russian Bear, my lifetime enemy.

The agent organized a sightseeing trip for volunteers, so half a dozen of us boarded a small, shaky bus and were guided around the city by a political lackey of the oblast. He was young, tall, dark-haired and enormously enthusiastic about the lies he narrated. He gorged on anti-capitalist bombast and his own self-importance, swamped by state mythology, like a man who never let his side down, or who had never read any history, other than the one he had been indoctrinated with. But the bus ride was fun, bouncing around the craters and ruts of the city, hanging on as he proudly told his story of the great Soviet experiment. Perhaps feeling it a step too far, he didn't endeavor to convince us of its superiority, since we could see the disjointedness by looking out the window. I'd say the streets were ridden with potholes, but that would be an insult to potholes; and I had read about the gulags. What overwhelmed was the sheer seediness of the place, with people, buildings and landscapes all convincingly grubby, like a strange, dystopian movie set.

But he took us to the customary locations, places someone from another planet might envisage as noteworthy: The Duke de Richelieu Monument, honoring Odessa's first mayor, standing atop the cinematic Potemkin steps. We glimpsed the Opera Theater, which seemed a monumental folly in Odessa, the second best in Europe according to the political officer, but we were deprived of access. We took in a statue of Lenin; then another one. Odessa was once famous for its attractive tree-lined avenues which, before communism, made the city a favorite year-round retreat for the Russian aristocracy, but in 1986 they looked dreary and barren, so blended in well. Its historical architecture was supposedly more Mediterranean than Russian, but everything carried a fittingly weighty, Soviet patina of grime, like a slow-motion traffic accident that had taken seventy years to arrive.

Odessa was cold, but not just from the weather. It was full of large residential blocks whose main features were broken windows, plastic sheets and filth. The city reeked of unbearable blandness and decrepitude. Everywhere the dirty concrete and peeling paint were made grimmer with the leaden skies. The government housed families in single communal apartments, where the residents suffered from overcrowding, and a fear of a knock on the door at night. I couldn't smell communism; I only smelled despair. Upon ridding ourselves of half the cargo we departed the Ukraine and set east for Georgia.

Batumi, the second-largest city of Georgia, had a small port situated in a subtropical zone near the base of the Lesser Caucasus. The *Fort Providence* berthed on the inner, southern docks. We sat there for six days as the grain slowly disappeared. The same sad, dark-green-coated sentries watched our ropes. We walked ashore this time, over the rusted railway tracks where the fence had decayed away, into the city, past the square housing blocks, like an old man with cancer, with the balconies dripping rust. We encountered few people along the broken pavement, but those we did had that same vacant stare, as if existing from day to day, enduring the pain of repetitiveness and the joyless determination of shift workers achieving quotas of widgets nobody wanted. They accepted it, a miasma of gloom and apathy. What other life did they know in a place where the government not only knows everyone's business, but everyone's mind?

We fell upon a large building, much like a grand hotel of a bygone era. It spoke of a different time. The five of us entered, jackets clutched close to deny the cold, and found the outsized dining room, filled with empty tables. In a sense of otherworldliness, a waiter in formal black trousers, white shirt and waistcoat appeared. We asked for beer, but we might have asked for a rocket ship to the moon. The concept of choice didn't exist; the only alcoholic drink was "champagne," so we ordered a bottle and sat at a large, round, white-cloth-covered table drinking some fizzy concoction and eating peanuts, the only food offered. A staleness pervaded the place. Now and then we glimpsed another face peering from the kitchen door, as if we were alien, which we surely were. Otherwise, we did not interact. We left the waiter a ten-dollar bill, and he seemed grateful but, like everyone else in Batumi, failed to crack a smile.

Batumi's exuberant commercial past had disappeared long ago, and no one cried when we set sail from a place that made us wonder if the sun would ever shine again. At least a few good people were employed to go there. It was a difficult time for shipping, it being a boom-or-bust industry. When business was slow, ships remained where they were, or steamed without orders to a near-market location, in this case "Land's End for Orders," the entrance to the English Channel.

SOMEWHERE BEFORE Gibraltar, in juxtaposition to our last port of call, we were ordered to the Mississippi River. Destrehan of St. Charles Parish, like a port nobody wanted, bless them, is a small community on the east bank of the Mississippi River, just north of New Orleans. We moored alongside a monstrous, shabby gray elevator sitting back from the surging water's edge, like a temple to the gods of agriculture, poised to disgorge thousands of tonnes of American bounty.

I had a free late afternoon, so, on a whim, I took a solitary stroll along the River Road with the April spring air mingling with the smell of the mighty waterway. Once over the levee, it felt odd to walk along a road while the river flowed southward above, but that is the engineering undertaken to tame the potent Ol' Man. The skies were crisp and clean, with a few fair-weather cumuli adding to the texture of quiet contentedness. After half a mile, as far as I could estimate, I came across a low wooden building with a "Budweiser" sign flickering in the window, so I stepped pensively inside. Some thoughts plunge into my memory as clear as the day they occurred.

The bar was forsaken, save for a young lady sitting behind the counter watching me with disinterest. I took a stool, ordered a beer and introduced myself. She appeared jaded and listless, as if her American dream had died in Destrehan. I sensed her reticence, but the bar was void of alternatives, so, as awkward as it was, I tried to promote conversation. On my second beer I discerned, "You don't appear happy, Sally."

"Where's yer strange accent from?" she deflected.

"Same place as me, London." I thought I should clarify, "England."

"I wished I was born somewhere else." She surprised me.

"You could always travel, take a vacation," I suggested, instantly recognizing the absurdity of the comment, especially when she muttered, "God willing." She was at an age when she might have expected life to have flourished, but the good suffer and the wicked prosper.

I ordered another, viewing the movement of her svelte, pastel-covered body as she leaned into the icebox.

"Do you believe in God, Sally?"

She uncapped the bottle and placed it on the bar. "Sometimes." She smiled the smile of the pained. The beer heedlessly loosened my tongue. I pointed out the absurdity of believing only some of the time, but she related the story of her sister's recent death from an illness she couldn't quite pronounce, and I couldn't spell. The morals imposed at a younger age are more powerful than ones learned later. Our conversation soared to heights only attainable with alcohol.

"Anyway, who made the Earth and the stars for us if not God?" Sally asked.

I don't know why the memory remained, other than the curiosity of sitting in a bar, austere and deep-rooted as it was, without the conversation of the sea. Sally, her dark skin burned ebony by the Louisiana sun, I sensed, had little opportunity to escape the indoctrination of her childhood. She scarcely understood what I did or where I hailed from, which made the conversation all the more pleasant, combined with her obvious allure. She caught me staring, a modest challenge.

"What are you thinking, John?"

"Nothing good, I can assure you, Sally."

I sensed God was not very interested in me. I headed back to the womb of the ship as the skies began their graying of the approaching evening. I wish I knew what happened to the people I met; there are some who cross our lives and leave an indelible mark. I hoped Sally would be treated well when the man comes around taking names.

WHEN A vessel loads dry bulk, like grain, the quantity loaded is assessed by determining the draft before and after, a process known as a draft survey. This was the basis for preparing a bill of lading, the receipt a captain signs affirming the quantity and quality of goods he is carrying on behalf of the shipper. The principle upon which they base the survey traces back to Archimedes. It's performed by reading the ship's draft at six standard points and then performing some tedious mathematics. Corrections for factors such as water density and non-cargo weight changes (usually ballast and bunkers) are made, before calculating the cargo weight difference in the vessel's hydrostatic tables, produced by the builder. Bills of lading signed, we turned in the river—no easy feat—and, with the 6-knot flow, shot down to the Gulf of Mexico and headed for the Panama Canal. Gullibly, I looked forward to the experience.

Captain M., like a reptile with a personality, interacted less and less, ensconced in his lofty suite, as if in a tree beholding prospective prey. He did what he had to do, usually with disdain and never with any humor, unless it was black and aimed at an easy target. Discontent from the lower ranks was the oxygen he breathed. I avoided confrontation, unless cornered on the bridge. But he'd missed my round turn in the Mediterranean, so his low profile had some benefit. His dark ire reached its culmination in a weekly inspection, when he encountered two street signs Larry had purloined in Destrehan as part of our efforts to revamp the lackluster bar décor. He gave us until Panama to complete the redecorating. He was also boring, so he had that going for him.

BECOMING A famous explorer today is harder because, well, haven't we discovered everything? The early-sixteenth-century conquistador, Vasco Núñez de Balboa was a Castilian pioneer, considered to be the first European to have crossed the Isthmus of Panama and lay his wondrously shocked eyes upon the undisturbed waters of the Pacific. Did he understand what he saw?

The Canal is a forty-eight-mile-long waterway featuring three sets of locks, several cuttings and artificial lakes, allowing ships of suitable size to transit the American continental divide. While we think globally of the Atlantic being east and the Pacific west, the general direction of the Canal is, paradoxically, from northwest to southeast, due to the anomaly of the isthmus's shape. My experience on the *Fort Providence* began one morning when I was summoned to standby on the bridge, tropical white uniform and all, and I expected to be there for the transit. We took the pilot and headed south with a straight run through the port of Cristobal and, soon after, arrived at the Gatún Locks, a three-stage flight lifting ships eighty-five feet to the lake level. I admired the professionalism of the operation. Truth is, no one enjoys maneuvering near all that concrete. Guided by a tug, wires forward and aft were sent to "mules," compact electric locomotives running along the lock, but there's only a two-foot clearance on either side, so considerable skill is required by the operators and all involved.

It took an hour for the dreamlike ascent, grabbing attention and feeling slightly surreal, but I disliked all those people on my bridge: pilots, captains, helmsmen, and tourists. As always, it was solemn and serious. We crossed the artificial lake formed by the Gatún Dam, and the standby dragged. The transit revealed little in the way of habitation, so it felt rather like crossing water deep in a lost jungle. Each mile revealed darker, spinach-green jungle surrounding muddy-brown water. I preferred standing a bridge watch alone, my own command, deciding, guiding the ship. Here I had a secondary role while the Old Man and pilot—in 1986, still American—engaged in professional dialogue, shackled together by their rank. From the damming of the lake, there flowed the Chagres River, a natural waterway having the unusual distinction of being the only river flowing into two oceans.

Afterward, we traversed the Gaillard Cut, an artificial valley carved eight miles through the narrowest saddle of the Isthmus. The humidity and mugginess mimicked that which had exasperated the original builders. The construction here remains one of the most staggeringly grueling engineering feats of the twentieth century, employing seventy-five thousand men. I couldn't imagine the hardship and toil required to create it. It went on and on, and I feigned attentiveness, for eight long hours. Like a job attaching strings to tea bags, the routine had quickly become predictable.

The single-stage Pedro Miguel Lock was our commencement of descent: thirty-one feet, the *Fort Providence* bridge wings oddly settling down to dock level. After dragging ourselves through, we transited the short, artificial Miraflores Lake, and then the two-stage Miraflores Locks, falling the final fifty-four feet. Then, we were traversing the port of Balboa, and Panama City's splendorous skyline, and the Bridge of the Americas, with the Pacific Ocean in our future. I accompanied the pilot, an affable chap, to the ladder, happy to see him go.

The Panama Canal is half the length of Suez, but it's more scenic (how could it not be?) and a lot more work. The size of the locks determines the maximum dimensions and the *Fort Providence* was Panamax, just able to squeeze through. Economically, the Canal eliminates some eight thousand miles of arduous voyaging around Cape Horn, and has become more strategically important to world trade than Suez, the closings of which had allowed shipowners to develop alternatives. There really are no alternatives to Panama. The Canal wasn't good by any stretch of the imagination, but at least it hadn't been a complete waste of time. It felt like a box ticked, another rite achieved.

The next day I turned my attention to the unusually large pile of mail from family and penfriends. Before the Internet, the discovery of people remote could be achieved with the long-lost concepts of personal and magazine advertisements. It had taken a while, unlike the instant connections of today, but I collected a dozen friends, happy to chat about their families and lives in places I had visited and plenty

I had not. I knew a young Hong Kong steward on the *Leonia* named Rico, who actually placed messages in sealed bottles and tossed them overboard every few days. I doubt the concept worked, but I connected with his attempted hollering of distress, the heady drug of a dangerous faint hope.

For anyone living remote from society, the distinctive interaction with others that a written letter evokes is genuinely positive. Telephone calls home were few and far between anyway, but the paper letter, read alone, slowly and thoughtfully, then reread, was a more gratifying medium of communication. I found that just holding the paper, scanning a photograph for clues, scrutinizing another's handwriting, were all stimuli to yield a calling out, like an SOS signal waiting to be heard across the enormous moat of loneliness. Correspondence allowed me to converse economically with females in Oklahoma, Peru, Denmark, the Philippines and other places. Did they correspond because I was English, or because I came from a wealthy nation, or because I was literate or because I had traveled? They allowed me to voice my opinion without hesitation or affectation; I avoided that awkward first glance and the misgivings of regret I had felt before. You could also break up without difficulty by mail; in one sense it was relationship building for cowards.

THEN THERE it was: the seemingly endless Pacific Ocean, largest and deepest, larger than all the land area combined. Magellan called it Pacífico ("peaceful"), in contrast to sailing through the stormy high-latitude waters off South America, and until the eighteenth century it was named in his honor. The *Fort Providence* headed for Japan, some twenty-three days distant. Anyone watching from the beach would see the tiny figure of our ship, shimmering mirage-like, disappearing

over the horizon heading, very alone, into the abyss. This was big-
league stuff.

Long, barren voyages promoted relaxation, performing maintenance, writing letters and catching up. The routine meant standard
watches and routine sleep, as long as nothing went awry. Bad weather
was not expected. Navigationally, we had a small drab box labeled
"Loran-C," another hyperbolic radio system using signals conveyed
by land-based beacons; about as useful as a broken mosquito net.
Fortunately, we had the sextants.

The wheelhouse at night is an enigmatic place, both familiar and
comforting, small and personal, and at the same time open and enormous, an overture to so many natural phenomena and chimeras.
There's no one at sea, really deep sea. People just travel across it. One
night, surprisingly unaffected by alcohol, after a comfortable four
hours of sleep, I took the watch on a clear, dark night. Somewhere
the low thrum of the engine dissolved in my mind. The visibility was
good, although a few scattered clouds hid a portion of the sky. It was
a fine night to contemplate and dream. Then, towards the watch's end
the light began to transform. The atmosphere of the morning came
creeping into me, magnifying the unexplained. The black sky slowly
melted behind some spreading stratocumulus to the south, as if the
first hint of the morning sun were approaching, but prematurely, and
from the wrong direction. Resting on the dodger, I watched until a
large, glowing-orange half-disk climbed slowly over the curvature of
the Earth, appearing at a break of a cloud, holding me transfixed with
awe. For a moment or two I stood breathless, unable to believe, eyeing
my first unidentified flying object. I shuddered, wanting to move and
call out, but I couldn't, frozen as if hypnotized for three or four minutes. Inside, I unexpectedly felt vulnerable, so far from home, all at sea,

where everyone relies on the slender steel hull and that engine going on forever; an ethereally dramatic effect that transcends understanding. If I were to ever believe, I imagined this was it. Then, abruptly, a hundred miles distant, the breeze freshened, and the cloud moved to the east, and the orange UFO identified itself as a heavenly body: the moon.

THERE ARE moments that impinge upon an individual, coloring one's view of existence, the eerie pull that the extraordinary can exert upon us. How inexplicable the sky must have seemed to the uneducated thousands of years before. Understandably, they believed the heavens revolved about the earth because the evidence lay before their eyes. I recognize how they found comfort in the life-giving sun every morning. They celebrated the passing of the winter solstice as it reached the nadir of its travels and returned to give them light, warmth and food for the new season. Justifiably, they celebrated the event, conferring upon the sun the acclaim of a returning god. I too, as a child, saw stars fall from the sky and couldn't grasp why. Since going to sea, I had striven to understand the relationship between stories of old and this huge imaginary blackboard of the firmament. It's when everyone else is asleep, one can reflect on the impenetrable questions. On suitable nights, the show grew profound.

I'd seen it before, but here, somewhere in the vast desert of the Pacific, it took on a whole new dimension. In a manner, I felt privileged, three thousand miles from humanities ubiquitous light pollution, to lean on the dodger and lift my eyes to the spectacle above; our own galaxy from the inside out, the Milky Way, a vast glowing river of light, the backbone of night, as the bushman called it. Galileo first suggested the enormity of what man had always seen without knowing. He understood, for the first time with his telescope in 1610, that the "cloud" comprised an uncountable number of individual stars—all the stars in the universe, he surmised. What we call the Milky Way is the thick edge viewed from our location on the fringe. It's hard to define how awe-inspiring the phenomenon is without invoking Shelley, or someone of nobler literary facility than mine. John Milton called it "a broad and ample road, whose dust is gold". It is astonishing the first time you see it clearly; the sheer number of stars just blows you away in wonder. In ideal conditions the scattered light casts shadows.

Only in October 1923 did we learn the shocking truth. Not only were there an enormous number of stars in the Milky Way, but one of them, flawless in my binocular view that night, was a tiny white smudge between Cassiopeia and Pegasus. Edwin Hubble proved not only was it not of the Milky Way, but, improbably, another galaxy in its own right, the light from which has taken two and a half million years to reach us. I could see Andromeda, the next closest big galaxy, looking ordinary, yet they say it contains a trillion stars. I stood and stared, emotionally seized, mesmerized by each moment, finding it intractably hard to avert my eyes, overcome by the utter enormity of the numbers involved.

On one of those nights I finally crystalized my heretical thoughts and the dizzying puzzle I couldn't engage nor reconcile since that hand had held me back in New Orleans. I have to admit, Sally, I'm a little confused. If the Milky Way contains billions of stars, some light from which has been travelling to our tiny suburb since before the beginning of man, and the Milky Way is just one of billions of galaxies, then the numbers are too cosmic to comprehend, like a mathematician tinkering with infinity. The human mind cannot grasp the impossible magnitude of the universe. How could I possibly believe a story based on us? How could an omnipotence care for something so insignificant as me? The earth isn't special—it turns out to be a banality; there must be trillions of planets. When the earth was flat and we identified a dozen astrological signs, then this concept may have made sense, but now I knew too much. I recognized a dozen stars well, like ancient friends, recurring as predicted every night, but they didn't gaze down on me, I looked up at them and I knew where they were and how I could use them. They were my personal relationship with reality.

The whole magnitude of God made no sense. Even Kurtz was a god to some. In a moment of elegant clarity, I realized life had no purpose, other than life itself. There were dozens of self-assured religions in India, so was Sally's any more meaningful? Darwin and Wallace were right; evolution is an undeniably suitable explanation, while religions are forever flawed, dwindling ideas based on mystic tales from when we prayed for the sun to return. You know the old story; we live on a planet made for us, and it's two-thirds water, yet we have no gills. It is an arrogant concept to believe the universe was made for us. Sally had her doubts, but even though her manacles had broken, she was still bound by the propaganda of her childhood. Seafarers used to be religious too, but that was before we had an engine. I still have a certificate of baptism, but it required more than a piece of paper, or a few words, to see the truth. It's an accident of evolution that we even consider these ideas.

At the winter solstice each year a phenomenon occurs in the night sky. The brightest star, Sirius (the "Star in the East"), aligns with the three stars of Orion's Belt (the "Three Kings"), and points to the birth of a new sun. It lingers for three days, then resurrects itself, and the days become longer, as in the stories of Horus, Krishna, Mithra and… Sally's Jesus. Observing the sky was like seeing God, and it was nearly all explainable. We know now that those four stars are billions of miles apart. Our lives are fleeting moments in a universe that doesn't care. I never lost my faith; I just recognized I never had one. My willing suspension of disbelief was exhausted. The burden lifted and I saw the truth all above me, and in that moment, I felt very small, very unimportant and very free.

THE *FORT Providence*, built by Hyundai in Ulsan, had seven hatches, the heavy steel covers hydraulically powered to lift and roll open. With a deadweight capacity of 64,584 tonnes, we had no gear, which made ports straightforward; most of the time, we just watched grabs or shore labor working. I had the rote CP cabin, and no complaints there; I was to learn later that more space didn't add in any meaningful manner to the lifestyle.

The long, relaxing summer trip continued. The news came through some days, distant and dreary: politics we didn't care for, sport we couldn't track and economics that didn't affect us. We sailed in our own lonely world, comfortably ignorant. Then, we awoke on April 26 with the news from Pripyat, four hundred miles north of Odessa, where a blaze and explosion had crippled the Chernobyl nuclear power plant. We felt safer where we were, like that postapocalyptic book by Nevil Shute. And, sadly, the Iran-Iraq War continued, with most Western observers bewildered by the geopolitics of the Persian Gulf, condensed into two nations quarreling over the twin burdens of oil and religion. The Tanker War escalated drastically, with attacks nearly doubling. To save the day, in a vacuum of consequence and responsibility, Ayatollah Khomeini issued a fatwa declaring that they must win the war by March 1987, so thousands more young men were fed into the epic conflagration. Perhaps when the money ran out, they might realize which century they occupied.

WHAT I saw in the sky continued to captivate. I couldn't remove from my mind the sheer enormity of it. One such phenomenon was a comet the Babylonians had been viewing since 240 BC. They saw the same phenomenon in 1066; we know because its image occurs on the Bayeux Tapestry. It has been viewed repeatedly throughout history, at regular intervals, but its predictability (periodicity) was not determined until 1705 by the English astronomer Edmond Halley. It's the only short-period comet that's typically visible to the naked eye, and there it was, low in the sky as we crossed the Pacific. I saw the fuzzy tail for a few nights; celestial, singular, extraordinary, and I was alive for this one special moment of the cosmos.

Our cargo of American grain was destined for Japan. These visits were quieter than before, away from the big cities, but I cherished walking the peaceful streets, visualizing how the people lived. I saw the flowerpots outside the delicate houses, the topiary gardens squeezed behind a wall, the tiny cars—always white—the quietness of the towns, houses with their doors open, bicycles left unattended; the old people, hardworking and proud, imprisoned by tradition. What had they been through? They lived in a different room of experience that I could never enter. It's the assault of the unfamiliar on the eyes. Clean, well-kept, safe, bright colors, and that propensity for adorability. We again bought Japanese beer from the vending machines, not for the taste, but because it was novel. Japan was frustrating because no matter how much I enjoyed the country, I knew I could never live there, as if I had just been peering through a window.

AFTER JAPAN, a reflection: from the day I saw the advert on the back cover of the *Careers Book*, I conjured a short inventory of places I had to see. Hong Kong topped the list. I had images of the towering skyline, a crush of lights with Victoria Peak in the background, neon illuminations and vertical signs, junks, sampans, floating villages, dilapidated old houses, the hustle and bustle of street vendors, police in Land Rovers, Anita Mui, Jackie Chan and Suzie Wong. I wanted to see and experience it. I tattooed it on my mind, like Valparaíso. I had never been, but I already wanted to live there.

Our orders were for Tap Shek Kok, which sounded mysterious and exotic, but was miles from Kowloon. All these years later, my memory fails to betray the reason we traveled there, but we berthed—with a biting antidote to all those soppy Hong Kong tourist posters—on an awful, overhanging dock, blustered by a strong current that continually strove to remove us. Nobody liked it, but the Old Man, in an uncharacteristic gesture of largesse, or perhaps erroneously, organized a launch to Kowloon in the early evening, so Larry, the boys and I rode the long, bumpy, fast launch into the harbor, prepared to be wowed. Who can know what's in a man's soul? If a kind thought ever crossed his mind, he did his best to hide it, but thank you, Captain M., for if you've never seen it before, believe me: this was the ride of one's life.

The skyscrapers appeared slowly enough; then passing Stonecutters, the whole harbor opened before us, as if stepping inside a giant Christmas grotto. We leaned outside the noisily bouncing boat, straining to take it all in: Hong Kong Island to the south, the buildings all lit in a blaze halfway to the peak, and ahead and to the left, Kowloon, grittier, but surrounded by a forest of apartment buildings, all alight, hanging precariously from every hillside. Everything of my seafaring life before had been a warm-up for something more compelling. We headed to the peninsula, opposite the island, to one of the world's most densely populated cities, Kowloon. Some labeled it the "dark side", an oxymoron with all those lights glowing passionately neon, caught between Western idealism and the Chinese mainland, between capitalism and communism.

I concluded during that epic ride, like an ephemeral moment, that this view, this place, where I had yet to step ashore, was already grander than New York, or Cape Town: a three-hundred-and-sixty-degree scene, so breathtakingly, eye-numbingly gorgeous, without rival. For the first time, I felt the word *awe-inspiring* appropriate for a man-made scene. The launch dropped us at the Kowloon Public Pier, and off we set along Nathan Road, the center of town, then to the west into Peking Road and Hankow Road, into a warren of neon-lit small streets, noticeably grubby. The air was heavy, like in many a city, mingling with the street sounds of traffic, gossip and unknown music. But the air smelled better at night, and the novelty kept inviting us in.

With only a few precious hours, what were we to do? We found the clubs where men sat around soft-edged circular bars while a semi-naked woman served cocktails. It was tepid and unoriginal, implying the industry had more money than ideas. The writhing naked flesh kept us watching because it had been a while, but by the end, we wished we hadn't bothered. We ate fish and chips in an English pub. And that was it. At ten o'clock, I had to grab the launch back to Tap Shek Kok and resume my watchkeeping drudgery. The frustration irked, but the only way not to lose sleep is not to go ashore. I had barely sampled anything of this wondrous place. No Chinese food, no shopping, no sightseeing, no sex. The next day, tired and feeling cheated, we set to the south, where the voyage had begun, carrying a simple promise: come what may, one day, I would return to Hong Kong.

THE SHIP sailed to Port Kembla in Australia, where, geographically, something special had occurred. In 1969, the *Sunday Times* organized a Golden Globe Race for the first person to sail around the world, single-handedly, nonstop. Nine competitors set out from England, including notable characters whom I admire more for their courage and eccentricity than anything else. The Scotsman Chay Blyth entered the race with no sailing experience, which might seem foolhardy and disqualifying. But they allowed him to compete anyway, suspecting he had the right stuff, because two years earlier he had rowed—implausibly—across the Atlantic.

The Frenchman Bernard Moitessier, abandoned the race, but circumnavigated the globe nearly twice, mostly in the Roaring Forties, setting a yacht record for the longest nonstop passage. Despite heavy weather, he contemplated rounding Cape Horn again, but put into Tahiti instead. He might have won the race, but rejected the idea of commercializing long-distance sailing, and ensconced himself in a nomadic life of solitude. The truth, like nakedness, is shocking. Loneliness can affect the mind, even when it's not total, as for seafarers on a long trip; we clung to the tenuous and vague friendships we had, secretly longing for the key to escape.

Donald Crowhurst represented the tragedy of the sea. Isolated, he was the last to depart England. After crossing the equator, he realized his boat was leaking sufficiently that to attempt the Capes and higher latitudes would be reckless. But he had borrowed money and promised so many people, the thought of returning in shame proved too much. Obsessed and delusional, he took the third option, and committed suicide.

The winner was Robin Knox-Johnston. The *Sunday Times* stipulated rules for the race, and I had nearly complied with them all. I had begun the voyage, and completed it, in Australia (I actually flew home from Japan two weeks later). The journey was continuous and in one direction, west. The distance traveled exceeded the equator's length; I had journeyed 26,922 miles. I had crossed the equator twice, and every line of longitude. (Hong Kong is 1° 42' west of Port Kembla). I had not traversed two approximate antipodal points, but the ocean and the voyage were indifferent to my hopes and fears. I was happy and justified in my reasoning and evidence, even if Guinness wasn't. It was a trip for the ages, my first circumnavigation, and we had set out with thirty persons and returned with twenty-eight (they had not replaced the two wives, sadly), which was considerably better than Juan Sebastián Elcano.

I was not an old man, but I was no longer young.

16

Cape-Sized

1986

The trouble is not that I am single and likely to stay single, but that I am lonely and likely to stay lonely.

—Charlotte Brontë

I T WAS the *Titanic* that awakened everyone, or perhaps before, when the shipwreck was conceived shortly after they invented the ship. In 1980, a maritime tragedy transpired that sent shock waves through the complacent British naval establishment. During the previous decade, between fifteen to twenty bulk carriers were lost annually. The incidents rarely, if ever, made the news. If I were cynical, I might suggest they probably flew flags of convenience and were manned by Filipinos. But, in September, an event created news: the bulk carrier *Derbyshire* disappeared on her fifteen-thousand-mile voyage from Sept-Îles to Kawasaki. She was four years old, manned by an experienced and well-qualified English master, officers and crew, registered in Liverpool, built by Swan Hunter of Newcastle, owned by the venerable and well-respected British company Bibby Line, and classed A1 by Lloyd's Register.

She had encountered Typhoon Orchid's 85-knot, brutish winds and sixty-foot waves off Okinawa. When the vessel failed to arrive, a search began, but was abandoned four days later. All forty-two crew and two wives perished, without a distress signal. Three theories sought to explain the loss, beginning, naturally, with crew negligence. Second, there had been a catastrophic failure at frame sixty-five (based on a sister vessel experience), where the cargo holds met the pump room; and, lastly, which seemed incredible, perhaps the seas had overwhelmed them, imploding the 30-tonne hatch covers, and carried the vessel down. Predictably, some were quick to impugn the crew, but in the investigation years later, the High Court concluded the *Derbyshire* had foundered when colossal waves had destroyed air pipes leading to the forepeak, triggering uncontrollable flooding and trimming the vessel by the bow. The court's conclusion suggested the vessel had encountered seas of such severity that the sequence of events—loss of hatch covers one by one, flooding and sinking—had all occurred within two minutes. She was the largest British ship ever lost, and I was traveling east to join her cousin.

I liked Japan, but goodness, it's a long flight from London. Weary on arrival, like a soldier going to war, and feeling lonely in the crowd, I was driven to Kimitsu on the eastern shore of Tokyo Bay, perhaps the largest concentration of industry in the world: an enormous six hundred square miles of well-protected refineries, chemical plants, steelworks and sundry other heavy industries. The economy was centered primarily on the large-scale rusty conglomeration that sat on a vast rectangular waterfront, jutting ten thousand feet into the bay, occupied by Nippon Steel. Here they crafted billets, slabs, rails, piles, H-beams and assorted other metal objects for homegrown industries. The whole smokestack area exuded an impression of dark gray and brown erosion, but the Japanese still made it distinct and somehow, at its peripheries, endearing, with giant signs of perfect model ladies advertising I know not what.

There she sat, the MV *E. W. Beatty*, vastly swollen, with the Nippon grabs—three of them—plunging in and out of her holds, stealing each load to deposit on the dock. They covered the whole area in iron-ore dust as if a simmering fire lay within, the powerful noise mechanical and booming. The mighty ship was awkward and unattractive. I climbed onboard with the enthusiasm of a petulant child going to school, the vessel rising slowly above me, gaining freeboard with every grab of ore. I knew the second mate, Ted, and he took me for a brief handover tour. It was familiar, both because Canadian Pacific's photocopier printed out each accommodation design, and because this was my sixteenth voyage. I truly didn't know where I was going, but I knew where I'd been, once a feckless youth, now a responsible man.

At the tour's conclusion, we found the bar; again, typical CP. Don't get me wrong, it was agreeable enough, just traditional. Ted opened the fridge door. "Ready for a beer?"

I considered the time, needing to sort the cabin, find some working clothes. "No, I'll wait." As I walked over to browse some cassette tapes, I heard the familiar metallic crack and gas release of the can opening. "Can you still do that, John?" I pondered for a moment, but with some fortitude, I left and climbed a few flights to meet the Old Man, about whose character he had cautioned me. He was thin, gray-haired and cadaverous, averting his eyes from my outstretched hand and nodding toward the open red folder on his desk.

"Sign there," so I bent and signed the articles of agreement, the document laying down the minimum victuals, hours of work, rates of pay and geographic limitations of the voyage, amongst other standards.

It was anachronistic, but it was what you did when joining a ship; it ritualized your contract under another man's command.

"I hear you're a tanker man?" he grumbled while rearranging an already perfect desk.

"Err, CP man, Cap'n." I was being slightly disingenuous, but with good nature. Life requires white lies, but not a hint of a smile, wry, ironic or otherwise, crossed his face in return.

"I don't like tanker men. Think they're superior. Make sure the routing to Richards Bay is set and check the distance. I'll check it later." He relished the squirming discomfort of others. I grasped this would be a difficult relationship, so I nodded and left.

Later in the day, he found me between cargo watches on the bridge, examining the charts and courses for the aforesaid Richards Bay in South Africa. He had brought notes of his preferred route through the South China Sea and Riau Islands. I didn't like it; seriously bad form, in fact. I didn't mind guidance; absolutely, I would have to discuss with him the general route, but this was nonsense, simply undermining another man's standing. I wasn't employed to draw lines, I was supposed to be the navigator, but his manner was curt and abrupt, and I was surprised again. I already judged him an utterly repellent character, and the promise of the coming months did not bode well.

But I settled in, as one had to, back on the chain gang. The thought of the Old Man wouldn't go away, like an irritating song called "obdurate shortsightedness" stuck in my head. It was employment, and the work on bulkers is generally less demanding than tankers. Sure, sometimes things happen, like with any other ship, but bulk carriers have a darker side. My previous experience in petroleum instilled in me some overconfidence, because everyone understands and avoids the likely dangers: sources of ignition, enclosed spaces, high pressures. Tankers were safe, I believed; they didn't break, they were very stable, and they were pretty much unsinkable, if they remained in one piece without a fire. Bulk carriers, like the *Derbyshire*, had a propensity to break in two, or sink once their integrity was breached, and, unlike tankers with their small, well-secured openings, bulk carriers, by necessity, had large open hatches each the size of a tennis court to allow the throughput of large commodities. Bulk carriers might lull one into a false sense of security.

The following day, the *E. W. Beatty* lumbered out of Tokyo Bay and into the Pacific, passing over the grave of the *Derbyshire*. She was Cape-sized, too large to transit the Suez or Panama Canals. Her dimensions restricted her to a handful of terminals commonly in the coal, iron ore and raw materials trade. It was twenty-three days from Kimitsu to Richards Bay, a splendid journey to acclimatize and avoid the Old Man with his compulsion to dominate and palpable craving to be respected.

Planning a trip from Japan to South Africa is intricate, but typically instigated with a simple premise: What's the shortest route for the vessel's maximum draft? Like any man, I wasn't about to ask for directions. Southwest through the Philippine Sea, passing north of Luzon, into the South China Sea fitted the bill perfectly. It would then be a straight shot across the Indian Ocean, skirting Mozambique, if it were not for the islands of Sumatra and Java impeding the route. We could have taken the congested Strait of Malacca, but why bother when between the two large islands lies the Sunda Strait, connecting the Java Sea and Indian Ocean. It has been a vital shipping route since the Dutch used it as the gateway to the Spice Islands, known for its irregular bottom topography, reefs and, oh, yes, the most famous active volcano ever.

The strait, often busy but rarely congested, is dotted with small islands, the navigation lights are helpful and the steep-sided coast-line shows up readily on radar. Anyway, if you want a recognizable landmark, just view the island from which rises a wispy plume of gray smoke. It used to be called Krakatoa, but it disappeared one day. In its place is the child, predominantly a submerged caldera, with three islands where the rim once existed, and a new cone, Anak Krakatau, forming itself since 1927. It remains active and ominous, waiting menacingly for the next Strombolian event.

THE TALE of Krakatoa is more than ancient: it is as old as the continents themselves. There are age-old tales of eruptions, but it had remained quiet since an enormous flare-up in 1680, growing slowly year by year in size. But, in May 1883, after rumbling for a few months, it finally reawakened.

Nearby residents grew concerned, but what could they do? Most sensed the noises were gradually growing in intensity, but few could imagine the catastrophe about to befall their lush, fertile land. Sunday, August 26 had been a suspiciously quiet day when, just after lunch, the sudden, sharp crack of an explosion shattered the peace. All eyes looked to Krakatoa. By mid-afternoon, it enveloped the area in an unnatural darkness, hot ashes streamed down and the volcano lit with an intermittent, fiery red glow. Waves crashed violently against the shore, ripping small boats loose from their moorings, to be dashed to pieces like fragile toys in a paddling pool. As the day evolved into night, the explosions continued. People panicked. Hot winds of flying cinder and ash pounded passing ships. Next day, the dawn never came, as ash and lightning filled the air and the eruptions grew more intense. Three terrible explosions shook the air, generating immense, powerful waves.

Then, at exactly 10:02 a.m., the unthinkable occurred: the most famous explosion of all time, the equivalent of a thousand nuclear bombs. Krakatoa exploded into nothingness with paroxysmal force, propelling nine cubic miles of rock into the atmosphere, like a giant jet engine aimed skyward. It destroyed its surrounding archipelago as it collapsed into itself, the caldera, completely transforming the Sunda Strait. They judge the explosion to be the loudest sound ever heard in modern recorded history, with reports of it being perceived three thousand miles away in Alice Springs. Anyone within ten miles would have been instantly struck deaf. Buildings five hundred miles away shook with the incomprehensible geological force, as pyroclastic surges traveled twenty-five miles across the Strait to the Sumatra coast. The eruption sent shock waves around the Earth at seven hundred miles an hour, recorded on barographs for days afterward. The antipodal recordings showed the wave circumnavigated the globe three and a half times over five days. Clouds of gas, fire, and smoke shot some thirty thousand feet into the sky when the rock cap broke. High-speed winds (the jet stream), carried aerosol particles that finally covered seventy percent of the Earth's surface, scattering light and turning skies inter-mittently blood red for four or five years.

Average global temperatures fell by as much as 2°F in the year following the eruption, and weather patterns remained chaotic until 1888. The detritus from the eruption reached Norway, where a news-paper article stated the "end of 1883 and the first months of 1884 had the most spectacular twilights of the last 150 years." The artist Edvard Munch produced at least four versions of his famous painting, *The Scream*, one of which showed the fiery blood-red clouds behind the yelling boy. At least thirty-six thousand people died, and many more were injured, mostly from the tsunamis—the largest ever recorded—that followed the explosion, their lives erased like waves flushing trash along the sand. In 1927, a new island, Anak Krakatau, the "Child," emerged from the caldera formed in 1883, growing about sixteen feet a year, from where I could see the trail of smoke rising into the air as the *E. W. Beatty* passed southbound.

LEAVING THE waiting catastrophe behind, we set southwest towards Africa. One afternoon the Old Man appeared on the bridge, his cabin life unendurable for someone entitled to control others. He set himself to some activity in the open chart room; I saw no point in engaging him. A minute later, he bellowed: "Second Mate!"

I strolled over. "Do you seriously plan on taking my ship this close to these obstructions?"

I'd read his notes, but his zigzag routing lacked logic, while the cartography was sound. Nonetheless, I reluctantly heeded his advice and rerouted the line further out, recalculating the whole voyage, but hey, that was his prerogative. I knew from his manner, the averted eyes, and the sniff of contentment, the only reason for the change was to make the change, to assert his authority. I wondered if he mumbled to himself in embarrassment when alone, like Captain Queeg.

Two weeks of meddling later, it was our good fortune to find land, let alone the place we were aiming for. We arrived off a little-known port ninety miles north of Durban. Ostensibly it's a small town in KwaZulu-Natal, located on a considerable lagoon. Henry Cloete, the notable historian of the Boars, declared it to have no potential as a future harbor, but he was mistaken. After the disastrous battle of Isandlwana in 1879, Admiral of the Fleet Sir Frederick Richards arrived, so they named the hopeless harbor for him.

In 1976 with its evident proximity to mineral wealth, the bay was recognized as a perfect location for the export of the area's riches. I thought Port Kembla was full-sized, but Richards Bay dwarfed it. The terminal was the largest coal export facility in the world, with an annual throughput of 66 million tonnes. There are fertilizer plants, iron ore and other stuff, but it's coal that dominates. The coal piles stretch for seven thousand feet, holding over 8 million tonnes, with five Cape-sized bulkers lined up loading, hatches gaping open like enormous chicks being fed by the mother conveyor belts, methodically and relentlessly gorging on the mineral wealth of eastern South Africa for export. Going ashore was a challenge that offered zero reward.

The coal came aboard precipitously, like an uncontrolled faucet. It all had to go somewhere, so after a day of continually tightening the ropes as the enormous load of solid black energy poured into us, relentlessly trying to vacate the ballast in time as a giant cloud of black dust engulfed us, we set out for Rotterdam, twenty-one days away. It's a long trip, but I was comfortable threading the twine along the ocean canvas between the two ports. My newfound understanding decreed that large bulk carriers led a slow and lonely existence, hauling vast quantities of dry commodities around the globe. I had my own tolerable room, clean, not luxurious, but comfortable, with my topical pinup on the wall; I just wished I might one day be Heathcliff to Kate's Catherine. The *E. W. Beatty* was a nine-hatch, 123,000-tonne bulk carrier constructed in Japan in 1973 and named for Sir Edward Wentworth Beatty (1877-1943), the first native-born president of the Canadian Pacific Railway.

I no longer attended the bar. The Old Man stalked it, like Jack the Ripper clearing the streets of Whitechapel. I was content to unwind in my cabin, slowly supping beer alone, writing letters to my growing throng of pen pals. They had become an essential fragment of my life, the people with whom it was safe to share my inner thoughts, the truth of loneliness which they and I understood. I wrote letters as a young man does when he's free to dream. We discussed correspondence and the lack of correspondence, about how our images and fantasies didn't meet our expectations, and in all of it, I tried to avoid any earlier propensity to befriend those of the same socioeconomic or ethnic persuasion. I was content with, and a better man for, my cosmopolitan friendships, finding humanity in an impersonal working world, but I must have known, deep inside, they were unlikely to be a long-term solution. I needed serendipity, not sparks of hope.

The ports just kept getting larger. I had been to Europoort before and felt an odd bond with the area, appreciating the cleanliness and elegance of something fashioned from nothing on such a colossal scale. Goodness, even those seldom-used industrial roads had been made of perfectly laid interlocking brickwork. The raw wind blew in from the North Sea, but on a sunny day the arrival appealed, like visiting a strong, healthy relative offering good news. Before the crude oil tank farms, we diverted into the mighty Maasvlakte, created in the 1960s by converting a once hazardous sandbank and reclaiming land from the North Sea, quickly becoming the premier bulk terminal of Europe.

The *E. W. Beatty* berthed at the far end to contend with the smaller 50-tonne grabs, which stole the coal from our hatches, dumping it onto the vast storage site of 7 million tonnes stretched out alongside us. For good news, Captain C. departed without fanfare, back to his vegetable allotment, back to the bowling club, back to his wife, where he no longer had the luxury of being insufferable, gone like the second post and half-day closing. He was so immersed in the stereotype you feared for his sanity, like Ahab. But he vanished, and every man jack breathed a gratified sigh of relief.

But making money meant moving. Too close to Maasvlakte is Europe's second largest port, Antwerp, by which I mean two watches, pilot to pilot. That's no time to do anything, other than work or sleep. The company was considerate enough to allow a few wives to visit and sail along, so couples stepped into the bridge; why not? I showed them the radars, one a modern Automatic Radar Plotting Aid (ARPA) that speedily and robotically displayed the course of targets and even alerted if it predicted too close an approach. Progress is generally a good thing, but this one filled my head with a cynical vision of technology and human stupidity. At deep sea, we could set it on specified limits and wait for a target to enter the spider's preset web. Goodness, the watch-keeper could nap, as if anyone would.

THE SCHELDT, a Belgian river, flows into the North Sea through the Netherlands, confusingly, near Flushing. It's the entrance to Antwerp. Oddly, I wanted to visit, not so much to see the city—although that might have been agreeable—but to experience the port itself, and per-haps understand a little of my heritage. The docks were a farsighted enterprise of growth the industrious Belgians had carved out beside the river quays, providing enormous space for the largest ships, but there remained fundamental drawbacks with Antwerp. First, there was the proximity of Rotterdam, with even better European connections to Germany, and second, the Scheldt has a tidal range of roughly twenty feet, adding untold vexation for all involved.

In early September 1944, with northern France won, Allied troops pushed into Belgium. The Twenty-First Army Group entered Belgium rapidly, spearheaded by XXX Corps, led by Lieutenant General Brian Horrocks, a hero of mine and my mother's—a teenager at the time—and met with little resistance. Horrocks was a tall, impos-ing figure with a personality to match, self-deprecating, with the ability to relate to superiors and the soldier in the field with the same con-versant passion, a trait Captain C. might have done well to emulate. Horrocks was a born leader; many men are not.

Attached to XXX Corps were elements of the 549th Electrical and Mechanical Company (perhaps thirty men) that worked to link generating plants on trains and ships providing local power under occasional long-range artillery fire. Visiting Antwerp was like a calling for me; one of the 549th was named George Winston Smith, my father.

In 1956, the government's Ten-Year Plan, instigated to alleviate the tidal challenge of the Scheldt, launched an unparalleled expansion boom northward with the construction of industrial complexes and the Kanaaldok. They improved access in 1967 via an immense lock, the Zandvliet, the largest in the world, finally opening Antwerp to the growth in modern shipping. The *E. W. Beatty* entered the vast artificial dock system, nearly eight miles long, roughly divided into three massive sections. Halfway down B2 we turned into Delwaidedock, a lesser section of a mile and a half long and three football pitches wide; more colossal stuff.

We supplied some South African coal, then shifted berth in the driving rain and gusty winds of a late Belgian autumn for the final delivery. The Old Man and pilot planned the move without engine or tugs, which might have been a good idea on paper, but became a long, scary night for those of us on deck; about as senseless as watering weeds, I thought. Warping is the activity of moving a (generally) small vessel with ropes attached to bollards. All very fine, in theory, but in practice, the activity became as stretched as the screaming ropes when applied to the *E. W. Beatty*. Everything holds until it doesn't, but being the officer, I felt obliged to step into the minefield and nonchalantly kick a few steel-tight ropes when necessary, as if to taunt them with my conviction of the operation. And, warp we did, some five hundred yards along the dock. Finally, we accomplished the move without disaster, but with much incident and unwarranted excitement.

Another night to remember that I would rather not have attended, but one must make a living.

Next day, strolling the deck with the chief mate, the air filled with dust from cranes grabbing the final dregs of coal, the new captain, with a refreshing brand of tact, radioed down with our post-Antwerp voyage orders. He solicited my assistance in finding the distance (bunkers would be required) and the location of a place named Huasco. We regarded each other skeptically to ensure it wasn't a hoax our new—surprisingly human—leader might be perpetrating. It turned out Huasco was in Chile, twenty-seven days from Antwerp, and probably still is. It took short shrift to assess the general route. The company had chartered the ship out, to send us—empty—nine thousand three hundred miles into another ocean the other side of the world. It would have been two thousand miles shorter via the Panama Canal, but we were Cape-sized. So that meant Cape Horn, the dark basement of the ocean, a passage reigning supreme over all others.

It's a long way from Antwerp to Cape Horn, and mostly over a vast expanse of unfathomable, endless sea. We would rarely be sighting land, but I relished astronomical navigation. I anticipated deep sea, the pleasantly uneventful routine of a long journey, the captivating night sky and its rhythmic cycles, for the solitude and time to reflect. The seas might change, but the sky never does.

THE NEWS from the Persian Gulf at the end of 1986 suggested Iran had the upper hand, its conscript army of cannon fodder having moved to within seventy miles of Baghdad. Attacks on tankers had begun five years earlier to deprive the other of their most important trade. Neither protagonist saw any issue with striking innocent third-party shipping, so they did. Attacks doubled in 1986 to over a hundred, which became an ever-increasing concern to foreign powers, particularly the United States.

I had been at sea now for nine years and had become, to all intents and purposes, a qualified man who navigated the largest ships. I mean genuine ships, not pleasure cruisers or weekenders; I did it for a living. By 1986, most seafarers were Filipino, with well-trained Europeans becoming expensive and uncompetitive. Most maritime nations applied cabotage laws to restrict others operating within their territory, but trade between nations was, essentially, unrestricted, and as ships got lost in the murky world between jurisdictions, shipowners raced to the bottom of the economic expense ladder.

Literature, popular culture and anthropology recognize the concept of a rite of passage. This primary function might include, say, one's first drink, first kiss, learning to drive or a significant change of status. I imagined it from a geographical standpoint. If I limited my work to the English Channel or adjacent continental Europe, I would have found myself somehow less worthy, as if I had cheated the very notion of being a seaman and all that its history encompassed. At sea, those rites of passage include crossing the equator and crossing the Atlantic and Pacific. I had realized those goals, and reached the antipodes by way of Suez and Panama, sailed through ice and the tropics, had seen Gibraltar, Cape Town and Hong Kong, but the big one, as far as any mariner is concerned, must be Cape Horn, long the most iconic maritime landmark. It's an otherworldly place at the extremity of the globe, hidden far away, where few have been.

We exited the Antwerp docks and left winter behind, heading south to a clear point off Finisterre, the extreme west of continental Europe, and then set south-southwest on a long rhumb line to a point off Rio de Janeiro. That's a comfortable two-week voyage. The weather and seas were good, the drinking sociable, and it was downhill all the way.

Navigationally, the sun and stars would guide us with a collection of my favorites: The Great and Little Bears, the vivid Vega and Capella. Nearer the equator, the startlingly bright Orion, its belt pointing to Aldebaran and the incandescent Sirius. Further south, the guiding lights were Alpha Centauri, Canopus and Hadar. I could see the galaxy with painful accuracy as it was thousands of years ago, but I couldn't see where I would be a few months beyond this voyage.

The pen pals made the difference, but I soon read all my letters from Europe, and we expected no mail until Chile. My burgeoning cluster of (fe)mail friendships worked for various reasons, most importantly relieving what Samuel Johnson called "a bleak and lonely solitude," emasculating all the anxieties and sorrows. For sure, it added to my knowledge of the world that I had acquired by traveling, like opening a cracked window wider still. Traveling, or moving had no influence on the relationships, and it was effective in diminishing what few prejudices I might have retained, resolving different versions of myself competing to be the real me. Perhaps the captivating benefit was the ability to have long, thoughtful discussions that took time to consider, without the fear of a face-to-face meeting.

After some weeks, we passed Buenos Aires, three hundred miles over the horizon, at about 35° south, roughly equivalent to Cape Town, Kwinana and Port Kembla. We persisted into the southern summer until there was no more summer, the stinging western winds slowing progress as the mighty bulker butted into steady seas on her starboard bow. At the 40th parallel, further than I'd ever been, the sky to the west dimmed into a dozen shades of gray, swirling and alive, occasionally scary and imposing. It appeared to suck the air from the atmosphere, and then the chilled southwesterly wind blew in with a vengeance as if calling us to our destiny. The prevailing winds here blow from west to east around the globe, virtually uninterrupted, giving rise to the Roaring Forties. Arriving at 50°, the weather picked up again; dark, racing clouds and frequent squalls obscured the horizon, the sky about to collapse under its own weight. Devoid of traffic, the radars wrestled with the whitecaps, cluttering their view, tracking waves with abandon because the robot had nothing else to follow. The seas became ashen and blown white, making awareness of anything else problematic. The wind is invisible, but to the accomplished seafarer, it is so obviously reflected on the sea.

The alternatives discussed for piloting into the Pacific were the Strait of Magellan, between the mainland and Tierra del Fuego, a major, although narrow, passage, which was in use for trade well before the Horn was discovered, and the five-hundred-mile-wide Drake Passage south of the Horn, where the Atlantic and Pacific Oceans collide.[44] Today, the Drake Passage, although liable to some seriously bad weather, provides far more maneuvering space. It being summer, I believe, made up the Old Man's mind. There is no significant land anywhere at this latitude, which allows both the unimpeded flow of the Antarctic Circumpolar Current carrying an enormous volume of water, and the near-constant, merciless winds, the Furious Fifties.

My plot took us west of the Falklands. Further on lay the Wollaston and Hermite Islands, at the tip of the archipelago which are now, confusingly, Chilean territorial waters. The Sixteenth-century English privateer Sir Francis Drake, during his westward circumnavigation, passed through the Strait of Magellan—the only accepted route at the time— into the Pacific. Before continuing north, he encountered a storm, and

---

44   The most southerly point of South America may be the Diego Ramirez islands, sixty-eight miles further south.

was blown south and east back into an expanse of open water, discovering in his misfortune that Tierra del Fuego, far from being the southern continent, was only an island of South America and an enormous sea existed further south.

After another few hours, there appeared on the right a continuous clump of gray hills with a duller background, dark and shockingly joyless. Next, some unnamed rocks exploded in white foam. It all looked like some large, continuous hilly range, but they were individual islands lost in the mist, sea spray and scudding clouds. The Pilot Book says it can snow any day of the year, and I wouldn't doubt it. Edging easy to starboard, there it was before my anxious gaze, ashen and somehow exquisite in its stubbornness, tiptoeing on the edge of oblivion, the light fading from the seascape. Squalls became frequent and severe, but the stony coastline, a steep slab of rock, backed by craggy, sawtoothed mountain ranges, remained steady on the radar. The terrain was entirely treeless, but lush due to the frequent precipitation.

Unexpectedly, we saw the small, fiberglass light tower of the world's southernmost lighthouse, a remote, magical oddity. Cape Horn! As half a dozen albatross, fabled good omens of seafarers, soared below, the clouds broke, and the sun streamed down in crepuscular rays, bathing the vista in ethereal light as if to announce our arrival amidst the sleeping spirits of the Horn; nature's marvel, like Philip Larkin's arrow-shower, somewhere becoming rain, or perhaps the tears of mermaids shed for all the lost souls. The unnaturalness of the Cape reflected the loneliness inside me. I appeared so small in this unforgiving universe.

At fifty-six degrees, the bracing winds whipped the seas into a marbled, frothy tempest while pushing the swell in a transcendent, rolling slumber towards the east. The *E. W. Beatty* took on a languid, lengthy roll pushed by the enormous swell as we aimed north, back towards the sun.

This was neither a long voyage nor a happy one, and "channel fever" surfaced once I sighted the conclusion. The waves became tiresome, like the voyage. The tensions slowly dissipated, but one was never secure until signed off articles. Canadian Pacific, eager to join everyone else in the rush to the economic basement, had determined to replace four junior officers with Indian nationals with similar (international) qualifications. I was nearing four months anyway. The dreams began: of returning to familiar places, sleeping, spending money, seeing the family, perhaps beginning a romance. The ship would dissipate in a few days as packing began and a sense of completion became closer. During this entire voyage, I had spent maybe twenty minutes in Maasvlakte ashore, conducting a draft survey. Other than that, I had spent the whole cruise aboard, living in what felt like a balloon slowly deflating, trapped in an industry unnaturally limited by global economics.

Huasco did not impress; rarely was a place so disappointingly viewed through the binoculars. We dropped anchor on a bright, clear morning, less than a mile from the shoreline. Everywhere was a rust-brown scrabble, ringed with anonymous, low gray mountains. It was dry and without life. Shortly after arrival, the agent's launch appeared in the open roadstead, and up came our reliefs, familiar but alien. We mingled awkwardly, having been instructed not to fraternize, so having little interest, we didn't. The whole episode, like the voyage itself, had the tone of obligation, and yet CP generously granted me study leave, maintaining my outlook slightly longer.

Landing ashore, we dragged our bags along the lengthy, dirty jetty beside the iron ore export facility, like traveling in steerage class. All that mattered was being on dry land, being safe and free from work.

They deposited us in a sleepy, nameless hotel, but the rooms were clean enough, and it was quiet and smelled of the real world again. Huasco, the city, was about as fulfilling as you might image. Quite obviously, a long way from anywhere and three hundred miles north of Valparaíso and totally, utterly reliant on that hulking black jetty made to export iron ore pellets. A small gang of local ladies, strictly second team, furtively offered themselves to either the itinerant workers or seamen; I couldn't imagine which was the better trade.

A few blocks from the hotel, strolling down the mournfully dusty road with a spaghetti western score on our minds, we found a bar with as much fizz as a flat soda, selling Escudo and Heineken to pass the time. The bus, surprisingly modern, departed at midnight and took eight hours, seven of which followed a twisting, lugging trail uphill; then the last hour, we cruised down into the large bowl-shaped valley of broad roads and fertile lands into the city center of Santiago, the capital. As the dawn rose, I spotted glimpses of the Andes and Chilean Coastal ranges flanking the city, but the hotel was good, the shower clean, and the soft bed called me asleep. About midnight, we flew back to London.

I returned to a good pile of mail from my far-flung friends, but in preparation for college, I calculated the sea time from my Discharge Book[45] and found myself four days short of the time required to sit the proposed exam. Joseph Conrad had fudged his time. This raised questions, some relevant to life, and some just irritating. The appropriate colored biro solved the problem.

A MONTH later, I took the scenic route down to Southampton on the sunlit south coast of England, a pleasant two-and-a-half-hour ride from my new house. The College of Maritime Studies nestled in the

---

45 All seafarers carry a compulsory record of their service in a Discharge Book.

bucolic suburban village of Warsash on the River Hamble. A mixture of old maritime-styled buildings and modern rectangular architecture, it had a first-rate reputation. Hampshire was, and still is, much wealthier than the decaying rust land where I had begun all those years ago in South Shields. Warsash was the land of boating and sailing clubs, women in hats and men in blazers. There comes a time when you do something for so long you can't imagine doing anything else, but I sensed somehow, I couldn't continue this career forever. Still, having come so far, I had to attempt the definitive academic assessment.

I embarked on my final studies, for a Certificate of Competency (Deck Officer) Class 1 (Master Mariner), the professional qualification required to serve as captain of a commercial vessel, of any size, any type, anywhere in the world. The term has been in use since the thirteenth century, indicating, in a guild's or livery company's terms, a person has achieved master craftsmanship in a profession. The curriculum encompassed, as you might expect, navigation, navigational aids, ship's stability, maritime law, engineering, cargo operations, meteorology and collision avoidance. But I also undertook a Higher National Diploma, medicine and a real-life ship simulator. My prior casual approach to learning would not work this time. This was no summer course in basket weaving—it was unremittingly demanding.

THE WAR in the Persian Gulf distracted people from the little they knew of the merchant navy. Thousands of ships plied the oceans, owned by major and lesser corporations, or small one-ship outfits going anywhere to justify the economics. Just like we needed the miners in the thirties, everyone in 1986 needed the seamen who carried ninety percent of everything; heroes passing unnoticed through life. I understood from my experiences at home, few had much idea of the life, or the people who populated it. The truth was, I embodied the epitome of proficiency and acceptable working conditions; the huge majority of vessels sailing the world were manned by cheaper labor—typically Filipino, Indian or wherever the next economically justifiable crew could be found—and were supported by the worst labor laws, unscrupulous manning agencies, only-for-profit owners, and governments who cared little because their voters didn't understand either.

A FEW years later, the Chinese-owned, Panamanian-registered Cape-size bulk carrier *Apollo Sea* departed Saldanha Bay, South Africa, fully laden with 124,000 tonnes of iron ore. The ship's agent contacted the authorities four days later to report the owners had received no communications. They discovered a small bunker spill only four hours from Saldanha Bay, this being the first indication that a disturbing event had occurred. The spill had distressed the local penguins, so the owners, prioritizing, denied responsibility. Later, it was apparent the *Apollo Sea* had suffered a catastrophic loss in five hundred feet of irreconcilable water, taking with her the entire complement of thirty-six. They conducted underwater video scans to positively identify the vessel lying on the sea bottom. Had the investigators the opportunity, determination or just good fortune to better observe the name painted on the stern in that underwater grave, they might have noticed, in faded outline, her previous identity: *E. W. Beatty.*

17

The Midnight Watch

1987–1988

I have absolutely no pleasure in the stimulants in which I sometimes so madly indulge. It has not been in the pursuit of pleasure that I have periled life and reputation and reason. It has been the desperate attempt to escape from a sense of insupportable loneliness and a dread of some strange impending doom.

—Edgar Allan Poe

IN THE spring of 1987, Kuwait asked the United States for military support from Iranian shipping attacks. They agreed their tankers would fly the American flag and travel in convoys protected by their mighty Navy. The US positioned four frigates, three cruisers, and a destroyer in the Persian Gulf, while an aircraft carrier and battleship sat outside, just in case. In July, the Kuwaiti supertanker *Al Rekkah*, ref-lagged and renamed *Bridgeton*, hit a mine, causing damage to the hull during the first convoy, thirteen miles west of Farsi Island. The vessel remained afloat with warships following in her wake for safety. They named the operation to protect tankers Earnest Will, like an Oscar Wilde character, and it endured for another year.

MEANWHILE, IN rural Hampshire, college passed in a pastoral haze of higher learning and subdued entertainment. I commuted home most weekends, until the work grew serious enough that I required every hour. I was possibly the youngest at twenty-seven, while many were in their thirties and older. I knew the curriculum would be tough. Eventually, the examinations had to be sat. Well, you know I have a propensity for assessment. Don't get me wrong, they were challenging, but I had been diligent and passed the "writtens." The oral exam, a concept conceived by Samuel Pepys to measure a man under stress, filled me with dread. All my powers of focus, memory recall and diagrammatic elucidation were worth nothing sitting opposite a human, waiting for me to invent an explanation I didn't have.

The undertaking began in a small room where they had installed a real-life magnetic compass, about five feet high, flanked by Kelvin's balls. The inside contained Flinders bars and other magnets; it's all very complicated. I had spent years learning how to correct the compass using these accoutrements and others, to eliminate errors of deviation caused by the vessel's structure. Yet in all my time at sea, I had only once witnessed an adjuster actually correcting a magnetic compass. After forty-five minutes of questioning, I reflected to myself, "That's it. I know nothing more about the compass. I'm dead."

The examiner nodded knowingly, looked at me with his bespectacled eye and drew a deep breath. "Well, let's move into the main exam room." I nodded meaningfully and hid my relief, remaining resolute, but glad to sit and exhale. Two hours later, it was over. I had mistakenly identified a tug pushing a barge alongside on the light board, but I was as likely to encounter that as a unicorn. I sat outside awaiting the catastrophic outcome. He called me back in.

"Well, Mr. Smith, you made a mistake with the lights... [yes, I know!] but I'm going to pass you..." I was no longer listening; further talk was inconsequential. You want something so badly it hurts, then you get it and there's an unfamiliar sensation of mental collapse, or vacancy. There were so many things I didn't know, so many assumptions I didn't recognize, but I had the license, a century after Joseph Conrad. For the last time in my life, I felt an obligation to a corporation—or perhaps exhausted, I plunged into the path of least resistance and called Canadian Pacific, offering myself for service. After congratulating me, they proposed I become a chief officer, an opinion with which I agreed. They proffered a bulk carrier in Australia, so, unusually giddy with enthusiasm, I began packing. The next day, they called and canceled because the cargo was on fire and they preferred the existing mate remain and handle the situation.

"But would you like to join the *Fort Rouge* in Rotterdam?" Quite frankly, no.

"You'll have to sail as second officer." Again, no!

However, I had tipped my hand. They had paid for college and required their pound of flesh. The corporation I had just complimented was now the department of numbing ineptitude, but I recognized I had to go.

A week later, back in Rotterdam, disgruntled and moody, I arrived at a collection of a hundred little tanks, from which some mysterious chemicals were being deposited into the pocket-sized tanker, corporate logo on the hull, Pac-Man on the funnel. That was it. It all happened so rapidly. From pastoral southern England, living regular hours like ordinary people, I was deposited back into an unearthly environment of steel, lubricating oil, grease, and—what the heck was that chemical smell?—the industrial, institutional aroma where nothing was natural.

The cabin was fine, typically bland. But then, I had to work, hour after hour; back to the insomniac's routine, day after day. Relaxation for the seafarer is taken in brief, treasured moments, but always with that shattering telephone dragging him back at midnight. I no longer accepted the irate bluster of others under stress. No one knows enough when they first board a ship. New routines, new cargo, the confusion of unfamiliarity. I settled with an act of sullen proficiency, relieved when we headed west into the Atlantic Ocean, sensing something special would be required to improve this voyage.

The bridge hit all the familiar notes, but on the chart room table sat a light gray box with a small cathode ray tube window and the name Magnavox Satellite Omega System. Technology moves so fast that today, it seems almost cute, like playing Ping-Pong on the television. But it was a revelation, and the end of my comfortable world. It fore-shadowed a future that any navigator worth his salt would cringe at. The system, developed by the US Navy for the Polaris submarine fleet, comprised satellites in polar orbits six hundred miles above the Earth. The grim box received the transmitted data and from its characteristics somehow calculated the ship's position, displayed as latitude and longitude; incredible stuff. How it accomplished this magic was, I'm sure, no trivial exercise, but let's keep it human. Coverage was world-wide, but a ship might be blind to view for hours. Positional accuracy was, incredibly, within a few hundred yards. I lost interest early on. A voyage I hoped might have been fine memory bait became a contest of human intelligence versus the box.

I had grown up using logarithm tables. I understood the science behind them, how clever men centuries earlier had striven to develop the theories and practice of celestial navigation and three-dimensional trigonometry. I had sat and learned it, night after night, and now a magic box that anyone with the common sense of up and down could use, sat blinking at us. I was unimpressed, and overqualified for a profession revolutionizing in front of my eyes. My motivations stopped making sense as the *Fort Rouge* began a tour of America in a grim Newark winter, then moved on south while I worked without enthusiasm.

THERE IS uncertainty as to where the name derives; probably of Indian origin, but just about everyone agrees it meant "Great River" or "Big River," which was apt then, and still is. It began before time and continues to remake itself over the ages. The modern delta, however, formed only over the previous seven thousand years, as deposited silt formed the limitless geography of bays, bayous, wetlands, barrier islands and watery land that defines the coastline today. Navigation of the Mississippi is a rite of seamanship required for a well-rounded education. There are three entrance channels, but everyone but fishermen use the Southwest Pass.

The river above the delta is so substantial its watershed touches thirty-one states. The lower of three distinct regions reaches from the sea to where it meets the Ohio River, a thousand miles away, but for most oceangoing vessels, the limitation was the Huey P. Long Bridge at Baton Rouge, with a height of only 113 feet. This was no longer the picturesque Old Man River of Mark Twain. The Port of South Louisiana extends fifty-four miles between New Orleans and Baton Rouge, and supports an enormous volume of commerce: petroleum, grain, corn, soy, chemicals, coal and sulfur, along with dozens of refineries and silos lining the river to export the natural wealth of America.

I had a difficult association with pilots, a profession as old as the sea. English law defines them as "any person not belonging to a ship who has the conduct thereof," which is informative, but not definitive.

It complicates a murky position. The captain has responsibility for his vessel, pilot or not, but in court he would have an awkward time explaining why his guidance was disregarded. They possess detailed knowledge of a particular waterway, e.g., depths, currents and tides, lights and signals at any time of the night or day. I respected the fact that they precariously embarked and disembarked frequently, which I knew to be nerve-racking stuff. All they generally ask is a lee and a safe ladder. Coming from deep sea, the pilot is where it all begins. I've seen good pilots and not so good, but whatever their social performance, the Mississippi pilots have a demanding vocation, especially at night.

Eighteen hours later, the dock. Maneuvering a ship through shallow water is a more difficult exercise than it might appear, involving some strange forces interacting between the ship, the berth, the river bottom and passing traffic. It also requires a considerable amount of well-coordinated (and it has to be accepted, sometimes dangerous) teamwork. Here we had another fuzzy area of responsibility, with the pilot communicating with shore personnel while the captain directed us. Not surprisingly, the largest port in America had compulsory pilotage.

I had seen the river before. Chemical and petroleum berths had replaced mile after mile of paddle steamers, antebellum houses and leafy plantations, along with their accompanying tanks and mysterious smoking objects, endless collections of barges, tugs and traffic. We had a complicated itinerary in small parishes screaming industrial excess. Each berth at each modest place was anonymous and indistinguishable, where one might gaze upon the tanks, railway tracks and asphalt. The horizon was flat as far as one might see: no houses, no life. The cargo work was strenuous, lengthy and depressing.

And what about this little melancholy ship? She was small, but the accommodation full-sized, like a man with a head too large for his body. She was one of four chemical and product tankers ordered in 1980, built by Sanoyasu in Japan. She had that swedged bulkhead design, making her modern, though aesthetically unpleasing. Her deck was a maze of pipelines and steel objects at shin height; all very functional, but an obstacle course for humans.

The atmosphere onboard was downhearted. People were friendly enough, and everyone did their job; I wouldn't expect less, but the fun was rapidly draining from the industry, reflected in the bleak and desperate mood of men trapped in a situation that allows neither a return to innocence nor a way up. The Old Man, sullen and sardonic, knew we'd be replaced by Filipinos soon, and he didn't mind. A few of us, younger perhaps, still had time. Roger Cordrey, the third mate, was one of those cheery people caught between late childhood and cynicism. I never saw him unhappy, and I was suddenly getting old enough to reminisce. Bob Welch was the fourth engineer, darker and laconic, but like Roger, a nice man to sit and chat with in the bar where beer was too often the usual comfort. Night after night we felt safe to expose all our grievances, our bitterness, lost hopes, mistakes, lost loves and feint desires. You learn who you are in this job—doesn't mean you'll like it. When not drinking, I spent evenings alone writing letters as if seeking an escape tunnel through an indifferent sea.

Just when I thought the voyage couldn't sink any further, they gave us orders for Suez. A million people live in Port Said, but Ferdinand de Lesseps's statue doesn't stand there anymore. Egypt had moved on. Was it as bad as I keep saying? Why, yes. And Jeddah was as miserable as last time. Unless you're destined for Mecca, avoid like the plague, the bubonic kind.

I don't remember Karachi. But as always, I loathed the midnight cargo watch. The shrill of the telephone shattering that bittersweet moment just before waking, a splash of cold water and stepping into a grimy boilersuit, breathing in the aroma of oil and chemicals. Down two flights of stairs, then stepping outside into the thick, sticky air of the tropical night, my eyes accosted by the startling glare of the floodlights and my ears overwhelmed by the screeching, screaming sound of the hydraulic pumps. A fresh breeze caressed me, but the hard, green steel overwhelmed my senses, all encompassed within an inky black void—the sea and the sky enveloping like an oily bubble. Half-asleep, stepping through the air lock, cracking my shin for the first time this watch; the control room reeked of oil, sweat, cigarettes and coffee. Right then, I needed to get up to speed and I was half-asleep. It had been a while since I had a run ashore for relaxation, and apparently, it would be a while longer.

On departure, I had faint hopes of heading further east, when new orders arrived with a dull thud we had not been expecting: "Load a cargo of caustic soda in Jubail." The mood distilled into a collective hush, which slowly grew into a murmur of gossip. Khor Fakkan, the waiting place, was less than two days away, while Jubail lay deep in the Persian Gulf war zone. Canadian Pacific generously offered personnel a choice of going or not. It was the first week of 1988. They had attacked 125 tankers the previous year by rockets, mines and gunfire. Forty-one seafarers had died. Yes, I had been there before, but it was different now—it was growing intense and unpredictable, with everyday news of tankers being hit. We rigged blackouts, and enforced them. People kept their thoughts to themselves, not in a display of stoicism, but because our beliefs might have been too vivid for discussion. I remembered I didn't have a will.

My grandfather died when I was eleven. He was a mischievous, wise, well-dressed and kindly man, a model of the type I wished marched alongside me in life. The survivors of war rarely talk of their experiences. During the slow disintegration of age, when he was becoming too ill to recognize, they moved his bed to the ground floor. I remember him waking during the day from some too-vivid nightmare, crying, "The guns! The guns!" fifty years after his war was fatally dustbinned to a history in jerky black and white. I'd read Wilfred Owen and Siegfried Sassoon. I knew war is neither heroic nor entertaining and wanted nothing to do with it, but I agreed to go, like so many others had to senseless wars before, because everyone else was going.

We were all volunteers again, accepting the inherent risk to maintain a wage, which is the same old story. After sneaking through Hormuz, the usually busy anchorages, transshipment and storing areas outside Dubai were strangely dark and quiet, like a walk down to the basement. We could smell the war, and no, we didn't beat to quarters, but into the fire we plunged. Small and empty as we were, we could follow the south and west coasts, doing our best to steer clear of Iran and likely dangers. We anchored during the day and ran at night.

I was ignorant of Jubail, but then, here it was, although from the dock, I couldn't see it. The town is perhaps seven thousand years old, the original inhabitants enticed by the natural harbor, abundant fish, pearl oysters, and potable water wells nearby. Like most of Saudi Arabia, nobody was interested until September 1933, when a team of geologists came exploring for oil. For years, the Kingdom continued on its way, isolated and independent behind its inherent natural wealth. Then, in thoughtful prognosis of a very different future, in 1975, a decision that only absolute monarchs can make was taken to diversify the economy away from crude oil income, like drawing pictures in the sand. Building began and continued to such a degree that in 1983 *The Guinness Book of World Records* declared Jubail the largest engineering and construction project ever attempted. Eight nations adjoin the Persian Gulf, and all produce crude oil, but the Saudis have 44 percent, which is kind of hogging it. The original village remained academic, like a sepia postcard struggling to pierce the fantastic surface, although I doubt they'll ever have a postcard industry in Jubail.

But at least it was safe. It was a place of epic projects and no people. No heart, no soul, just the mandatory wailing mosques in a far-off distance amongst the leprous-colored buildings, a place where it's not worth laying grass. They called it a strategic position, but anywhere is strategic if you move the map. We thought of it as a world of utter sterility. The Saudi customs and religious police boarded to scrutinize another lifestyle, while any attempt to justify the ensuing intrusion of privacy was perfunctory. Jubail was like a well-wrapped present that disappoints when opened. In the relentless bleakness and immense scale, I finally questioned: What the hell am I doing here?

The *Fort Rouge* sat on the sparkling new dock, and we had showers tactically placed on deck in the event anyone came into contact with the cargo. They issued us special gloves and goggles, and in rushed the caustic soda (NaOH). It's used in industries like the manufacture of paper, textiles, soaps, detergents and drain cleaner, and can cause severe chemical burns and permanent blindness. I left feeling as if we had never been there, with the electricity of war in the air, and joined a convoy outbound, safely in the crowd, protected by Her Majesty's warship *Boxer*, a svelte Type 22 frigate, her gray, thin skin pulled tight over her ribs, all rectangles and odd, ominous devices poking out, like a heavily armed eggshell. Some military personnel helicoptered over to visit, while the warship scooted around, seemingly bored with the tempo of it all.

Two days later began what I used to enjoy, a long voyage across the Indian Ocean to Australia, with Roger and me obtaining noon each day by sun sights, but the HAL 9000 in the corner now tainted the adventure. It felt like show-up-on-time-and-cash-your-check stuff. The mighty Alcoa had a deep-water jetty in Cockburn Sound, Kwinana, just north of the BP refinery, where they made over 2 million tonnes of aluminum each year in a complicated process involving bauxite and caustic soda. Like glitter from an old Christmas card, Boomer showed up again. The reunion was unlikely to end in cuddles and compliments, but at least he brought some charisma, and like a weed, he was sort of growing on me.

A WEEK before Japan, they advised us of our Filipino replacements, just like the prior trip, joylessly nailing the coffin lid of the British Merchant Navy closed. Roger, Bob and I sat in the bar most evenings, chatting and conjuring up capers, like Great Train Robbers, not like girls discussing important nothings. With a fractured world outside, we found common ground, tapping into our collective primal solitude and uncertainties. We were bitter, cynical, weary and disillusioned. Should we run the ship aground? Should we put something in the fuel? Alcohol says something about a man before he gets to say it himself. Eventually, we agreed to enjoy a few days in Hong Kong on the way home. The office was cooperative in organizing flights and a discount at a good hotel. We flew out of Osaka. The overriding feeling of the voyage: purposelessness, so I departed determined to improve the situation.

IT'S CALLED the "Pearl of the Orient." I was tired, like one is from an economy flight of more than an hour. But as the aircraft fell lower on that long approach to a place I longed to revisit, the images of the wonder city became clearer amongst the hills. The wings danced in the light, caught by the turbulence; the buildings came closer, revealing a thousand lit windows. We slowed dramatically. Goodness knows what the height might have been, but it was lower than anyone thought comfortable with all that concrete jutting into the air. Then it happened: a sudden bank and turn to the right, the aircraft tilting onto its wingtip, aiming for Kai Tak, hanging, with that eerie feeling of falling from a great height. I saw the cubic one-block city-within-a-city, thousands packed together, an isolated element within the urban landscape of Hong Kong. It was a white-knuckle ride that every air passenger arriving in one of the Earth's most densely populated places cannot forget.

Bob, Roger, and I took a bulging red-and-white taxi, luggage on our knees, from Kai Tak Airport to downtown Kowloon, passing the seemingly endless rows of high-rise apartment blocks. We checked into the Peninsula Hotel, about as empire-iconic as could be, like one of those frightening dark blue squares on the Monopoly board. Above the lobby were six stories on three sides around a splendid fountain, on the corner of Salisbury and Nathan. As dusk fell, from the entrance we gawked at the endless towers of flashing, sparkling neon which define the Hong Kong skyline of densely packed high-rises across Victoria Harbor: ROLEX, Coca-Cola, OMEGA. Neon is to Hong Kong as blue bobbies are to London and vending machines are to Tokyo. It was a short evening, so we ended up a block from the hotel at a club in the basement of Mohan's Building on Hankow Road. It tired us, so it seemed appropriate to not overdo the drinking. Kowloon can swallow the unperceptive tourist, particularly when the sun goes down. We agreed to hit the streets on the morrow, fit and ready.

The next morning, stretching from the shock of a good night's sleep, we walked up Nathan Road, seeking breakfast, and found a gourmet hot dog bar. This wide boulevard is the main commercial road through downtown, packed with honking cars, double-decker buses, crowds of people all about their business and lost laundry hanging on the street wires. We avoided the pushers shifting fake Rolexes (I already had one) and vendors selling cheap suits. Overhead, the hanging Chinese signs are so much neon bunting, each hiding something magical and mysterious inside, the whole conglomeration as atmospherically compelling as it was viscerally thrilling. We took the incredibly cheap and historic Star Ferry across the harbor—a ten-minute ride—to Hong Kong side, watching the skyline unfold before us. The green-and-white icon was celebrating its centenary on the route between Tsim Sha Tsui and Central (Kowloon to Hong Kong Island) in 1988. On arrival, we walked.

Determined to be touristic, we set upwards to the Stone Slab Street, known for its uneven pavement of granite steps, in pursuit of shopping, where the scale of the city loomed over the humans. Hong Kong is irregular, since the island is dominated by steep hills. Central Street Market was the oldest, full of licensed hawkers selling good and inexpensive stuff for the tourist dollar. It was hot and tiring. I bought the holidaymaker items I thought appropriate and, in the evening, we cleaned up and found food and beer off Nathan Road. Bob and Roger, their brief stay completed, flew home the next day, but I decided to linger longer in the enigmatic city.

I thought I had the social preference for men, but that might have been due to their numerical preponderance in my life. At the mercy of my capricious desires, with the ache of frustration and no longer willing to pay the non-discounted rate at the Peninsula, I moved a block away to the Mariners' Club, a curiously blue building on Middle Road. I'm sad to say the Missions to Seaman is not the same as it once was, but I should also credit the organization for being religiously based; ecumenical, in fact. It was spartan, and clean, like my cabin on the *Fort Rouge,* but smaller.

I took a relaxing tourist boat out of the ramshackle beauty of Kowloon into the harbor, and west about the island to the Aberdeen fishing village, a quaint and charming place far from the jostling crowds, like another world. There were rows of junks and sampans, and some houseboats where the fishermen and their families lived, going about their daily routines in a picturesque scene, with the unexpected touch of modernity nearby. Even in 1988, it had an otherworldly feeling of a Disney replica in a modern city, screaming, "Get out of our way, we're heading for 1997." Grasping the irony of a mariner enjoying a boat ride, I hunted elsewhere, and when you can't find what you need in Hong Kong, there's only one place to go.

The intimidating citadel of Chungking Mansions sustained thousands of people from a hundred countries, who lived and worked in a confusion of relative lawlessness. When walking east on Peking Road, one is confronted by the buildings' visage: huge and gray, rows of soulless windows and precariously overhanging air conditioners, looming like the Ministry of Truth. But what you see is only a fifth of the whole enormous place. Like impressionist art, you had to squint to understand it. They built it in 1961 as a residential building, but by 1988, it had morphed into a shock of unearthly proportions, containing countless low-budget hotels, brothels, curry houses, noodle shops, tailors, and foreign exchange offices, a sleazy center for drugs, gangs and criminal activity, a haven for cash-driven enterprises, small and large, and the noise, smells and fluidity of life.

Teeming, run-down and ultimately diverse, it simultaneously attracts and repels. People either peered inside and spun away or walked purposefully within. Inside was a glittering and jumbled confusion of shops, food stalls and money changers. It seemed to go on forever, perplexing, hallucinatory and thrilling. The five blocks were connecting only at the murky, oppressive lower bazaar, refuge of hippies and a microcosm of a global market. In this warren for trade, food, prayer and sex you could exchange currency, buy electronics, get a massage, meet colorful characters and eat cheap, delicious food, all in a constant flux of traders, shopkeepers, asylum-seekers and policemen, ever changing yet always the same. Globalization, as an economic term, had recently emerged, but a good school would be Chungking Mansions. Triad influence appeared nonexistent because the Mansions were international, even cosmopolitan. The language of business included Chinese, yes, but was predominantly English, and the triads didn't speak English. If Orwell had gone to Hong Kong, he would have been down and out, with the dogs, in Chungking Mansions.

THAT EVENING, I met Bang in a noodle shop. She had another name, but I could never pronounce it. She had a delightfully crooked smile, the very slightest limp of awkward grace, which she declined to explain, and a wince-inducing English accent, but she moved with youthful elasticity that enticed. After cocktails at The Stag's Head on Hart Avenue, we understood any emotional development would die in the dust that night, and since I couldn't get her into the Mariners' Club, we returned to Chungking, where she found a small room on the tenth floor for what she termed "panky-yanky." Her enthusiasm for the language just broke it more. The elevators—never enough of them—rose to a myriad confusion of hotels and dormitories piled upon themselves in this impossible seventeen-storied muddle. Bang, leading the way, bought an odd, stark sheen to the picture postcard of Hong Kong, as we mated with enthusiasm.

When I awoke, I discovered I had fallen in love…with Hong Kong. I learned from Bang how to buy and eat noodles, the best place to exchange dollars while shunning fake notes, and the areas nearby to avoid. She showed me the Kowloon-Canton Railway Clock Tower, which I had already seen. The world imperceptivity changed into a richer, more mysterious one in her clutches. After two days of meeting in the Mansions (I never knew where she lived), I asked her if it was possible to visit the Kowloon Walled City, when she casually revealed she had an "aunty" in residence.

FROM WHEN the Chinese built a small fort to deter pirates in the Song dynasty, to when they ceded the near-perfect harbor to the British in 1842, until the British rescinded the contract later, until the 1980s, as Hong Kong prepared for a very different future, there had been an isolated, disconnected walled place, a city within a city, near the airport in Kowloon. For most of the twentieth century the British and Chinese were unconcerned, while it remained a strange, forgotten residence of refugees, squatters, and outlaws.

The uncontrolled building of three hundred interconnected towers crammed into a seven-acre plot of land, the Kowloon Walled City was, by 1988, home to perhaps forty thousand inhabitants—no one knew exactly. Amazingly, many residents accepted living there, even without sanitation, safety and sunlight. The immigrants brought their professions and vices, and for much of the twentieth century, it was the most densely populated place on Earth, booming as refugees and small businesses arrived to take advantage of an enclave without law, where you didn't need a visa, a license to operate, nor to pay any tax.

THE TAXI took us east towards the airport, to Tung Tau Tsuen Road, which at street level was not dissimilar to other, seedier parts of Kowloon, the lovely rotting essence of Hong Kong, mini-tower next to mini-tower, all waiting to be eclipsed. This was a rare occasion, mingling with the less advantaged of a foreign place, and then only because I had Bang, and afterwards it made me sad and ashamed I had rarely accomplished the task. We alighted and stepped unknowingly from British Hong Kong to the unknown place, a filthy pavement overhung with a thousand signs, drooping residences, plant boxes and wire. I beheld the twelve stories of ramshackle buildings teetering above, and the mingling smell of cooking meat, fish balls, ginger, chili and a thousand other spices.

"Come, come," beckoned Bang, as she slipped into a gloomy alley between a dentist and a Chinese health spice shop, so I followed her into the vertical human labyrinth. We were inside a dark "street," four or five feet wide. I called to her to slow down as my eyes acclimatized. We were standing on wooden boards over running water. Ahead were the lights of shady open shops, a step or two above. Bang spurred me on as water drops lost their fight with gravity. I could see wires, so I kept moving; this couldn't be good, but the sprightly Chinese woman egged me on, deeper and deeper into a street scene by Hogarth.

I heard scampering below, but the prime suspect remained hidden. When I caught up, I insisted on holding her hand before some stifling disorientation overtook me. We scaled stairs, some dark and dingy, then the next ablaze, like Piccadilly Circus. The sights and sounds accosted me from every direction: an open door showing a machine clunking fish balls into a large tin bowl, then a ceaseless barrage of distant cries and cauterizing banter from behind a steel door, then a tiny shop selling cigarettes, soft drinks and incense, and behind a curtain the relentless clattering of the mah-jongg table.

We climbed again through shadow and light, the world alive with perplexing sounds and stranger smells that came and went with each few steps. The higher she led me, the less dark and clammy the walls became. The houses were cement boxes or wood-and-tin shacks. A man with blond hair might be rare, but Bang reassured. She seemed to know the route and stopped to briefly engage a woman washing clothes in buckets.

She rapped on a steel door and slid it open, calling as she stepped inside. Beckoning me into the tiny, chaotic room, she ushered me to the small bed, to take a seat with an old lady while she watched a black-and-white television in Chinese, looking like she never trusted happiness. Her aunty, meanwhile, was standing over a one-ring stove, boiling an unknown dish, while an obligatory fan creaked back and forth. Bang and her aunty chatted raucously and openly until they mentioned me; I know because they stared my way. I shared a Coke with Bang while the sharp, staccato Chinese interplay continued, and the elderly lady kept watching the television as if we had never arrived. She'd covered the walls of her bedsit with pictures of family, plastic flowers, shoddy, hanging electrical connections, a Chinese calendar, and red stacked bags of contraband or necessities; I couldn't tell. The fragrance overwhelmed, a mixture of cooking, incense and roach spray. They were poor but content, because they knew their place. Like a Franz Kafka novel, the irrational became rational.

The Kowloon Walled City was one of the few times modern man has attempted, without forethought, an anarchic, laissez-faire society, a symbolic place of resistance. And it worked, but was destroyed a few years later—not from within, but by the Hong Kong government, in preparation for 1997. They built the prosperity of Hong Kong on the backs of people who lived inside the city within a city, who toiled in silence, asking little in return other than to be left alone. The fragility of the building was juxtaposed with human life, but the people had hope. It wasn't a slum—it was a community. It reaffirmed to me what I already knew deep inside: there were so many people born in less fortunate circumstances than me. I saw, but I didn't see. Their feelings and thoughts were unknowable in a brief dalliance.

Hong Kong was exotic, but my casual carnality with Bang would not make soothing reading, and I'm sad we never really said goodbye. She disappeared the next day, and I resolved not to seek her; my feelings and emotions were just out of reach again. The city's upcoming political ambiguity was as troubling as my moral complexities. Hong Kong keeps the casual visitor at arm's length, but holds you in its grasp too. It's a peculiar, mysterious, magical place that might be expected to sink beneath the hype that surrounds it, but I implore you: beg, borrow or steal a ticket, but get to Hong Kong before it becomes Singapore. Perhaps it's too late, and maybe that's a good thing. And the *Fort Rouge*? The wireless had been slowly killing the adventure of going to sea, seizing decisions from us, and satellite navigation offered up the coup de grâce.

Life has a decidedly unsatisfying flow. England always seemed fresher when I came home, especially to my own house. Canadian Pacific was done, escaping the ship-manning business, replacing expensive British staff with Filipinos, and I understood that. I didn't blame them. So, was that it? A three-day, semi-cathartic experience with a young Asian lady? No, I recognized I needed to find some emotional footing to finally become a well-rounded man.

Somewhere, somehow.

18

Something Happened

It's a bizarre but wonderful feeling, to arrive dead center of a target you didn't even know you were aiming for.

—Lois McMaster Bujold

CANADIAN PACIFIC as an employer was no more. They were nice enough to invite me to London four years after we first met. I had nothing but gratitude, but it was over. Those in the office were polite but distant, in the manner people are when they're about to give you bad news. It wasn't a shock. The manager thanked me in that style corporations do with someone they don't know; another number. But he thought my qualifications and experience perfect for a job opportunity with Esso; I was "just what they were looking for," developing their foreign flag fleet. Esso International Shipping Co. Ltd. was Exxon's idea of a new fleet of (admittedly old) ships, trading worldwide without the irritating restrictions of unions, expensive European crews and first-world legislative limitations. I drove to Southampton for a perfunctory interview; they were agreeable and promised a quick promotion. They stressed a few things: the money was good, very good; they only ran supertankers—extra-large ones; and the trade would include the Persian Gulf. I was stepping back to where I began, in the messy footprint of crude oil. I accepted the offer, but left suspecting they might have added, "Choose your next step carefully."

Barely a month after Hong Kong, I flew to Gibraltar, which I'd been wanting to see. The landing was nerve-racking stuff: approaching from the west over the Bay, the aircraft turning sharply for the too-short runway, avoiding nothing more solid than a political line on the map. From the airplane steps, I saw the rock, statuesque and sublime, stark gray and green against the brilliant blue lunchtime sky. I wanted more, but sadly, we were driven directly to a waiting launch.

The empty, imperious supertanker idled quietly, her blunt, bulb-less bow protruding clear of the ocean, a smokestack cloud belching above, disfiguring the pristine sky. She was leaden gray, with old tan derricks and a disjointed house lacking bridge wings. The unusually raised forecastle seemed an afterthought. The hull suffered the usual mechanized scraping, rusty marks from lightering, tugs and fenders somewhere far away. She lay there woefully, as if asking, "Do you think you can handle me?" She reeked of solidity and permanence, like a floating nuclear bomb shelter; brutish, cold and alien, but with the comforting reek of inert gas.

The eighties oil tanker was a planet-girdling transporter of energy, built for nonstop voyages from supplier to consumer. Kockums AB built this one in Sweden, two years before the *Lampas*, one of eight of her class. She was launched the SS *Esso Demetia*, and had spent the previous few years British manned, shuttling cargoes from the North Sea to Fawley and Europoort. It had been grueling work for them. I understood the long hours working cargo, piloting in confined waters, but now Esso was setting her free as it had designed her; long journeys at 14 knots, day after day, week after week. The British crew went ashore, and a Filipino replacement boarded, taking their duties, along with their inheritance and legacy, as the British Merchant Navy circled the drain. We, supposed foreign-flag mercenaries, replaced the British staff and became inexorably bound together for the first time.

We took the bulky, ugly brute east to Sidi Kerir at the northern terminus of the Sumed pipeline, and loaded a cargo for Fawley. There, two miles across Southampton Water, where I had completed my schooling, sprawled the Esso refinery in idyllic Hampshire, a vast and complex machine. The ship held acclaim, too, being the largest in the world with bow and stern thrusters for maneuvering alongside. We used tugs anyway.

Wherever it was, there was always work, the midnight watch and the cargo control room, with that certain feel spaces continuously occupied by men accrue. It was functional in the extreme, furnished with the few essentials needed to make those on duty self-sufficient throughout their watch. The chairs were battered, stained and second-hand. The room smelled of hydraulic oil, and the Kockums equipment was a concoction of ingredients thrown together without the benefit of any serious consideration of logic; an oil-polluting, machine-shredding calamity waiting to happen.

As we completed the work-up voyage to Fawley, nobody was clambering for the subsequent orders of our real destination, but they arrived anyway, like we knew they would.

I wasn't the only one who thought the Suez Canal—boring as it was—should have something eye-catching to celebrate its importance, other than a bland monument at Ismailia. When nearing completion in 1869, French sculptor Frédéric-Auguste Bartholdi strived to convince the Egyptian government to erect a sculpture named *Egypt Bringing*

Light to Asia, at its Mediterranean entrance. His plan was to build a lighthouse in the form of an ancient Egyptian female fellah, or peasant, robed and holding a torch aloft. Egypt had more pressing problems and ignored his lobbying. So, Bartholdi, considering an alternative, fell upon the bright new nation across the Atlantic, and the monument has since become known as the Statue of Liberty, and remains reminiscent of an Egyptian peasant girl. So, Port Said never got its robed lady holding a torch to guide ships in, but New York got the emblem that has since defined it.

MEANWHILE, THE Iranian terminal at Kharg Island became "Exocet Alley," after all the Iraqi attacks, so they shuttled cargoes down to Larak, in Hormuz, supposedly out of Iraqi range. However, one day in May 1988, contrary to military doctrine, Iraqi fighter-bombers actually reached the distant island, striking five tankers, including the world's largest ship, the *Seawise Giant*. She sank in shallow water, taking sixteen crew members with her. The gravity of entering the Gulf was now palpable.

Arriving at Khor Fakkan was now routine, but I didn't pretend to like it. We sat for a few days with the armada of empty tankers waiting to enter. This was the deal, along with a 100 percent bonus. There were few options. We entered through the Devil's lair, sandwiched between friendly Oman and unfriendly Iran, in a dark, gray, brooding hulk lacking maneuverability, and unable to hide along the coastline. We were vigilant but relaxed. We practiced, yes, but we were long-time professionals and everyone could don breathing apparatus and man a hose. By 1988, the Persian Gulf was a teeming theater of operations for Western navies and weekly attacks. The Royal Navy's Armilla Patrol focused on the southern entrance, leaving the Americans to guard the northern Gulf. Insurance rates spiraled higher, while the repair yards in Bahrain and Dubai couldn't keep up with the work. Owners of aging fleets, flagged for convenience, saw the obvious chance to make money. For us, everything we had revolved around the safety and integrity of our surroundings, the ship, but we felt powerless in the face of a seemingly hidden enemy who might arrive from anywhere at any time. I was young and full of life, so I was ready for war, but I didn't aspire to being Exxon's first martyr.

THREE DAYS in without incident, we arrived, without pilotage, beginning about fifteen miles west of the port at the Ras Tanura light buoy. It was an open roadstead where ships found their own way. In the eastern province of the Kingdom, it comprised Ras Tanura and Ju'aymah (the "gift of God", aptly). It was summer, hot and humid. For an instant of geologic time, the startling titan of an industrial age met the residue of the Paleozoic for a world spinning ever faster. Not surprisingly, it was enormous. Ras Tanura, the busiest oil port in the world, could export more than six million barrels a day. The terminal berthed eight supertankers simultaneously at the offshore jetty.

The berthing pilot boarded, planning to bring us in safely and economically. The main goal is not to miss and have to return for another approach; three hours at least. In a neat series of maneuvers, so slow they're unseen by the naked eye, he brought her parallel to the sea island, then let the hot, gentle wind and tugs gently push our beam squarely into our allotted space. This was big-league stuff, and it only took three hours to secure the wires. Before the completion of mooring, the cargo-transfer arms were secured. Two miles distant on the tear-drop spit of land, a tank farm of thirty-three million barrels fed the waiting ships.

The infrastructure is the largest in the world, naturally, but also its Achilles' heel; this core economy of scale leaves it highly susceptible to blockage of the Hormuz strait, where it all had to go. Ras Tanura existed in a world of its own making, where the spiritual and the technological lived together, lending it a compellingly elusive sense of time and place. Fanatical beliefs encouraged utopian heavenly fantasies steeped in the sixth century. We might as well have been on the moon. It needed something to divert attention from the relentless faith, squashing any interest that survived the brutal religious process. What one remembers is the blinding, sweat-producing 120°F air, and the pain of the dark red deck, transmitting heat into your body like a microwave, where hard fixtures are too hot to touch. Every time I entered the control room, I inhaled another pint of icy water.

THE LOADING process, distant, mechanical and devoid of human interaction, was as fleeting as we expected; the oil rushed in faster than we could vacate the ballast, a perilous time for the tanker man as the two commodities hurriedly took their natural routes with a few valves keeping us from a Sharia cell term. We didn't break six hours on, six hours off. After three hours' sleep, I took the watch at midnight on the morning of June 11, 1988. I spent six hours scurrying around the deck, topping off tanks. Rick, the chief mate, with a receding hairline, a mercenary like everyone else, was gregarious and knew his business. He had, as they say, "been around." I learned from him that Dr. Martens were stylish. He closed each valve remotely; a measured process, involving hoping beyond hope that the tiny switch activated as designed— they sometimes didn't. At six a.m., we were done, but I still showered and crashed, just in case.

An hour later, the shrill call, "Yeah?" waking my fresh, clean body from the cool sheets.

The third mate, "John, standby on the bridge, I'll take aft."

And then the protracted unmooring and turning operation.

My day improved six hours afterwards, when I took the pilot down upon clearing the berths. Two hours later, Captain Dan, a cheerful and experienced Irishman on the wagon, went below, leaving me to the long exit channel, setting east towards the iconic Ras Tanura light buoy, where we had arrived. Finally, well into my own watch, by mid-afternoon I was alone. But I felt good; we all did, leaving the dull but anxious place where photos of a female arm in the *Daily Mirror* were considered pornographic. The visit offered little, except intense work, crude oil and the infrastructure for moving it, now fading behind in the murky haze of the desert.

The war had slipped our minds briefly, replaced by overexertion and sleep deprivation. I set the ship further east fifteen miles for the light buoy, lazing in the temperate water like a sentinel, between safety and the forgotten vulnerability of the open Gulf. I spotted a container vessel heading south, and felt nicely placed to negotiate the buoy and follow. The weather was fine, a thin haze, but less than usual, with slight seas of no importance to the *Esso Demetia* plowing deeply, powerfully, through the water. The bar would be opened by six, and I needed a drink.

Then the alteration of course, letting the heavy, quarter-million-tonne tanker swing languidly, relentlessly, around the light buoy a few miles to starboard, slowing to a natural heading behind the container ship three miles ahead, like balancing one of those ball-inside-a-dome games. I switched her back to auto, and set a course, 105°, a balanced effort to distance ourselves from Iran while avoiding the shallows off Bahrain and Qatar, just another two million barrels heading for the spigot of Hormuz.

I let her settle down, checked the compasses, completed my log and reconciled the blissful final fifteen minutes of an eleven-hour standby, relishing the thought of that bubbling, foaming amber rising to my lips. It had been eighteen hours since I had slept. I took a seat, skimmed through a Lloyd's magazine and glanced forward as the container ship crept ahead. I perceived a dozen or so small dots to port, far away, fishing vessels—nothing of concern, and yet I felt a vague unease. I was tired. I flicked a few pages, then glanced again, to starboard, ahead, to port—the innate, natural action of the lookout. I couldn't shake that damn feeling, but the answer was cooling in the fridge. I'd sleep well this evening.

Strange, some fishing boats had clearly moved. I looked again. Ha! Fast fishing boats. Very odd. Feeling fatigued, I stepped down, picked up the binoculars and took a closer peek at the "fishing boats." I was rusty on panic, but something wasn't right. I strove to rationalize the image. Fuck! Is that really what I'm seeing? Two fast, gunmetal gray, open boats, perhaps thirty feet long, each with two ominous, long pipes above the men, bouncing on the chop. I didn't believe it could happen to me, but the realization assailed me in that instant, and almost in a trance, I lifted the small, plastic cover and leaned on the danger-red panic button with a prearranged signal. *Blaare—blaare! Blaare—blaare! Blaare—blaare!*

As the alarm reverberated through the house, I stared again at the two boats aiming directly towards…me! Assessing myself the prime target, I tore towards the rear exit door just as the Old Man, fresh from a shower, broke through, and we suffered the first thumping—bang!—then another—bang! I slid and leaped down each half flight with the careless facility of long practice and a fast descent into pure fear.

Another and another tremendous, deep thump! somewhere resonated and shook through the ship. Reaching the lowest companionway, I fell upon the boiler-suited and hard-hatted, mustering complement. A tremendous jarring, distant bang! and then bang! Missiles were hitting us as the injured leviathan pushed on regardless. Walkie-talkies were squelching, some were readying breathing apparatus, and the men began forming squads as Rick ordered. Another bang! And bang! I suffered a brief cataplexy attack, brought on by the emotional shock, and collapsed to my haunches, unable to support myself, placing my hands over my face. I wanted to curl into a ball and disappear in the claustrophobia and the sense of inevitable, awful doom. The feel of each express train rocket shuddered through the house. So, this is how it ends? Perhaps the reader won't identify with your hero's realization that comes with a self-recognition of human failing, but I was teetering on the edge.

"Where's the Old Man?" someone asked. Squatting on the stairway in shorts and Hawaiian shirt, I felt absurd and impotent. Another bang! I wanted to don an orange boilersuit and participate, become a member of a larger team, safe in numbers.

"On the bridge," I acknowledged. Then, seeing the frightened faces reflected in my eyes, I evolved in that moment, merging the blurred moral lines of heroism, self-preservation and duty.

"I'll go back," and turned to climb. I hesitated, then clambered on, quicker, the spirit oozing back into my bones as if I were being inflated with a bicycle pump. I had to do this. Someone had to pilot the ship. Reaching the bridge, I slowly, cautiously, pushed open the door. "Captain?"

"Here." I slipped round the chart table on all fours, and there he was, hiding beneath the center binnacle, between two instrument panels. Stretching higher, momentarily relieved, I saw the boats speeding away forward on the port bow, but then I witnessed what I'd always dreaded—a fire, forward; sparking and jumping, as if electrical. Between the fire and me were two million barrels of low flash point, light Saudi crude oil. This was bad, very bad, but then, as Captain Dan struggled from his hideout, we both stared wide-eyed to my left and saw flames leaping and curling up above the bridge wing from somewhere below.

My heart faltered; my brain was senseless with inputs I'd never comprehended occurring in real life. No school prepares one for this. "John, rig a hose!" Aroused from my fearful trance, once out on the wing, I unbolted the door, tumbling out the hose, threading the cap. An AB arrived and we ran it towards the flames. We stood back from the rising inferno and lashed it to rain down upon the conflagration.

Hear me out for a second. I understand the common spiritual quandary, suffered by many, believing one is in hell. It occurs when, say, the bank account enters the red, or one loses employment. But if you know, without a shadow of doubt, you're in hell, then you're standing on a blazing supertanker full of crude oil.

INSIDE THE bridge, "I need to know where we are, John?" At the radar, I found the light buoy racon intermittently glowing, but it was beginning to fade astern. Captain Dan radioed down to manage the fire teams on deck.

On deck: the missiles had struck the port slop and port bunker tanks below a storeroom, promoting the inferno that leaped up to the bridge wing five stories above. Of the two fire teams, one attacked from the main deck, led by Rick and the bosun. Third Mate Peter Brown, a young, anti-establishment type, along with the pumpman, led the second team, tackling it from the rear. They led the fire teams because there was nobody else. People can be tougher than they realize when determined. They used high-pressure water hoses on fires being stoked from oil spilling out from multiple holes in the hull. The fire blazed, engulfing the deck store containing acetylene tanks and paint cans. From there the flames roared over the boat deck and the accommodation to the bridge wing, where they danced on my last nerve.

I stared aft and beheld the sea ablaze for a mile astern, as the crude and bunkers poured out. Amongst the flames the remains of the port lifeboat floated like a funeral pyre. On the bridge, an AB took the helm. I continued tracking the position, which became problematic with the racon fading. We swiftly discerned a need to alter our attitude toward the wind, alleviating the pressure on the fire teams, but that would mean turning southwest and entering the renowned shallows of the Gulf. They ran the starboard lifeboat out to embarkation. The forward sparking fire had been extinguished by pulling a breaker, or just lack of fuel, while the fire teams concentrated on the boisterous fire aft, which seemed unlikely to run out of energy. I seriously believed this to be the end. We needed a lot of luck.

Keeping busy wasn't difficult. The problem was trying to rationalize the intent to remain against the obvious metaphorical and literal ticking bomb. Captain Dan, understanding the fire lacked control, alerted authorities and requested assistance on Channel 16: "Pan-Pan, Pan-Pan, Pan-Pan, this is the *Esso Demetia*..."

The radio message "Pan-Pan" is the international signal for a state of urgency. I listened, slack jawed. Was he speaking Martian? His decision disturbed me. Surveying the situation, seeing the lonely starboard boat as our only exit, while the supertanker, fully laden, careened on regardless and the fire roared skyward, I supposed the situation some-what more urgent. Receiving no response, he motioned me to the radio and, before considering if this was a limb I wanted to climb out on, I broadcast the awful well-rehearsed message: "Mayday! Mayday! Mayday!" Being shot at concentrates the mind.

Ras Tanura Port Control came on, asking, absurdly, if oil had spilled into the sea. I replied it had, lots of it, but the conversation deteriorated into legal nonsense about responsibility. I had surrendered the airwaves to Arabic chatter and officialdom, when, exceeding all my dreams, I heard a deep, American Midwestern voice: "*Esso Demetia*, this is the American warship. Do you require assistance?" Captain Dan took the VHF and explained the situation while I resumed my navigational duties, and dusk engulfed us, leaving the vessel as a glowing bonfire in an enormous inky void.

The firefighting continued with feverish bravery, the teams cooling the burning storeroom and surrounding areas. They astonished me, and maybe themselves. The team led by Rick released the vessel's foam supply from the two nearest monitors, blanketing the aft port deck, but that was a one-shot deal, like two well-shaken cans of Reddi-wip. Then, seemingly from nowhere, a roaring wind appeared on the star-board bridge wing. We stepped out to be confronted by the power-ful spotlight of a military helicopter only feet above us. A crackling speaker boomed down: "Do you need medical assistance?" Captain Dan, bracing against the down thrust, waved his hands; as yet, we suffered no casualties. The helicopter roared away to the east, while the dirty, belching smoke plumed into the night like an apocalyptic demon, and the nocturnal sky fell like a portcullis.

Engine room: I had loathed the few occasions working below; the constant vivid lights and the din of the roaring boiler and whining turbine, but mostly I had an aversion to not seeing events transpiring, forever understanding the outside world through telegraphs and telephones. The engineers must have dreaded my first alarm, then the long episode of being hit, deep inside their steel box below the waterline, speculating on events outside their control. What if a shell hit the engine room? What if the fire couldn't be controlled? Throughout the night, every order was fulfilled; the engine kept turning (thankfully), the steering responded, the foam was released. When we requested inert gas to pressurize the port slop tank, it all worked, and it had to.

Without rehearsal, this was life happening in front of me. The fire raged, seemingly unquenchable. Dense shadows, streaming light: the world was alive with fantastically bizarre sounds and eerie, violent ghosts that night. We zigzagged languidly to relieve the heat on the fire teams and then, as if from nowhere, the "American warship" arrived like Johnny-on-the-spot, standing a mile away, keeping station. He didn't offer firefighting assistance, but advised he would evacuate casualties. However, for us, his sinister, battleship-gray existence forever checked our fears of the gunboats returning. We were safe, as long as we could dampen the fire, and the fire teams were slowly—barely—confining it. It was one of those yearlong nights, transcending the political swill of the day, cutting to the bone, letting us touch, however briefly, the hard reality of war. The public has no desire to puncture the mythic, heroic narrative of combat, but I can encompass it in one word: terror.

Captain Dan and I donned boilersuits, alleviating the frustration of playing my part like a beach tourist. By midnight, after all that water and foam and inert gas, and all the zigzagging to defray the cruel, relative wind, the fire was quenched, and good riddance! It had taken six hours to quell the bitter scent of burning petroleum. The American warship had stood by, watching and waiting for an evacuation that never came. It was a close-run thing, like Waterloo. Earlier that day, three Iranian gunboats stalked a German ship in Hormuz, killing a Filipino seaman and injuring two others with the same anti-tank missiles. The paradox for me was that those six hours had been both exhilarating and exhausting. People never feel so alive as when they are at war.

We limped on to the island of Bahrain and anchored, at the same time declaring it a port of refuge and general average. We anchored and rang "Finished with Engines." The helmsman, after ten hours of duty, finally relaxed, with our appreciation. The warship vanished as rapidly as it had arrived. I feel obliged to quickly explain: one of the inevitable issues of carriage is running into an unprecedented circumstance. Even while we are prepared for adverse conditions, helpless situations are more common than we suppose; the nature of the business. When a ship cannot continue its voyage, the main concern is to muster the ship, its crew and the cargo out of imminent peril, to a port of refuge. It's a maritime right. In common law, the concept of general average is the sharing of costs by all parties concerned with the common maritime adventure necessary to complete the voyage, which seems a model of equitability and reason.

At five in the morning, against all the dictates of my recent academic achievement, I left the bridge unmanned to visit the bar. I inhaled one cold beer and felt a little freer, as my band of brothers, debriefing in rowdy voices, released the tension in both celebration and relief. I wanted to be a cog in the wheel, to be part of the team, like the survivors of Rorke's Drift. It was the struggle that had kept us going. Back on the bridge, a hazy dawn emerged while I fought to remain awake. I'd been working for thirty hours straight, and I was drunk with fatigue. Time moved in increments of five minutes. My ability to focus, alertness and concentration slipped away. I paced to remain conscious. If I so much as closed my eyes, I would be asleep.

AWAKING FOUR hours later, I found a British warship had anchored nearby, the Leander-class frigate HMS *Scylla*, like a small sentinel watching over a wounded whale. History says the gunboats had shot twelve rocket-propelled anti-tank shells, nine of which struck their target. The American helicopter had tracked their wakes to Iran. A busy Lloyd's surveyor came aboard and declared we could continue to Khor Fakkan only, where we would need to affect temporary repairs. Holes patched, they ordered us to Singapore. We partied en route, staff and crew, together; our camaraderie deepened. It was the first time I felt the strange, disjointed national barriers lowered since I had sailed with Ching. Lines between social classes blurred and disappeared amid the fire, while imperialism and racism mutated into the glow of equality and teamwork in a crew mess room party. The firefight had been a magnificent achievement, accomplished with our own form of heroism, worthy of celebration, where different characters fought their own battles, intertwined to win for the common good. Singapore might just make it all worthwhile.

SINGAPORE, MY old friend, the place I longed to be, but this was too much work. The preparation for dry-docking took three weeks, toiling six hours on, six hours off. Plus. It encompassed a lightering, a long delivery to the Esso SBM and crude oil washing, and more crude oil washing. We knew back in Fawley the equipment didn't function as advertised, but we were content to check the boxes; a paperwork cleaning, safe in the knowledge that the next cargo blanketed everything. But they had called our bluff. The monster had to be cleaned. We set out somewhere into the South China Sea and spent a week water washing until it seemed there could be no water left. After inerting and gas freeing, we entered the tanks and failed any achievable standard. With typical late-in-the-day Exxon thinking, back at Jurong anchorage, they employed a hundred locals—mostly a large gossip of middle-aged women—to dig out 400 tonnes of sludge. Finally done, a month after arriving, a pilot guided us east to the Johore Strait, the snaking waterway between Singapore and Malaysia.

To the north of the island, Sembawang would be a sleepy residential area were it not for the extensive dry-docking facility. Hidden away, it is an eighty-six-hectare shipyard, which seems unusually out of place in suburbia, far from the concentration of yards to the southwest. It remains a physical legacy of empire, when we had the Maxim gun and fought against feudal clans armed with spears and black magic. It stretched for two miles along the northern coast, and in 1975, a hundred million dollars upgraded the facility with a new Premier Dock—1,260 feet long—to which we headed.

IT'S A mile from the dry dock along Admiralty Road to entertainment. It was a good walk to stretch our legs, to breathe in the rain, Saga trees and orchids in a stroll through suburbia. This was no humble part of town, or perhaps there's no poor Singapore left; Lee Kwan Yew had eradicated it. The walk fulfilled in itself. The humid late afternoon, and the stroll past contented middle-class houses and fauna, was like a steamy eastern replica of England. The peacefulness washed over us with every leisurely step.

At the termination of Admiralty Road, where it met Sembawang Road, there stood a colorful collection of ten businesses, mostly bars and restaurants. Without reference, we entered the first one, like so many of Southeast Asia: open fronted, cheap plastic chairs and tables, bug-killing lights, some anonymous pop Muzak, a smiling bar server and cold Tiger beer. We settled in for a customary, open-minded chat, celebrating the indomitable human spirit within the brutality and arbitrariness of war. The ship, being high and dry, absolved everyone of any thought of having to return to "take care of something." We had no fear that night. We were free. Rick and 'Lecky, having set their limits lower than mine, returned late, while I disappeared in some drunken haze to a suburban den of immorality. It felt good to be back!

Have you ever had one of those mornings, seven thousand miles from what used to be home, waking up in some dark house alone—fully clothed, thankfully—stumbling out, finding your way to a road you half recognize, far from the tourist city, looking at your watch—seven a.m.—and not wanting to know? Few feelings surpass strolling alone, touching the dawn air, breathing deep, feeling free. I liked the sensation of a tropical morning before it brushes its teeth, the succulent mossy taste of the air before it becomes oppressive. At that moment I knew I would never live in England again. I walked past a house of suburbia, small BMW outside, and thought, I could live here, I could live anywhere. Maybe I should junk this career, find a new one and settle down.

THE DRY-DOCKING was important and very expensive to someone. There were insurable repairs—lots of them—but when an opportunity arose, they added retubing the superheater, affixing anodes to the ballast tanks and some tank recoating, painting the hull, laying out the anchor chains, and blinding off the now-nonfunctioning, bow thruster. I oversaw work on deck, on the bridge and any other place where a man carrying a clipboard could waste some time. The sultry, clammy air made everyone warm, wet and uncomfortable. Singapore has only one season—summer.

Dry-docking creates an extreme mess. The process covered the entire deck with containers, air hoses, hydraulic lines, men with portable tools, large fenced-off holes, smoking cabins and a never-ending column of workers coming and going. In the dock, large hydraulic lifts raised men for high-pressure cleaning, sandblasting and painting, which takes time on a supertanker. The yard was humming with labor, perhaps a dozen vessels in dock or lying nearby, finishing off. They undertook considerable cosmetic work, including a revamped corporate logo on the funnel under the ill-conceived notion that anyone would see it. Exxon would change their minds the following year. Inside the hull, a nightmare of buckled plates and twisted girders had to be replaced; at any one time, a hundred different projects were being worked upon. I could fully appreciate the sheer size of the yard, attempting to walk from the Premier Dock to the main gate; fortunately, bicycles were available.

ONCE MY body had acclimatized to real life—not working eighteen hours a day—I settled back into comfortable, overseeing and monitoring mode, and decided I needed back into Singapore proper. That meant shopping in Lucky Plaza for electronics, cheap souvenirs and music; back to Orchard Road, where the large trees added shade and shelter from the blistering equatorial heat, and where the tourists live, moving from one nice establishment to another, like visiting moguls. But after Hong Kong, Singapore seemed slightly flavorless, now accepting a global audience, as if one step away from an exhibit at Epcot.

Yes, I found the occasional lady of abandoned character, usually in the bar at the Tropicana, Singapore's first entertainment complex to feature a topless revue, on the corner of Scotts and Orchard Roads, where Lulu once performed—fully clothed, I'm told. Usually, we just visited the bar downstairs, full of Filipinas, Malays and Indonesians, or the Red Lantern down at Clifford Pier while drinking Tiger beer. Sometimes we just found a good restaurant and a cool drink and took in the beauty of the Asian lady in situ, conscious of the fact that it all felt so familiar and wondering if there was any more to it. It was a boom time in Singapore, with plenty of expats filling the bars with money to spare. Nobody noticed, but on August 8, 1988, Iran and Iraq agreed to a cease-fire.

AFTER THREE weeks and a gleaming new coat of paint, they refloated and pulled the ugly, though shiny, leaden-gray beast from dock and parked it nearby. We had large new areas of steel gleaming on our port side where the holes once were, the deck remained a mess, and we had no electricity. They connected shore power, but it was insufficient to run the air-conditioning the first night; indispensable in the sultry Singapore heat. With our home about to sizzle into the evening, the company agreed to billet everyone in a hotel for the night. Over the moon with corporate benevolence, the entire complement cleaned up and boarded a bus for downtown. Two volunteers remained to assuage any salvage complications, while the rest of us, once at the foot of the gangway, discarded rank, all heroes together again, Filipino and Britisher, sharing stories of our visceral, nerve-shredding, pulse-pounding experience a month before, the stories growing longer and longer, like the one that got away.

The bus dropped the fourteen crew at the Miramar Hotel on Havelock Road, across from the Singapore River, close to People's Park. On that steamy early evening of a tropical night, with the city sounds and the cool, welcoming, bright glass doors of the foyer, I would have been glad to follow. But they took the staff a short ride to even more glamour at the downtown Marina Mandarin Hotel on Raffles Boulevard. A tall, glistening façade surrounded by shady green vegetation with an oppressively domineering art deco foyer, like a scene from *Metropolis*, newly minted in color. It all screamed opulence and overdone elegance, with outside elevators to watch the pretty people riding up and down.

My bathroom had a fake-gold telephone, but I had nobody to call. Nick, my replacement, and I decided on a quiet beer somewhere outside. We could have walked to Raffles, but we took a taxi to the Shaw Center, a buzzing focus of the nightly tourist business, all gleaming lights, sticky air, bustling taxis and people, people everywhere, six abreast on the broad pavements.

Tired from a long day, Nick and I walked up one floor to the Jockey Pub, a cool, cocktail and beer place, a sort of expat, oil business bar where one could play darts or pool or relax at the square-shaped bar amongst the like-minded with their girlfriends. One could typically find a friendly chat with a visiting or resident Brit or Australian. We stood at the corner drinking Heinekens, letting the heat and toil of the day seep from our bodies, chatting as one does about the usual nothings, a sort of informal handover from one navigator to another, the inside junk in which no one else was interested. Then, I lost my train of thought, my eyes settling on a divine apparition directly across the bar.

"Hey, Nick, see that girl over there."

"Where?"

"Over there, she keeps looking at me. She's gorgeous!" as if I needed to convince him, while suspending the ordinary laws of time and observation.

"Yeah, whatever. One more for the road?"—an offer I rarely declined. People were talking, but their words grew incomprehensible, like background noise. She watched me. Though this wasn't a completely unanticipated event, she looked at me differently. She, in her white dress and smile, lit up the room. I took the extra drink to console myself as she departed with friends. When Nick and I left shortly afterwards, there she was still—on the sidewalk—climbing into a taxi and, good grief! as it pulled away, she gazed back at me standing at the curb, forlorn and devastated, feeling I had just missed the possibility of a lifetime.

NEARING THE end of our dock schedule, the following night a few guys sought a volunteer to fill the taxi from Sembawang. "Where shall we…?

"The Jockey Pub!" My insistence won the day.

And there she was again, with a girlfriend, her beauty and personality all-consuming. We stood smiling across the bar, the two girls seeming to bounce with sexuality and joy. I bought them drinks (two double Courvoisiers—yikes!), and they joined us. "Hi, I'm Jacky!" I couldn't remove my eyes from this Thai Madonna as we chatted, her broken English the only fence between us, attempting the modest societal matters, like listening to other people talking. All I wanted was this diminutive, wonderful lady, her flawless, saffron-tinted skin open to her cleavage, revealing a heavy Buddhist chain, her radiant eyes all expression and glint. We closed on each other like a slow-burning fuse. Her slim, petite body, topped with wavy midnight-black hair, hung below her shoulders, while her diamond-encrusted ears framed a so-cute, slightly broken nose from a long-ago kickboxing tussle, and those beguiling, twinkling eyes—they shouted yes without her saying anything. Once we touched, everything else slipped away.

An hour later we were cuddling in a taxi, seeking a hotel for the night, when I realized I wasn't carrying identification, a mortal crime in Singapore. The driver, understanding the predicament with the pragmatic wisdom of his profession, found a small-time and grimy area that Lee Kwan Yew had somehow overlooked, closer to the city's emotions and impulses, a dark certified low-life street, lit only by the light of open doors and dubious neon signs. This wasn't right. Then it hit me: "…Take us to the Miramar Hotel on Havelock Road."

I walked in, sure and purposeful, for my first attempt at playing grifter. Jacky glided to the lounge while I approached reception with my newly written, semi-guilt-free, fraudulent lines. The receptionist interrupted, "Oh, *Esso Demetia*, that's fine, Sir, no ID required. In fact, you get a fifty percent discount." I shall leave the drawing of the night's inescapable conclusion to the reader, suggesting the addition of soft, background saxophone music.

And so began nights of bliss with Jacky, while every morning I rode a taxi back to Sembawang. Finally, the departure day arrived, and I found something tugging at me, affecting my conversation, drawing me into reflectiveness; something—what the hell was this?—for the first time in my life, I felt like letting go, jumping off this spinning world, turning back the clock and reliving the previous week over and over again. I had a job, well paying, a career if I wanted it, but something—something—was tugging me in some unknown direction, affecting me like never before. Yes, I liked the physical relationship, but I enjoyed taking her out to dinner, holding her hand. When I held her in my arms, her obsidian-haired head fit perfectly under my chin.

We departed Singapore, the ship reeling from the havoc wrought by handing over millions of dollars to a dry dock company; complete disarray. But the hull looked shiny, and we had a new corporate logo, but the same name. The final night, I dropped Jacky at Chancery Lane, where she lived.

"Can I write? Will you write to me?" I asked.

"Yes. I will. Come back, John, yes?"

I made the mistake of looking rearward from the taxi window, seeing her standing there alone, seeming lost and forsaken, all dressed in blue, her hair falling down across her face in the light breeze. We had meant something to each other for a bare week; Christ, my eyes were watering, what was the matter with me?

THE *ESSO Demetia* headed out of Singapore with my head elsewhere, like a dream I didn't want to awaken from. We tested systems; the pumps, the pipelines and all manner of gear in the engine room, as if I cared. When leaving dock, you really have to hold your breath the intakes are tight, the stern tube isn't leaking and all the tank plugs have been reinserted. We set northwest, drearily back to the Gulf, and Esso promoted me to chief mate, which was nice; an unexpected elevation for someone who a decade before was an innocent and ill-favored boy. We all returned to Ju'aymah in a well-protected convoy; now it was no longer necessary.

I had a new cabin, too large to be useful, but when not drinking, I found time to lie around admiring it, listening to music I had bought in Singapore, pen-scratching letters to the family and a dwindling parade of pen pals who suddenly meant much less. Overwhelmingly, my mind was on Jacky, as the ship steamed west to another world, leaving her a thousand miles behind. Where was she at this moment? I knew she traveled back and forth to Bangkok. Was she safe? Was she thinking of me? I tried to imagine her as I penned letters to innocence, euphoria and the sheer joy of living.

Ju'aymah was, predictably, the same, but I wouldn't say a pointless enterprise. There's nothing wrong here other than…everything! It was repellant to me: the stress, the heat, the sheer remoteness of the place, the pointless religious fervor, the lack of beer. Now, as chief mate, I faced the insane quirks of a Swedish builder trying to please Exxon's design idiosyncrasies in the control room. I should have known from the very first day I saw it. Too much equipment failed to function properly, or controls were inadequate, apparently made by an intelligence with no idea how life on Earth actually worked. Balancing the cargo safely in the tanks was undertaken with a loading computer predating the Commodore 64. We didn't even have spreadsheets. In a mass panic towards the end, I overloaded the ship, sinking the load line. But I lied, the Old Man shrugged, and we sailed the sublime six-week voyage to America. I drank and set my crew to the endless task of cleaning the post-dry-dock mess. I rather liked the dull routine of existence, and it gave me time to consider my future.

THIS WAS her first visit to America. The Coast Guard had developed their inspection routines significantly, so I set the crew to the details the uninitiated took seriously, like well-painted signs and clean decks. The unworldly young man who had ascended that ladder to the *Lampas* all those years before was the same one leading here, now self-assured and competent.

But I still had to deal with this eccentric and enigmatic ship. A week prior arrival I pressure tested the crude oil washing system, lost control of an uncontrollable cargo pump, over-pressurized the lines, and passed oil through the deck block-valve, mis-replaced in dry dock. The oil tore forward through a lignum vitae manifold cover, resulting in an impressive, gushing black fountain of oil, like a fireboat in New York Harbor exploding from the manifold. The incident presaged events. Two days later, the chief engineer transferred bunkers from forward to aft, and the tank overflowed. We had to stop this time to lower a boat and manually clean the hull.

Then events went seriously wrong at LOOP (the Louisiana Offshore Oil Port). The *Esso Demetia*, safely having blundered through its Coast Guard inspection, lived up to expectations and leaked oil to the surrounding water as we pumped ashore. After endeavoring to bluff our way through the legal ramifications, we had a two a.m. fire alarm, but most of the engineers were too drunk to awaken. I balled out a few of the latecomers; "I'm up, everyone's up." Fortunately, it was false alarm. My relief arrived, took one look at the huge, thirty-six-inch deck valve he would have to take out and reverse, and flew home. They evicted us from LOOP in disgrace, like the final scene of a Werner Herzog movie. Three days later, Esso found a gullible replacement, and I helicoptered ashore with others, departing the ill-omened and irredeemably ugly ship.

THE TANKER War had compelled a sharp drop in shipments, and a consequent rise in oil prices. Iran lowered its price to offset higher insurance premiums, and, consequently, the global oil price actually declined during the 1980s, exposing the absurdity of it all. Our fight with the fire, a minor extra in the epic, might have succeeded, but the war had raged on. Over 320 seamen were casualties; wounded, missing or dead; the real price of oil. War changed me, but isn't that what it's for? I had nothing bad to say about Exxon—everyone else would do that the following March.

I never met the leading actors of that night again. In my opinion, every man jack was courageous, in his own way, with his own fears. The leaders showed determination, courage, the ability to make a decision under stress, and to endure physical discomfort. We were collectively left with a potent and emotional glimpse into the fog of war. On the bridge, those long hours were an intense and oppressive experience. Captain Dan impressed. The word "leader" comes to mind—effortlessly. He cast a composed and saintly sheen over the proceedings, and I understood the Master Mariner qualification was not about paper examinations, but character.

The encounter done, desperately searching for an adjective both descriptive enough to encompass the experience, and distinctive enough to convey my jangled senses, I concentrated my soul on the life-affirming meeting with Jacky, who had aroused in me strange emotions I had not before encountered, setting my heart racing more than the fire. My cynicism of life began slipping away. I was born and grew up into a man I never liked. It was time to decide the final version of me.

Against all conventional wisdom, this time I was going back. Back to Singapore.

19

Serendipity

1989

When I saw you I fell in love, and you smiled because you knew.

—Arrigo Boito

THERE'S NO starting and stopping: the basic affairs of life endured. For years, my psyche had been declining faster, with an occasional incident slowing the drift, but then this most peculiar sensation, this obsession called love. So, this is what it feels like. Jacky had captured my faculties of vision and thought. It had been a tough seven-month voyage, like a four-hour movie. Arriving home, I slowly opened letters in order of interest. Some were from warmhearted friends, but I saved the best for last, and opened the delicate, blue-and-red airmail from Singapore. Her English prose was all over the place in strange, dripping-Thai calligraphy, but the words were positive. She wanted to see me again. It might fail, but I was being pulled—without protest—into the next giddy chapter of life, like a flower groping towards the sun. I went back this time, and it made all the difference.

AND IT was all I hoped it would be. Day after day, we played tourist; the zoo, Sentosa, the aquarium, the shopping malls, the Jockey Pub, Newton Circus and our mutual fondness for hotel cocktail bars. We drank every night and lay in bed until noon. All of my innate sarcasm and cynicism were wasted on Jacky, so they drifted to the rear of my vocabulary. I visited the street where she lived with three others. It was a large, comfortable house in a curiously leafy suburban road in the Novena district, just north of downtown, with a pile of shoes in the doorway. We camped in the Miramar Hotel, naturally, until they greeted me by name every day. The images are secure in my mind: her tight jeans, the short blouses, the Taywin shoes, the scents of Badedas soap and Poison perfume, gold everywhere and an unquenchable ability to smile and laugh at the little surprise moments of life. I had never felt so happy and contented. She made me feel uncomplicated, unstressed; I was proud to hold her hand. The longer we were together, the harder going became.

I'd earned three months' vacation and I took it, every last day. Exxon had a habit of finding me as I kept moving between London and Singapore. The telex came—it might have been made of newspaper snippets, like a ransom note. With respect to Epicurus, I had to work. The tiny Exxon subdivision who employed me operated very large ships, four of the world's top ten. The mad rush to construct ever bigger ships in the 1970s had halted. Many were laid up, some abandoned on a beach in Poland or Bangladesh, and a few, like the *Seawise Giant*, temporarily out of service.

TO SAY I lacked enthusiasm was the prime understatement of my life. It was quiet that late evening at Gatwick airport, and I noticed them easily enough; a third engineer and his junior, drinking at the sizable, oval bar in their sub-alcoholic addiction. Finally, I walked over and a recognition struck me before I could say, "Good evening, gentlemen."

It was Wick, from the *Litiopa*, with less hair now, much of it beginning to gray and he'd lost his perfect tan. He finally recognized me as we familiarized.

"A bit young, aren't ya?" said the youthful one, like a boy the ugly girl might have won in a raffle. Wick was, by his own admission, a reactionary. Years in the engine room and drinking and not very good food had marked him, made him bitter toward the new, well-educated men who had risen above. His resentment stemmed from what was coming: a Filipino or Indian replacement, and then what? There were only so many jobs on the ferries.

After another ten minutes, he questioned again, "You're the chief mate?"

A NIGHT in a hotel, like so many times before. This was Malta, gray and stony, like it always had been. I really didn't want to go, but, hey! John, you have to work; like Orwell said, one must function in society, one had to contribute to capitalism. I saw little alternative. Another launch at dawn, like the firing squad, the boat bouncing on the chop, and there in the near-distance, the lead-gray apparition of the mighty supertanker, the largest I ever saw. Good grief! It was half the size again of the *Lampas*. Like that day in Ras al Khaimah, I was the same, but different. Twelve years later, I remained young, but I had grown so much. Then we were there, bobbing up and down near the scenery-enveloping behemoth, solid and immobile. It was a long climb, the longest ever, while our bags went aloft on the derrick hook. We alighted, breathless, on the rusty-red deck and I took in the enormous panorama of the Ultra Large Crude Carrier. It ignited no emotional response. I had grown assertive to replace my timidity. Awash with dark moodiness I found it tiresome and shrug-worthy.

The net landed; Wick identified his suitcase and a Filipino AB grasped it. A man in an orange boilersuit stepped open-handed to me, "Hello, I'm Peter. New fifth engineer?"

"Er, no, I'm the new fucking 'Arry Tate and I haven't had my breakfast yet." His eyes widened slightly, digesting the incongruous sight of a twenty-eight-year-old chief mate on the leviathan. The AB released the bag and asked for mine. The obvious sometimes merits utterance; like the SS *Esso Mediterranean* itself, subtlety and delicacy had avoided this one.

I met the captain, an old-style Exxon man, who wore a gray uniform, while radiating an awkward blend of calamity and amusement. He was also dangerously optimistic, like a man who doesn't know what's going on. They called him Bunbury, after Oscar Wilde's fabricated man. Regrettably, we went to Suez. Annoyingly, Bunbury required the bow clear of the water at sea, while it had to be in-water for the Canal. A simple notion, but someone had to do it, and we consumed an immense weight of bunkers running the huge turbine pumps. The grim, fittingly dark ship labored in and out of Suez. I saw little (because there was nothing to see). No, I spent a day and night with the pumpman (my crucial man), shifting ballast in and out to satisfy Bunbury's bizarre, aquatic streamlining hypothesis. The pump room, deep down in the belly of the beast, hardly seemed big enough to contain the pumps and giant angles of enormous pipelines squeezed and convoluted inside. I hoped beyond hope that we would not have to replace a valve down here.

The charterers—Saudi Aramco—sent us, naturally, to Ju'aymah. It was quiet, banal, empty, frenzied and drab. It was the same again;

another panic, a straight thirty-six sleepless hours of work. The loading was tense, grinding, fearful of something breaking or leaking, never-ending—in the night it really mattered. I took the legal drug coffee; others took more potent options. The only connection between us and them was the radio, a surreal correlation between the industry and their religion and morality. We loaded three million barrels of Saudi's finest and the ocean groaned under our weight.

Upon leaving, a strange feeling of transparency overwhelmed me. As hard as it was to imagine, the time had come. That very evening, sitting in my cabin having a comfortable beer with the second engineer, I raised the thought of giving it all up. "Resign? Esso won't care." But I rather thought they would. Bunbury didn't take it well, as if he were at fault. Coincidently, they had appointed an extra junior mate, which precluded me the slow, metronomic-like routine of watchkeeping. I turned to day work, for the manager, an irony if there ever was. The desire to fast-forward was irresistible, so in the evening, not surprisingly, I set to drinking; and you know I rarely had a positive experience in the alcoholic family.

THE BAR, symbol of masculinity and emancipation, became a retreat of detached merriment, the only place to be free. Beer—like scopolamine—doesn't lie. There was nobody new to talk to, no nonworking passengers, no newspapers. Random thoughts flitted through our minds but they'd all been spoken before. They were mostly agreeable characters who only reminded me of better ones on better ships. We drank until it didn't matter anymore, our casual lies of civility lulling us into a false sense of camaraderie, while I counted down the time by the pull-rings of empty cans on my finger each night.

If they treated any other drug this way, it would outrage politicians. Alcohol is a strange lover. Soon after imbibing too much, we regretted it, yet we still came back for more. Nobody knew it intoxicated us, but that was about to change. When not socializing I found the habitual loneliness of my grand cabin, but now it just distressed me. My wanderlust was tempered and I penned letters to Jacky. On Sunday mornings Bunbury conducted the time-honored tradition of inspections, dragging me, the chief and the bosun with him, but it was better than wet Sunday afternoons in England. On regular days I sent the crew out in the never-ending battle against rust. When feeling good, or topping up the inert gas pressure, I went out early to take in the beauty of the morning sky altering on a vast open horizon. Although there is typically nothing to appreciate, there's always something to see—the incongruity of the hard, dirty steel, ship amidst the pristine beauty of the limitless ocean. It felt splendid for a few minutes.

Unbeknownst to us, while on that remote five-week passage, an error of navigation occurred on the other side of the world, initiating a political scandal, the ramifications of which were to change the life of going to sea for everyone; not always for the better.

ON MARCH 24, just after rounding the Cape, the news broke. It went in one ear and out the other, but I feel obliged to comment. I should not speculate as to how much oil was spilled; the arguments continue, but it was substantial. They called the ship the *Exxon Valdez*. The legend of the drunken sailor has served the shipping industry fittingly over the years, and Exxon wasn't about to miss an easy target. It distorted a complex incident, with many incriminating causes, into a simple story of human weakness. Broken radar, missing equipment, missing oil-spill workers, falsified tests, the blatant disregard of the law—all these made a disaster not an accident but an inevitability, one the industry had been sailing too close to for too long, and with which I was intimately familiar. Granted, the captain had been drinking, but shortly before midnight he had handed over control to a competent and qualified officer of the watch. Narrow waters, true, but the third mate had traversed the route many times. I sense nothing illicit here. Minutes later, the vessel missed a turn and hit Bligh Reef. Then it became complicated, with failures on the bridge and ashore, plus the disastrous cleanup operation that ensued. But there's one aspect of the *Exxon Valdez* disaster that rarely made the headlines. Big oil and the drunken sailor were easier targets—new and old stereotypes together.

I was familiar with a major contributing factor. When the ship departed the Alyeska oil terminal, its crew had completed a grueling twenty-two hours, loading North Slope crude oil. I knew the regime well; it was the same as Ju'aymah and everywhere else. The burden upon the three mates was particularly intense. So heavy was the workload, none of them appeared to have had sufficient respite to legally man the bridge when the tanker departed. I had suffered the same routine a dozen times myself. There were few restrictions on the working hours of a merchant ship. The chief mate told the *Anchorage Daily News*, "This is just normal to me. If you want to be the chief mate, this is how you will work. If you want to be a second mate or a third mate, this is how you will work." Before this day, everyone at sea worked until the work was completed, while ship managers relentlessly reduced personnel.

More questionable, and slightly off-subject, was why Exxon added their name to the ship's side in the first place. The owners of the pipeline consortium and overseers of the oil-spill cleanup organization—particularly BP—obscured their names from the press, but everyone knew the name of the ship. I never understood why companies affix their name or logo to ships the public will never see. Hubris, I suppose.

WHAT CAN I say about the improbably vast *Esso Mediterranean*? It was one of the largest vessels trading in 1989, 457,000 deadweight tonnes. She had some standard Exxon design peculiarities, but the Japanese had handled it better than the Swedes. They floated her in Kure, Japan, in 1976. Most everything worked as it should. The loading had been a rapid two days of stress and anxiety as the oil rushed in to our 99 percent limits, but I knew the discharge would be lengthy, fragmented and stressful. Sixty miles offshore the Sabine River, the lines on the chart designated a federally approved lightering area. A few days out, as we headed there, I reminded Bunbury I was expecting a replacement.

The concept of lightering one vessel to another had been around for a long time. By 1989, it had taken on the manner of a large, specialized, commercial business, essential for the economy of scale so crucial to moving petroleum. The benefits included a reduction of draft to enter a port, or to trade part-cargo ownership, or in this case, to allot the oil to smaller vessels physically acceptable for US port entry—the *Esso Mediterranean* being restricted to a handful of ports worldwide.

The smaller vessel (perhaps 100,000 deadweight tonnes), approaches the larger one from the starboard quarter,[46] while both are making way, at about 4 knots. When half a mile astern, they parallel each other at a distance of one cable (tenth of a nautical mile). As you might imagine, this is achieved cautiously and slowly. As they close the distance, once the lateral gap is correct, heaving lines are hurled across the tempestuous, frothy waters between the two. Maneuvering really large ships,

---

46 The approach is almost always from starboard due to the phenomenon of transverse thrust—the opposing forces of a propeller acting laterally, much magnified when going astern.

without tug assistance, is challenging and anxiety-inducing, with the strange forces of interaction influencing the motion of each. Then the time-consuming, perilous mooring begins. Like others, but with the berth we're embracing moving. Sounds irrational, and it is, especially in anything other than perfect weather conditions. To add risk, the whole highly stressed process often happened at night, just to make sure no one had sufficient sleep. The ships were held ten feet apart with four low-pressure, pneumatic fenders about twenty feet long, like soft rubber ducks between a mother hippopotamus and baby. Once secured, the cargo transfer proceeded while the smaller ship wobbled about, accompanied by thunderous, metallic and ominous screeching sound effects from the wires and fenders.

We lightered six times in two weeks, which sounds easy if you say it quickly. The work was demanding, while we went about our little affairs. On and on the tiresome chore continued, disconnected from reality, like being stuck in the wrong lane. Exxon asked me to remain and tank-clean back to Suez, but I wasn't listening to a bar of that song. Finally, they found my relief, and I took the long walk down the accommodation ladder, with each step abandoning more of the *Esso Mediterranean* and, I convinced myself, my ebbing career. The ship had been hard, cold and cumbersome; life with Jacky was fun and invigorating. There was nary a lifelike character on the whole voyage, so I escaped for another world.

SERENDIPITY IS an odd concept. It's difficult to find and even harder to explain. For me, it was an aimless, random search without knowing where I was going, nor what I was seeking. Once accepting that orderly processes have their limitations, what I finally sought could only be achieved by restless, undirected rummaging. What were the chances of having walked into that bar so many months before? I joined that ship and accepted I might never find what I was seeking, and the discovery of whatever it was somehow intuitive, yet when I saw it—her—I somehow, instinctively, knew I had to hold on, go back, again and again. She was the one I had not been seeking, and now I could not let her go.

I had seen the east, and felt it calling. I headed to the bronzed yellow faces, the black hair and eyes, clusters of Chinese, Malays, Europeans and half castes; the unique city a bag of assorted, artificially flavored humanity, and back to Jacky, soothing my eyes and spirit. I was unsure of the next step, but I was free. I learned Thais talk of food between eating and cooking, and they are very receptive to the camera. We returned to the Jockey Pub where Jacky's effervescent charm captivating all eyes and made me proud. I met her German employer, Klaus, an importer of suspiciously nontariff, nonregulated gold from Bangkok. He said I should see the world, and I said I'd already seen it.

In Singapore, I reflected on the two momentous and simultaneously occurring events, so dissimilar, yet auspicious. I was in love with Jacky, and the sun was sinking on my maritime duties, I believed, a career bookended by the *Amoco Cadiz* and the *Exxon Valdez*. Finally, I thought of myself as a fully developed man. I had learned self-reliance, morality and a sense of duty. For each moment of joy, for each satisfying watch, there had been so much hard work and boredom, but the life had shaped me. I had achieved much, geographically and professionally, but living with Jacky, I realized that the manner in which one lived life, especially with a partner, was far more important.

I had learned so much in twelve years, and I had changed. Originally, I lacked perseverance, fidelity and constancy. The idea was not to waste the time I was given, and I regret only a few instances—my participation in the dreadful practice of cleaning oil with water, the drinking and driving, the daily throwing of trash into the ocean, the evasion of taxes, and some other minor acts you might have noticed, but I regret more the things I didn't do. I've worked up to owning my mistakes and feel far from being morally bankrupt. I learned to live without the supernatural. When I was young, my mother told me of many different religions. I resolved then not to be misled by sentiment into beliefs with no evidence. Mum, I've not appreciated you in my head, nor in my heart, as much as I should have.

I had learned that war is apparently long boring stretches of inactivity and then shock and fear, while its essence is death. War was no longer something philosophical for me. I had faced it myself (in a remote corner of the playing field), but in the end, all the inspirational, feel-good heroic moments felt earned. As soon as I left home, scratching at my English anxiety, it was my duty to see the undeveloped world, and I saw my fair share. I had trusted it might give me hope, but that wasn't the case. English boys used to go to sea to rule the world, but now young Asian men were going to keep their families alive, for much less reward. I had learned that places I had read of were not so remote and impersonal as I once believed.

In those early days, I doubt Jacky understood my work. Like others, did she wonder what happened to a ship after it faded over the horizon? How could anyone understand without reference? The industry was, and remains, something the average person never sees nor understands, yet it hauls to them every gallon of liquid, every commodity tonne and every widget they use. Those who man that industry are never seen, rarely appreciated, too often never missed, and nobody visits their grave. They live a life in which loneliness is taken for granted, where the sea magnifies their personal struggles. Their absentee lifestyle often leads to divorce and detachment from growing children. I met so many, many good men, and am forever in their debt for the knowledge, strength and sheer joy they instilled in me.

Exxon tracked me down some precious weeks later, during the best days of our lives. Well, it was their hotel, I suppose. The scratchy voice on the telephone relayed the essence of their manning dilemma and asked if I might return—just for one trip? All my money seemed to have disappeared without my really knowing where it went. Warily, my mind set to the commercial need, as I gazed upon the half-naked, golden-skinned Madonna lying beside me.

Afterword

O N A dazzling sunny day in 1998, a full moon and high tide filled a spare stretch of dirty beach in Chittagong, Bangladesh. Lead cutter Hakkim, in his dirty, scuffed-blue hard hat with black goggles attached, stood in the mud, watching with others. Most dressed in oil- and mud-stained rags, barely meeting the description of clothing—they would do the heavy, mind-numbing, backbreaking work, but Hakkim felt good in his blue jeans and shirt. And he wore shoes.

All the men, and some women, were employed through contractors for the Kabir Steel company. They had no medical facilities, no compensation for being unable to work, and no training. They lived apart from their families who remained in the nation's interior—these were the lucky ones, earning, in grinding hopelessness, a dollar a day for backbreaking work to carry the thousands of tonnes of steel up the polluted beach, day after day, for perhaps six months, while their families lived in poverty and hunger. The striking women in colorful saris, sullied with the grime of the trade, were to carry mattresses and furniture up the same slight incline.

They stood in the 120°F heat, the acrid smell of the nearby streets and the fumes from burning steel just along the beach, filling the air, to watch the giant red ship grind itself up onto the beach, pushing a small but relentless tide ahead of it. Her paint still looked good, but her engine had become too expensive to run, and the politics of America had overtaken her time. The men stood ready to begin the long, arduous task, ready to feast on the bones. The name on the bow wept *LAMPAS.*

AND ME? The sea had been good, because it made me a man. Well, it didn't take long to make the single best decision of my life. There's a last time for everything and I would not sail with Exxon, or anyone else, again. I always came back to myself, because I know what I've done. Life at sea was a challenge that has made any other work since just easy to do. I had, serendipitously, found love. I had found Jacky, stood up and said what I meant. I proposed to Jacky in the Miramar Hotel cocktail lounge, with no idea how or where we were going to live. We married in the Bahamas and became Americans, and have since retired to Washington, D.C. For this year's thirtieth anniversary I'm considering taking Jacky somewhere exotic. Valparaíso, perhaps.